Hero of the Republic

J. Madison Cutts, Jr.

This photograph of J. Madison Cutts, Jr., was taken circa 1893.

Hero of the Republic

The Biography of Triple Medal of Honor Winner
J. Madison Cutts, Jr.

Rick,

Thank you for your friendship
and support.

Best wishes,

By

Bing G. Spitler

BURD STREET PRESS
SHIPPENSBURG, PENNSYLVANIA

Maps drawn by author.

This Burd Street Press publication
was printed by
Beidel Printing House, Inc.
63 West Burd Street
Shippensburg, PA 17257-0152 USA

The acid-free paper used in this book meets the guidelines for permanence and durability of the Committee on Production Guidelines for Book Longevity of the Council on Library Resources.

For a complete list of available publications
please write
Burd Street Press
Division of White Mane Publishing Company, Inc.
P.O. Box 152
Shippensburg, PA 17257-0152 USA

Library of Congress Cataloging-in-Publication Data

Spitler, Bing G., 1947-
    Hero of the Republic : the biography of triple Medal of Honor winner J. Madison Cutts, Jr. / by Bing G. Spitler.
        p. cm.
    Includes bibliographical references (p.) and index.
    ISBN 1-57249-222-8 (alk. paper)
    1. Cutts, James Madison. 2. United States. Army. Infantry Regiment, 11th--Biography 3. United States. Army of the Potomac--Biography. 4. Medal of Honor--Biography. 5. Cutts, James Madison--Trials, litigation, etc. 6. Courts-martial and courts of inquiry--United States--History--19th century. 7. Virginia--History--Civil War, 1861-1865--Campaigns. 8. United States--History--Civil War, 1861-1865--Campaigns. 9. Soldiers--United States--Biography. I. Title.

E492.4 11th .S65 2001
973.7'455'092--dc21

                                                        2001035046

Dedicated to my father, Robert Lee Spitler, businessman, public servant, and loving father

In memory of Hazel Catherine Spitler

Gentlemen of the committee. It is of a strange order of Divine Providence that while on the 18th day of June, 1863, one Captain Hutton picked a quarrel with me which led to his own final discomfiture while it returned to his regiment, with a sad and sorrowing countenance and almost a broken heart, one who before that time had been a happy warrior, the man of sorrows, precisely to a day, one year afterwards, on the 18th day of June, 1864, fell as was supposed, mortally wounded, a universally acknowledged hero of the Republic. All this not great for a day and his role for an hour, but after the most conspicuous and distinguished services in a long series of battles, and in the very act of tendering specific, conspicuous distinguished, and successful services of that kind which are the pride and glory of a soldier, and are in all nations recognized by the highest and noblest rewards and praise.

Congressional Records
Fifty-third Congress
United States of America

Contents

Illustrations and Maps

Preface

By the end of the 19th century, many of the weary veterans of the American Civil War had joined their comrades who had given their lives during the great struggle. For many years after the war, the government took stock of its heroes and recognized the most gallant, living and dead, with recognition of the highest honor the nation can bestow on one of its soldiers, the Medal of Honor. Established by an act of Congress in 1862, the medal signifies action in battle "above and beyond" the call of duty. During the great rebellion, the medal was awarded for various feats of gallantry. Most medals were awarded for capturing an enemy flag, and most of those as a result of the last major engagement of the war, the Battle of Sailor's Creek, where the rear guard of Lee's tattered army was overwhelmed. Whatever the reason, those so honored have earned the deepest respect and admiration of every American.

Out of more than 3,400 Medal of Honor winners, 1,520 medals were awarded to men who fought in the Civil War. Of those, 20 were actually awarded two Medals of Honor, for gallantry on two separate occasions. Precedent established after the Civil War ruled that no recipient should receive more than one medal.

The Medal of Honor is an entity unto itself, and it carries the same level of honor and glory regardless of the number received. It would be unfair to bestow a higher honor on recipients of two medals because it would diminish the great value of those who received only one. On the other hand, it should never be forgotten that there were some that once journeyed to the edge of oblivion, survived, and chose to return for a second or even a third time. Truly, the character of those men is to be admired and recognized.

One such man was James Madison Cutts, Jr. He was born to the Washington aristocracy and, with his Harvard law degree, showed great promise for law and politics. He chose instead to join the Union army as a private at the outset of the Civil War. He received his commission as a captain in the regular army and displayed bravery and valor throughout his military career. While Grant directed the Army of the Potomac against Lee during the last year of the war, Madison Cutts so conspicuously distinguished himself in battle that he was called "Hero of the Republic" and later was awarded the Medal of Honor for gallantry in three separate battles. His story is unique to our country's history, and as fascinating as any novelist could have imagined.

I came to know of James Madison Cutts, Jr., in the summer of 1992 while reading Carl Sandburg's *Abraham Lincoln*.[1] As I read the brief account of Lincoln's pardon of Captain Cutts and of how the young man went on to win a triple Medal of Honor, I became very curious. What did he do to be awarded the triple Medal of Honor in a war that epitomized valor and glory? Has anyone ever written about him? Is he in the history books? If not, why not? Is there still family left? If so, where are they? I wondered whether it would be possible to trace his actions through the war. And finally, the ultimate question, where is the medal now? From that point, I started a journey that has led me to this end. It has been a wonderful adventure that has enabled me to reconstruct the days of his life.

Acknowledgements

I am most appreciative of the support I have received over the years from my friends and relatives. Their continual inquiries kept me going at the lonely times when the end was well beyond the horizon. It is to these friends and members of my family that I say, thank you. I would, however, be remiss if I didn't mention a few of those who contributed in some special ways to the writing of this book. My fascination for the American Civil War started one day in Mrs. Hickson's seventh grade social studies class at the School Street School, in Ramsey, New Jersey. It was Margaret Hickson who introduced me to the War of the Rebellion, spoke of the intricacy of strategies, and how battles were won and lost. In a matter of just a few days, she planted a seed that has lasted a lifetime. Many others, such as my brothers William, Benjamin, and Robert, as well as relatives and friends Daniel and Patricia Angeline, Daniel Farmer, Magdalene and Joseph Van Dalsen, John Graham, Jennifer Logar, Christopher Pappas, Mary Person, Ann Spitler, Michelle Graham, Johnny Powell, and Wayne Temple helped me stay the course. My son, Scott, his wife, Amy, and their daughter, Emily, provided much-needed inspiration and encouragement along the way. Mr. William Lind, archivist, the National Archives, was invaluable in providing me with information, support, and an occasional visit to the inner sanctum of the National Archives. My editor, Eugene Moore, provided the literary and grammatical strength necessary to make my writings legible. He accepted his role quietly, either by nature or knowing the unquestionable challenge that lay before him. I cannot fully express my gratitude to the grandchildren of Colonel Cutts, Harriet Cutts Lundquist, and James Madison Cutts, IV, for providing me with insight and support. They opened their homes to me and helped make the dream a reality. Above all, it was my best friend and wife, Joyce, who tolerated my many hours of research, writing, and frequent trips back in time. Without her steadfast love and caring, this work would never have been completed.

Author's Note

Many sources were used in the effort to reconstruct the life of James Madison Cutts, Jr. Fortunately, there was his extensive military record at the National Archives as well as the *Official Records*, family records, the Library of Congress, and most significantly the *Congressional Records* of the 52nd and 53rd Congress dealing with his attempts for relief. Finally, although small in numbers the personal comments, letters, and memorabilia of the Cutts family were rich with insight into the man.

To trace Madison Cutts through the days of the Civil War, it was necessary to establish a connection between his movements and those of his military units. Except for the time he spent as aide-de-camp on the staff of Gen. Ambrose E. Burnside he served with his regiment. In the last year of the war, Madison Cutts' regiment, the 11th U.S. Infantry Regiment, made up the First Battalion, the First Brigade (Ayres' brigade), the First Division (Griffin's division) of the V Corps. In the absence of direct information regarding his exact location on the battlefields, the author refers the reader to the closest military unit of the V Corps which best establishes his location.

Chapter I

The Family

James Madison Cutts, Jr., was born the second child of James and Ellen Cutts on October 20, 1837, in Georgetown, District of Columbia. His name honored his father and his great uncle, the fourth president of the United States. The family would call him Madison. With his birth Madison joined his older sister, Rose Adele, to complete the family. The two children joined the ranks of the civilized world with a fortunate genetic balance of their mother's incredible beauty, their father's strong constitution, and a high level of intelligence from both. The Cutts family lived on the hill in Washington, D.C., where the elder Cutts had been reared. They were of modest means by Washington's social standards yet prominent in stature and position. As soon as Madison was able to understand, his father spoke to both of his children of those family members who came before them. The Cutts family had a proud heritage in America, and his father often shared it with his children.

The original Cutts families of Madison's line came from Richard Cutts, Esq., of Grondale Abbey, Arkeden, in the county of Essex, England. Richard, a supporter of Cromwell during the English Civil War of 1640, feared revenge should the royalty prove victorious. Knowing the severity of the situation, he encouraged two of his older sons, John and Richard, to leave England for America. They had heard of the rights granted to Capt. John Mason and Sir Ferdinando Gorges with respect to land in the northern part of the colonies, and they developed a plan to move there. Although they would go to America for secular reasons, they were considered dissenters from the Church of England.[1]

The two brothers soon emigrated. In 1646 they settled in the area known as Strawberry Bank on the Piscataqua River in what is now Maine. Upon arriving in America, they had dropped the letter *s* at the end of their name, probably in fear of what might happen if King Charles I defeated Cromwell. Ambitious and hard working, they immediately set about to achieve the success they had dreamed of in the new land. They worked together to build a business, and quickly became successful by harvesting the forest and the sea.

In 1648, not long after the brothers had reached a degree of stability in the new land, another brother, Robert, and a sister, Anne, joined them. With Robert's arrival, the brothers now had the means to expand their operations by making him a representative to conduct their business at the other end of the trade. Robert's first assignment was to travel to the island of St. Christopher, located in the northern part of the Leeward Islands in the eastern Caribbean, to establish a business there. He sold the fish and lumber from his brothers and purchased West Indies goods to send back to them. During this time of trade, Anne married John Shipway, a merchant residing in Strawberry Bank, who played an important role in the Cutts' business venture.

Robert married a young woman while living on St. Christopher, but she died within a short time. Not wanting to remain on the island, he moved to Barbados, where he continued to serve as a merchant and representative for his brothers. With their business flourishing, Robert returned to Portsmouth, New Hampshire, where he remained in the family business for a period of time. After a while, Robert, who was always looking for new business opportunities, created a shipbuilding business in Kittery, Maine, across the river from Portsmouth. He built a large number of ships in his yard and continued to increase his wealth. With friends of influence in high places, he later became a justice of the peace. Robert married for a second time to Mary Hoel, the daughter of a clergyman, and they had a son whom they named Richard. Robert died at the end of June 1674, leaving his wealthy estate to his wife and son.

Robert's son, Richard, continued to live in Kittery where he eventually married and fathered 13 children. Richard became a man of great respect in the area. He had gained from his mother a large estate on nearby Cutts Island. With that and other resources, he continued to grow in wealth and later served seven terms as a selectman. He died in or around 1735, leaving his legacy of public service to his son, Richard.

Richard Cutt, Jr., who had been born on April 5, 1693, was an intelligent young man, held in high regard in the province. He married Eunice Curtis on October 20, 1720. Around the time of his father's death, Richard decided to add the letter *s* back onto the end of the family name to make it Cutts. In 1745, the War of Austrian Secession began in Europe, with France and England once again bitter enemies. The conflict quickly spread to the New World with the French capture of Cape Breton, Nova Scotia, by forces from their fortress at Louisbourg. Immediately, the British rose to meet the threat. To protect themselves and their valuable empire in North America, the governor of New York developed a grand plan for the capture of Louisbourg. He commissioned William Pepperell, a merchant, to lead a force of colonials to execute the plan. Richard Cutts, with the rank of major, joined William Pepperell's regiment. The siege of Louisbourg began on May 5, 1745, and ended with the French surrender to the British on June 17.[2] After serving in the militia, Richard returned to Kittery, where he continued as a respected member of the community. He served in a variety of elected positions including the legislature of Massachusetts.

Richard and Eunice Cutts had a son named Thomas whose early years were spent as a clerk in Kittery. At the age of 22, Thomas traveled to Saco, Maine, where he learned the trade of a merchant. Because of his persistence and an uncommon aptitude for business, he quickly grew wealthy. He became a shipbuilder as well as a leading merchant in the area and until the time of the American Revolution, traded extensively with the British. In 1776, with the outbreak of the Revolution, Thomas joined the Continental Army where he achieved the rank of colonel in the 3rd New York Regiment.[3] Thomas and Elizabeth Scammon Cutts married before the Revolution and had eight children, including a son named Richard who was born on July 28, 1771, on Cutts Island, Saco, Maine.

Richard Cutts, a brilliant child, was born into a family of prominence and wealth. He was graduated from Harvard Law School in 1790 then quickly followed his dreams of commerce and navigation. He traveled to Europe and eventually built a successful shipping business, which provided him with the means to participate in the government. Service to the country by this time had become a great family tradition. Richard became one of the family's youngest to enter politics. In 1801, at the age of 29, he was elected to the House of Representatives of the United States. He came to Washington greatly admired and soon built strong relationships with his associates in the Congress. With the wealth provided by his ships, he built a beautiful home in Washington opposite the northeast corner of Lafayette Park.[4] He proudly continued the family heritage of public service in Congress under the Jefferson administration. It wasn't long after his arrival in Washington that he befriended Secretary of State James Madison. They developed a friendship, which was most enduring. Madison's wife, Dolly, an attractive and lively woman from Virginia and Pennsylvania, took a liking to Richard. As the matchmaker, she was instrumental in bringing Richard together with her favorite younger sister, Anna Payne. Anna came from a long line of patriotic Americans including the Washington and the Jefferson families.

Just before their wedding both Richard and Anna had their portraits painted by the famous artist Gilbert Stuart. Anna Payne's portrait was interesting because of the story behind its creation. During the course of the painting, she and Stuart became entangled in a discussion surrounding the most expressive part of the human face. Stuart indicated it was the nose, while Anna insisted it was the eyes and mouth. The following day Stuart arrived early and, as a joke, reshaped the curtain in the background of Anna's picture to resemble an exaggerated replica of his nose. Delighted by the prank played on her by the famous artist, Anna would not let him paint over it.[5]

Richard and Anna married in 1804 and were well positioned in Washington society. They attended virtually all of the social events at the executive mansion and were an integral part of the government. When not in Washington, they traveled to Montpelier, the Virginia home of James and Dolly Madison. Richard served his country through six terms in Congress. In 1812, he stood with the great leaders of the country, sacrificed his personal wealth, and voted for war with England. With the outset of the War of 1812, Richard risked and eventually lost his fortune. In June 1813, President Madison appointed him superintendent general of military supplies. Pres. James Monroe later appointed him to the position of second comptroller of the treasury, which he held until 1829. He never regained the wealth he once had had in shipping; nevertheless, he contributed greatly to his country and his family. The beloved Dolly Madison spent the latter days of her life in the house built by Richard across from Lafayette Park. Richard and Anna had four sons and two daughters. The first child, a son named James Madison Cutts, in honor of the president, quickly became the president's special joy. He gave James a uniform and a navy commission as a midshipman, which he held until 1821.[6]

James grew up, as his father had done, in the presence of presidents and many of the day's most noted and powerful leaders. Educated in Washington he was considered quite a catch for the local society beauties except for his lack of wealth. He eventually secured employment in the Treasury Department as a clerk. A well-disciplined young man, he quickly earned the respect of all who knew him. In the early 1830s with the encouragement of Dolly Madison he began courting the beautiful Ellen O'Neale who lived in Washington with her aunt.

Ellen was the second daughter born to Thomas O'Neale, a prominent Irish Roman Catholic landowner in Maryland. Her family heritage included her uncle, Bishop O'Neale, and connections with the Lees, the Randolphs, and the Calverts, all prominent families of the New Republic. Not a wealthy family, the O'Neales lived on a small plantation in Rockford, Maryland. When her parents died Ellen and her older sister, Rose, were taken in by their aunt, Mary Miller, who operated the Congressional Boarding House in the Old Capitol Building located at First and "A" Street in Washington, D.C. The Old Capitol Building had been built to house Congress after the British destroyed the Capitol during their raid in 1812. Some time after the Capitol had been rebuilt, it became known as the Old Capitol Building, which was turned into a boarding house.[7] At night the most powerful men in the government, including John C. Calhoun, Henry Clay, Daniel Webster, Martin Van Buren, and John Tyler, surrounded the two young women. For the most part, the residents at the boarding house were from the South. They spent hours in the parlor discussing the business of government, states' rights, and the question of slavery. Ellen, too young to spend much time in such talk, watched her sister actively participate and develop a true love for the Southern way of thinking.

The men found the young women a delight—particularly Rose, who soon became the object of many of the younger men's dreams. Rose had many suitors including congressmen and other government officials. Although Rose attended a great many social functions, without wealth and family connections she had difficulty being accepted by Washington society. The development of Rose and Ellen O'Neale became strikingly different. Maybe it was because Rose had a greater awareness of the unfortunate death of her father, killed by a slave, maybe she believed the words of the firebrand Southerners at the boarding house, or maybe it was a combination of many things. For whatever reason, Rose developed an undying loyalty to the South and became a determined supporter of the Southern cause.[8]

Ellen, being less political, grew up oblivious to the cyclone that swirled around her. She attended school in Georgetown where she developed into an intelligent and stunning beauty. She longed to do what most young women dream of doing in their youth. With the help of the crafty matchmaker, Dolly Madison, James and Ellen soon fell in love.

In 1833, James married Ellen Elizabeth O'Neale, in Washington. The couple spent their honeymoon at Montpelier where they received the blessings of James Madison. They remained there for some time before returning to Washington.[9] They were considered a beautiful pair, with Ellen being considered one of the prettiest women in the capital.

On December 27, 1835, Rose Adele Cutts was born to the couple in the house of her grandfather. Bright and beautiful, she, too, grew to become quite familiar with the social scene in Washington. She was known as Adele to those outside of the family; while those close to her referred to her as Addie.

Two years after the birth of Adele, Madison was born in Georgetown. He was a fine young lad who promptly won the hearts of his parents, his big sister, and the grand dame of Washington, his great-aunt, Dolly Madison. If Adele was called Addie, then it was logical to refer to Madison as Maddie.

The two children were extremely intelligent and, through the strength and disposition of their father, encouraged to develop themselves to the fullest measure. In her youth, Adele attended parties at the executive mansion with the granddaughter of Pres. John Tyler. She enrolled at the academies in Georgetown where she found great enjoyment in all of her classes, particularly French.

His parents enrolled Madison in the Emerson Institute, which, under the firm leadership of Principal Charles Young, initiated his formal education.[10]

Madison was the favorite of his great-aunt Dolly, who lovingly referred to him as "my little Madison."[11] In her later years, she enjoyed having him near her and delighted in his youth. Dolly, regarded as the social center of Washington, regularly received the most important people of the time, including every newly elected president of the United States. She often had the likes of congressmen, senators, and other great and powerful men of the day at her receptions. At these receptions she would have young Madison standing by her chair, helping her greet the guests. He became so well acquainted with the famous Henry Clay that he often referred to the tough old man as "Cousin Henry."

Madison grew to love and trust his great-aunt intensely. Several times during her later years at her birthday parties, and at the prodding of his cousin Anna, he would ask, "Auntie, how old are you?" She replied by giving the same age every year. As a result, for years Madison believed that she had the ability to remain at the same age forever.[12]

Sometimes the energy level of the youth proved too much for Dolly. When in the late afternoon she needed to rest, she would send Madison out to Lafayette Park, telling him to keep an eye on the statue of Thomas Jefferson, which was then standing on the executive mansion lawn. She told him, "To keep an eye on the statue and to come home when Mr. Jefferson hears the dinner bell ring and goes in to eat." The young boy, with undying devotion to his aunt, would sit for hours watching the statue. He finally matched his aunt's wit when he reasoned that inasmuch as the statue can't hear, it never hears the bell ring, he logically deduced; so, he realized it never goes to dinner![13]

During these wonderful days Madison thrived in the environment of history, love, and kindness of the notable people who surrounded him. He greatly admired his aunt, crediting her wisdom, strength, and grace as the most influencing factors of his youth. She taught him of the nation's Founding Fathers, all of whom she knew in person, which developed in him a respect for honor and instilled in him a devotion to duty. He learned about the history of the United States from one who had lived it. Several times during his youth the family traveled to Charlestown, Virginia, where he played with his cousin Charles Washington, a nephew of Pres. George Washington. He felt the honor, even at his young age, in holding the gold medal presented to General Washington by a grateful Congress. He felt the same when he visited his cousin, William Washington, at Fredericksburg, Virginia, and held the general's sword. These made lasting impressions on him while it strengthened his commitment to maintain the honor of the family.[14]

Dolly often spoke of the glorious days when the Republic was born with Madison by her side. She had the ability to captivate the young man, and he listened and absorbed all that she said. He cherished his time with Dolly and carried her wisdom, character, and sense of historical presence within him all of his life.

In the last years of her life, Madison realized his beloved aunt was poor and destitute. He often brought small amounts of money to her from his father. He delighted the day he was sent to her by his father as an advance courier from the Senate chambers to tell her Congress had voted to purchase the remaining Madison papers from her for $20,000.

His father was not a wealthy man, holding only a clerk's position in the treasury. He was, however, a man of pride, great personal strength, and dignity. He brought up his children to appreciate the beauty of life and the value of integrity and honor. They were taught the lessons needed to take their place in Washington society and encouraged to always maintain their family's honor. As the children were growing, the family frequently had noted guests in their home, including Henry Wadsworth Longfellow, John Quincy Adams, and Charles Dickens. Many of the guests remarked about the striking beauty of Ellen O'Neale Cutts, Madison's mother. As Adele and Madison met these great people, they developed a keen sense of self-confidence in the presence of famous and powerful people.

In 1845, Madison and his family mourned the loss of his grandfather, Richard Cutts. Although Madison didn't know it at the time, he could have taken great comfort in the words regarding his grandfather written after his death by the Honorable John Quincy Adams:

> *The memory of the Hon. Richard Cutts of Washington, D.C., deserves from his friends and countrymen a more detailed notice of his career of life than a mere notice of the day and hour of his decease. He has been for many years distinguished by the confidence of his country in many stations of honor and trust, legislative and executive, and has faithfully performed all their duties....He gave a firm, efficient and undeviating support to that [Jefferson] administration and to that of his successor, Mr. Madison, until the close of his first term, on the 3d of March 1813, having patriotically sustained by votes, non-importation, non-intercourse, the embargo, and finally war, as measures called for by the honor and interest of the nation, although ruinous to his private fortune...as thus it did, reduce him to poverty.*[15]

A few years after the death of Richard, Madison's father progressed in responsibility to the level of senior clerk in the U.S. Treasury, where he was greatly respected for his abilities. During his father's years in the treasury, he frequently came into contact with and befriended many of the nation's great leaders, including a number of brilliant military officers. Being quite intelligent, he understood both the events of history and the bureaucratic nature of Washington. His associations with the military provided insight and understanding of the war with Mexico. Madison certainly watched his father with admiration as he wrote the book *The Conquest of California and New Mexico by the Forces of the United States in the Years 1846–1847.*[16]

Two years later, in 1849, Dolly Madison passed away, thus ending Madison's cherished relationship with her and closing an era of Washington history. Young Madison had been left with a sense of devotion to and an understanding of the role people could play in the life of a country.

Later in his youth, following attendance at the Emerson Institute, Madison enrolled at Georgetown, where he stayed until he was 18.[17] Madison had grown into quite a striking young man. He stood 5' 10", with brown hair and brown eyes and overflowed with self-confidence. Disciplined, intelligent, quick-minded, fair-tempered, likable, and mature for his age, Madison was the kind of person whom people, especially the ladies, wanted to be around.

In 1852, Madison went from Georgetown to Providence, Rhode Island, to attend Brown University. While in college he studied the liberal arts, joined the boxing team, and became an accomplished horsemen. He was a brilliant student, delighting in his studies. It was here that he was first introduced to Cervantes' *The Adventures of Don Quixote.* The hero of La Mancha became Madison's favorite, and he held sacred the honor and chivalry of old. Madison believed that virtue was a powerful shield against all injustice in the world. As he developed, this would be his guiding light and code of honor. In his sophomore year at Brown he became a brother in the prestigious Brunonian Chapter of Alpha Delta Phi Fraternity. Alpha Delta Phi was founded in 1836 on the principles of academic excellence. During the first five years of its existence at Brown University, its members epitomized dedication to learning; of the first 30 members of the fraternity only four didn't achieve election into the honored Phi Beta Kappa Society. To be a member of Alpha Delta Phi during that period was to be recognized as one of the top students in the school. In 1841, the fraternity elected to deactivate rather than submit to lowering its standards to compete with the newer fraternities on campus. It remained inactive until a group of students with the same high standards as those in the original chapter elected once again to achieve affiliation with the national fraternity. By 1851, the Brunonian Chapter of Alpha Delta Phi was again alive at Brown, with goals and objectives nearly identical to those of the chapter at the time it was founded.

Madison's intelligence and command of arts and letters made his membership into the Brunonian Chapter imminent. Joining the fraternity at the first opportunity, he upheld its mysteries, its brotherhood, and its tradition. Proud to be an "Alpha Delt," he would, often, in his mind return to Providence, the Brown campus, and the fraternity.

While Madison was involved in his studies, Adele became the leading light of Washington society. Whatever her family lacked in wealth, Addie made up for in her beauty and charm. She became acquainted with virtually all the prominent men in Washington and most of the wealthy younger men. Once Adele, when believing she had found a proper suitor who was too afraid to ask for her hand, cleverly dressed as a common maid for a masquerade ball and asked her beau, from behind a mask, if he could use a housemaid. He replied, "No, I already have a woman in mind for that!" Adele dropped the mask and announced, "That is the end of that!" and the relationship was ended.[18] It was not long afterward that Adele would be won over by someone whose abilities matched her own. In the summer of 1856 she became acquainted with Sen. Stephen A. Douglas and, to the surprise of all of Washington, Adele agreed to marry him.

Douglas, born in Vermont in 1813, had become a prominent lawyer in Illinois. He was elected to the House of Representatives in 1843 and then to the Senate in 1847. Douglas had married his first wife, Martha Denny Martin from Mississippi that same year. They remained happily married until Martha died from the complications of childbirth several years later. He truly was one of the most respected orators and most powerful men in Washington. But now the ladies of prominence began to question his marrying such a young woman, even though it was the beautiful Adele. The wife of Jefferson Davis was the most spiteful saying, "The dirty speculator and party trickster, broken in health by drink, with his first wife's money, buys an elegant, well-bred woman because she is poor and her father is proud."[19] Madison, on the other hand, was thrilled the day in 1856 when he was told that his sister would become the wife of the senator from Illinois. He had long admired the great Douglas and, even though his sister was less than half the age of the senator, he was excited at the thought of their marriage.

On November 20, 1856, Thanksgiving Day, at the age of 20, the beautiful Adele married the 42-year-old senator at her father's house in Washington, D.C. Their marriage ended one of the most absorbing discussions of society in Washington. After her marriage, Adele quickly took charge of Douglas's sons, Stephen A. Douglas, III, and Robert M. Douglas. The boys took to her and soon accepted her as their mother.

During their youth, Adele and Madison watched their Aunt Rose O'Neale achieve great prominence within Washington. She was most admired by the men who came into her presence. Anyone of importance knew her, and her beauty and charm captured the hearts of many. Often she was asked to give her hand in marriage, but to no avail. It would require a special person to capture the heart of the intelligent and determined Rose O'Neale. It also would require a person of status and means.

In 1850, Rose O'Neale finally found a man that could provide her with the life she so desired and married the wealthy Robert Greenhow. Robert, a lawyer, from a prominent Richmond family, was working as a translator and librarian in the State Department at the time of their marriage.[20] They remained in Washington for a short time and then traveled to San

Francisco, where Robert started a law office. He purchased land on speculation near the city's marina district and became quite prominent. It was a time of great opportunity, and Robert and Rose had the money and the ability to make the most of it. Unfortunately, Robert met an untimely death when a walking bridge gave way beneath him in early 1854.[21] After her affairs were put in order in California, Rose returned to the city she loved, Washington, to pursue other interests. She was well off, and had the ability to develop her interests in politics. Rose established a group of political friends and associates within the government who came to her for advice and political favors. She created one of the most powerful organizations yet to be seen in the capital where she mediated disputes, recommended people for office, and exerted influence on policy makers.

Rose O'Neale Greenhow became an accomplished lobbyist in Washington and—because of the nature of her work—a bit of a scandal. She amassed a tremendous amount of power through her access to important people by manipulating information obtained through her "girls." Rose had a number of beautiful women working for her performing dubious functions relating to the care and comfort of her guests. She entertained most of the politicians and bureaucrats of the day, and it was not uncommon, in the late hours of the evening, to see Pres. James Buchanan's carriage in front of her residence. Rose had become one of the most powerful women, if not persons, in the city. She held great influence in the government of the United States from the president on down.

In 1857, President Buchanan appointed Madison's father to the position of second comptroller of the treasury, a move that for a short time was surrounded by controversy. Some thought that the appointment came as a result of the influence of Senator Douglas, but in reality he had nothing to do with it. Madison's father had been widely respected for his abilities and was well qualified for the position, but because he was Douglas's father-in-law, political bickering developed out of the matter. Soon after the appointment the president published a letter stating that Douglas had nothing to do with the appointment, thus the fury was gone. Most likely, the appointment came at the insistence of Rose, whispering in the ear of the president for the benefit of her sister and brother-in-law.

The entire Cutts family, including Senator Douglas, attended Madison's graduation from Brown University in the spring of 1857. He earned a master of arts degree, and upholding the great tradition of Alpha Delta Phi, was inducted into Phi Beta Kappa. He was also given the honor to deliver the commencement oration, which became a defining moment for him. In his speech, *The Responsibilities of the American Citizen*, he presented to the world his philosophy of life. He referred to three key elements that the American citizen must possess: self-denial, integrity, and patriotism. He related to the audience the stories of self-sacrifice by George Washington and the other Founding Fathers in the early days of the Republic and how their efforts led to the birth of the nation. Second, he spoke of the need for integrity and how it gives dignity to men and to nations. And lastly, he spoke of the individual citizen's patriotic duty to go beyond regional interests and embrace the welfare of the country. He used the principles from this speech as the basis for his actions the rest of his life.

Madison left Brown University as other young men, honorably molded by the hands of that noble institution. After graduation Madison, following his grandfather and other members of the Cutts family, entered Harvard Law School. There he served under the tutelage of Professors Joel Parker, Emory Washburne and Theophilus Parsons, relishing in their guidance.[22] He spent his time at Harvard much to himself. He focused his activities on studying the law and "established a reputation for application and ability."[23]

Adele elected to take a role in her husband's reelection campaign of 1858. This probably was the first time a candidate's wife actively participated in her husband's election campaign. She had the opportunity to meet Douglas's challenger, Abraham Lincoln, at the start of the campaign and came to know him well while they were together during the famous debates. Their meetings were always cordial and warm, with Lincoln treating Adele with kindness and respect. Adele thought Lincoln to be quite intelligent and charming, and she enjoyed his homespun comments and manners. Senator Douglas was sent back to Washington in the fall and there began to strengthen his support for an 1860 run at the presidency of the United States.

During Madison's time away, the Catholic community in Washington completed the construction of a new Roman Catholic Church located at 19 "I" Street NW, which they named for St. Aloysius. Above the altar Constantine Brumidi painted the first communion of St. Aloysius for which Adele had posed as the saint's mother. President Buchanan, Senator Douglas, Rose O'Neale Greenhow, and the entire Cutts family attended the dedication ceremony for the church, which took place in October 1859.[24] Everyone in the family and the congregation looked upon the grand painting with pride and reverence.

In the spring of 1860, Madison couldn't help following the political events of the presidential election. It all began with the Democratic nominating convention in Charleston, South Carolina, in April of that year. The slave-state representatives presented a motion that slavery should be allowed in all new territories as accorded by the Constitution. This caused a great deal of concern, because support for the measure was impossible for the free-state Democrats; but its failure meant the destruction of the alliance between the Northern and Southern Democrats. With the failure of the motion, representatives from Alabama, South Carolina, Mississippi, Louisiana, Florida, Arkansas, and Texas left the convention. The remaining delegates adjourned to meet later in Baltimore.

Seeing the demise of the power base of the Democratic Party and fearing a Republican victory in the election, a group of influential citizens from both the Democratic and Republican parties met to nominate a compromise ticket that could be supported by voters in both the North and South. They nominated John Bell from Tennessee for president and Edward Everett of Massachusetts for vice president. It also was hoped that these two would play a major role, as compromise candidates, should the election be thrown into the House of Representatives.

On May 16, the Republican convention was held at the Wig Wam in Chicago. There the relatively unknown Abraham Lincoln received the party nomination. The Democratic Party met in June and faced a crisis again when the delegates from Virginia walked out, along with other slave state and some free-state representatives, over the admittance of new delegates from Alabama and Louisiana. The majority of the Democrats stayed and nominated Stephen A. Douglas for president and Herschel V. Johnson for vice president.

The fracture of the Democratic Party continued with the nomination of yet another group of candidates from the dissenting Democrats who had walked out of the convention in Baltimore. They gathered shortly thereafter and nominated John C. Breckinridge from Kentucky for president and Gen. Joseph Lane from Oregon for vice president. With their nomination and the primary doctrine of their party, slavery or disunion, the strength of the Democratic Party evaporated and with it the chances for Douglas's election. Still, Douglas would not give up. The only chance for him to get elected was to pull together all the moderate members of the different factions of the Democratic Party. If the vote split among the Democrats, Lincoln would surely win; and with a Lincoln victory the disunion of the United States would become a greater possibility.

In the summer of 1860, Madison graduated from Harvard and was again elected to the position of honor of giving the class oration. Presidential candidate Stephen Douglas used his brother-in-law's graduation commencement as an excuse to return to New England and start his presidential campaign.[25] With the whole family present, Madison delivered a speech titled "The Profession of the Law as an Element of Civil Society," and with its conclusion so ended his formal education.

Shortly after Madison's graduation, Douglas invited the young lawyer to serve as his personal secretary for the upcoming presidential election, an opportunity Madison readily accepted. He not only admired his brother-in-law as a great patriot and politician but also had come to love him. Although they were different in age and upbringing, both had an unrelenting love of country and of the law. In addition, their common love for Adele held the two together as relatives, professionals, and brothers. The chance to serve Douglas in his greatest hour was a privilege for Madison, and he took to it with enthusiasm. Over the years, through close contact with the noted politician, Madison had learned a great deal about politics. Stephen Douglas, the master, delighted in sharing all he knew. Madison, not yet 22 years old, had become the personal secretary of one of the most popular men for the presidency of the United States.

Douglas, Adele, and Madison worked hard during the summer. Concluding it was not enough, in the fall Douglas decided to travel through the South to gather support from the clearer-thinking Southern voters. His party, comprising of Adele, Madison, and several others, began its journey from Centralia, Illinois, and traveled down the Mississippi River to Memphis. From there they moved on to Huntsville, Alabama; Nashville and Chattanooga, Tennessee; and Kingston, Atlanta, Macon, and Columbus, Georgia. On November 2 they arrived in Montgomery where Douglas made a speech to a hostile crowd who began throwing eggs, one of which struck Adele. Madison found it difficult to hold himself back in such situations but did the best he could to protect his sister and the presidential candidate. Unfortunately, the day did not improve. While members of the party were at the dock preparing to sail to Selma, the deck of the steamer on which they were standing collapsed under the load of a large number of well-wishers, sending Adele and others crashing to the deck below. Although Adele was not seriously hurt in the accident, she required several days to recover. Douglas continued the campaign trek while Madison remained in Montgomery with her. On November 5, Madison telegraphed Senator Douglas to let him know that he and Adele would soon be leaving Montgomery and would meet him in New Orleans. The entire party reunited in New Orleans just in time for the election. In a matter of hours after the votes were tabulated, the telegraphs began to sing with the results of Lincoln's victory. The weary campaigners stayed in New Orleans for a time to rest from their strenuous ordeal.

Later, while traveling en route to Springfield, Madison confided to Douglas that he thought he would settle in St. Louis to see whether he could start his legal profession there. His brother-in-law was saddened that they had not won the presidency, because that would have allowed him to keep Madison by his side; but at least he could do something to get him off to a good start. So Douglas wrote a letter of recommendation to his friend in St. Louis, the banker James H. Lucas:

Memphis, Tenn.
Nov. 26, 1860
My Dear Sir,
Permit me to introduce to you my friend and brother-in-law
J. Madison Cutts, Esq. who is about to take up his residence
in your city. You will find him a young man of education,
talent and integrity. I commend him to you as worthy of your
entire confidence, and shall feel grateful for any courtesy and
services you may render him. Very Truly Your Friend
S. A. Douglas[26]

Almost immediately following the election, the Southern states began the process of carrying out their threat to break up the Union. It was a time of triumph and anger, of hope and fear. Madison was not disillusioned from the experience. After bidding his sister and brother-in-law good-by, he stepped off the steamer at St. Louis to start his career in law.

Chapter II

A Call to Arms

When Madison arrived in St. Louis, his prospects were as fresh and bright as an early morning sunrise, and the opportunities appeared to be endless in the busy frontier city. He carried with him the recommendations of the great Senator Douglas. It was a time of excitement, and he was ready to establish himself as a lawyer. Madison called on James Lucas, and presented his letter of introduction. After a few days of inquiry, Lucas had established contact with Basil Duke, Esq., attorney at law, and shortly thereafter brought the two men together. Duke had been practicing law in St. Louis for 12 years and had developed quite a respectable practice. In 1858 his younger cousin, Basil Wilson Duke, joined him. Since the younger Duke's ambitions were more focused on politics than the law, it was a good decision to welcome Madison to the firm. Thus, Madison's legal career began on Chestnut Street in the Kennett's Building, in St. Louis.[1] Almost immediately, he befriended the younger Duke.

Duke presented quite a contrast with Madison, who had spent most of his life in the East. Basil, a young aristocratic lawyer from Kentucky who had recently graduated from Transylvania College in Lexington, looked forward to starting his law career so he could marry the lovely Miss Henrietta Morgan and start a life with his intended bride. Both men were of moderate size, with Basil slightly taller and thinner. Equals in intelligence and discipline they both had been reared in the highest social circles of their respective areas. They both were regarded as fine upstanding gentlemen of the most honorable intentions, and both were natural leaders. As lawyers they not only shared each other's ideas about cases but also confided in each other regarding the great debates of slavery and secession. In the fall of 1860, the presidential election had captured the attention of the nation. The Lincoln-Douglas debates several years before had set the stage for the questions of states' rights and slavery that had been confronted in the recent election.

Madison's views were strongly Unionist. He felt the South should continue to compromise if necessary to keep the Union together. Basil, actually, favored Breckinridge, but knew the compromise that Stephen Douglas offered as a candidate was the only way the South could keep the country from electing the extreme Abraham Lincoln. Therefore, Basil openly supported Stephen Douglas for president.

With the election of Lincoln and the talk of secession, both of their plans began to take a new course. With the news from the South of "secession if Lincoln takes the oath of office," and some states not intending to wait even that long, war became imminent. Madison regretted Douglas's loss and knew that his friend, mentor, and brother-in-law was probably the only man in the country who could have saved the Union. Even though Douglas showed great insight and courage in making the campaign tour, the question had been immediately answered when the ballots were cast. But Madison resolved to support the new president and to uphold the Union with all his heart.

Now, with states seceding from the Union and other Southern states vowing to do the same, the talk of war was in the air. In January, Madison elected to join a drill squad in St. Louis known as the "Wide Awakes," a group of about eight hundred strong Union sympathizers. This organization had been established by Capt. Nathaniel Lyon of the United States Army to counter the pro-secessionist movement that was widespread in Missouri west of St. Louis. The Wide Awakes practiced military drill in the evenings under the guidance of regular army officers and were provided weapons from the army arsenal. The troops in the drill squad received a heavy dose of drill and military instruction. The drill came easily for Madison. His father had stressed discipline and order since his early childhood. Madison's father had worked his entire life in the treasury and, like a fine-tuned watch, built his life around regimen, attention to detail, and discipline. He often encouraged Madison to conduct himself in the same honorable manner. Madison took pride in his patriotic heritage and his blood relationship to George Washington. Of course he also was proud of James Madison, whose name he bore, and of the many great things he had done for the country. As time passed, it became more evident that the tide of events was pushing the country to the brink of war. Many of the young college students were communicating with each other and vowed to join the army in the event of war. During the months following Lincoln's inauguration, Madison made contact with his friends and brothers who had graduated from Brown University. They agreed that if it came to war, they all would volunteer together to serve the Union.

In February, Basil Duke and several other Southern sympathizers started their own drill team, called the "Minutemen," and it quickly grew to about four hundred men. Since they had no weapons, the men elected Basil to go quietly to Montgomery to appeal to the Confederate government for weapons and support. On April 6, Basil began his clandestine trip to Alabama. Successful in securing the weapons, he traveled back to St. Louis where he narrowly escaped being hung as a spy by Southern sympathizers. Basil elected not to go into the city but to return to Kentucky.

Lincoln had played a waiting game with the Southern radicals by not going out of his way to cause a showdown. He did, however, indicate he would maintain all Federal installations along the coast of the United States. If the South attempted to take control of the Federal installations in the Southern states, Lincoln would be forced to take action against them. Not wanting to make the first move, Lincoln ordered the forts to be supplied with whatever they required and waited for the Confederate response. It wasn't long in coming. The firing on Fort Sumter in South Carolina and its subsequent fall forced Lincoln to act. He took immediate action and called for 75,000 volunteers. As the first shots were fired on Fort Sumter, Madison began to execute his plan to meet his college associates in Rhode Island. He immediately sent a telegram to his friends, telling them to do whatever they could to sign him up with the 1st Rhode Island Volunteers. As he made his plans, word was sent saying that many from Brown University had enlisted and that he should attempt to join the regiment in Washington, because they were scheduled to move there before the regiment was formed.

With the fall of Fort Sumter on April 13, 1861, the world was turned upside down. Madison found himself settling his affairs in St. Louis and making plans to return to Washington. He had known for some time what he would do if it came to war between the states, and he read intently the news of the actions that followed the fall of the fort. It was interesting and quite warming to hear that Senator Douglas paid a call on Lincoln on April 14 to confer and to provide unquestionable support for the president.

St. Louis was filled with concern because Confederate sympathizers had seized much of the state government. The Federal soldiers moved quickly to secure armories and stores of rifles and ammunition and to maintain stability until order could be established.

Madison promptly began to gather his belongings and to schedule the closing of his legal practice. Before he had finished his legal obligations, he went to the U.S. Armory to say good-by to the officers of the drill team. Madison had become acquainted with Capt. John Schofield and had developed a friendship with Capt. Nathaniel Lyon. These two Federal officers were leading the Wide Awakes drill teams. With Captain Lyon's help, Madison had attacked Hardee's *Handbook* with all the energy of a Harvard law student taking an exam. He read the drill with a passion; and when he had questions about leadership or tactics, he went to Lyon for the answers. Captain Lyon, a United States Military Academy graduate, had experienced battle firsthand in Mexico. He gladly helped the intelligent and dedicated Cutts to absorb the strategy and tactics of battle. Madison liked Captain Lyon because they thought and acted in much the same way. Both were energetic, quick to make decisions and to take action, strong willed, and they were fanatics when it came to the preservation of the United States. When the time came to say good-by to Captain Lyon, the captain jokingly asked Madison, upon his departure, to put in a good word for him with President Lincoln and to ask the president to make him a general. Madison said he would if he saw him, and they parted as friends.

Leaving St. Louis put an end to Madison's plans to build his fortune and rise to the heights of his profession. Now, all that would have to be set aside until the secessionists were defeated. Anyone with a pounding heart could not help being caught up in the excitement of uniforms, great armies, and the glory of battle. As he left St. Louis, he was preoccupied with thoughts of fighting, honor, duty, and the incredible historical events that were about to unfold before him. He could not imagine the many roads he would travel before the conflict was finished, but he looked upon the times as his opportunity to play a role in the making of the United States as his ancestors had done.

From St. Louis he traveled east, stopping in Springfield, Illinois, at the home of his sister and Senator Douglas. Douglas, who for so long spoke of understanding and compromise, now threw all his support to the president and in doing so greatly added to the cause of the Union. He had returned to Illinois shortly after the fall of Fort Sumter to ensure that the state would remain in the Union. He called for all of his supporters to stand firm and to support the president at all costs.

On the evening of April 29, 1861, Madison joined the senator in his study to discuss his trip to Washington and enlistment into the army. Following their conversation, Douglas wrote a brief note to President Lincoln and asked Madison to deliver it in person to the president upon his arrival in the capital. When he had finished, the senator gave the note to Madison to read.

Springfield
April 29, 1861

My dear Sir

    This letter will be delivered by J. Madison Cutts Esq., the only brother of Mrs. Douglas, whom you may remember to have met some years ago in Chicago. He is a lawyer by profession, a man of talent & attainments, and in every respect worthy of your confidence. He goes to Washington to take a hand in the defense of the Capital and the Government. He will be able to give you any information you may desire in regard to the public sentiment and condition of things in this state, as well St. Louis, where he resides. I found the state of feeling here and in some parts of our State much less satisfactory than I could have desired or expected when I arrived. There will be no outbrake (sic,) however, and in a few days I hope for entire unanimity in the support of the government and the Union.

    I am very respectfully your servant.

                              S. A. Douglas

    His Excellency
        A. Lincoln [2]

This was Douglas's way of establishing a position for his brother-in-law in the army. Following their meeting, Madison boarded the train and continued his journey to Washington.

When he arrived at Washington, he found the city buzzing, as he had never seen it before. Flags were everywhere and everyone spoke of war. Men gathered on street corners, speaking of the prospects of battles and the inevitable demise of the secessionists. There existed a great and almost universal spirit in the people for the preservation of the Union, except for a few whom sided with the secessionists. They were quickly shouted down, and in some instances physically beaten by patriotic bystanders. As he hurried to his parents' house he could see soldiers at almost every corner. He looked for the 1st Rhode Island and learned that they were living in temporary quarters in the Patent Office. He planned to join them as soon as he saw his parents and delivered Senator Douglas's message to the president.

His father and mother were proud of their son. They were "War" Democrats and fully supported the Union, but were obviously concerned for their son being placed in harm's way. As a high-ranking member of the treasury, Madison's father knew what was required to establish a large fighting army. He knew that it would take men, time, money, and training and even that didn't insure victory. Madison, caught up in the passion of war, simply looked forward to his opportunity to serve his country.

The war presented a difficult problem for the entire family. Over the past generations, the Cutts family had spread its roots from the North to the South. Several family members had married people from Virginia and other parts of the South, which split the family as it had the nation. Madison's uncle, Richard D. Cutts, had joined the Union army as an officer and was assigned to the War Department. His Aunt Rose, however, maintained her strong support of the South.

After meeting with his parents, Madison walked to the executive mansion. Once there he saw a large number of people waiting for an audience with the president. He immediately recognized one of the men, John Hay, from his days at Brown. Madison and John had been friends at Brown, and they enjoyed college life together. Hay was two years behind Madison, graduating in 1858, and he had a reputation of being an ambitious and intelligent man. Madison knew of Hay as a potential member of Phi Beta Kappa, and they often met when the activities of the Alpha Deltas crossed paths with Theta Delta Chi, Hay's fraternity.[3] Following his graduation from college, Hay moved to Springfield, Illinois, where he became acquainted with Abraham Lincoln. When Lincoln required a secretary during his campaign for the presidency, he had hired John Hay.

It was Hay who directed Madison to President Lincoln's office. Madison, who reported to the president with dignity and respect, had met Lincoln once before in Chicago. In a business-like manner, he quickly handed Douglas's letter to the president and explained his mission.

After Lincoln read the note, Madison fulfilled his promise to Captain Lyon and suggested that the president make the captain a general. It was probably a moot point since many of the West Point graduates were quickly being recommended for higher rank. Feeling a sense of accomplishment, Madison had finished his work as a civilian.

His obligation to his friend and mentor completed, he moved to the Patent Office, where the 1st Rhode Island Regiment was stationed. On May 3, 1861, he finally joined the Rhode Island Volunteers. It was official when his name was penciled in on the already established roster of Company C. He was issued his uniform and immediately took his place in the column for drill.

On May 7, when Maj. Irvin McDowell returned to the unit, Madison was officially sworn in as a private, Company C, 1st Rhode Island Volunteers, under the command of Col. Ambrose E. Burnside. Within his company were several close friends from Brown. Alexander Taylor, '56, was there along with Francis Goddard, '55, and his brother Robert, '58, Moses Jenkins, '55, Charles Smith, '59, John Brown, '60, and James DeWolf, '61. They had been a close bunch in school, taking advantage of all of the social activities that their fraternities and the city of Providence could offer. On the other hand, it could be said that their academic standing and the membership of several of them in Phi Beta Kappa fraternity in some way balanced their bon vivant behavior. Other acquaintances were in the other companies, and they all felt reassured knowing that their friends were close by. The unit drilled almost constantly and after a few weeks began to look reasonably accomplished. Madison continued to review books on the tactics of war. He was quite confident in his abilities and knew that he would make a good soldier. John Hay found time to visit and was impressed with the manner in which the Brown alumni conducted themselves. Hay later wrote his sister about the men of the 1st Rhode Island Volunteers:

> *When men like these leave their horses, their women and their wine, harden their hands, eat crackers for dinner, wear a shirt for a week and never blacken their shoes—all for a principle— it is hard to set any bounds to the possibilities of such an army.*[4]

Within a short time after arriving in Washington, the regiment had established Camp Sprague at Gale's Woods, about a mile north of Washington, and settled in for instructions and drill.

In mid-May Adele sent a note to Colonel Burnside, requesting permission for Madison's immediate leave to attend to the ailing senator from Illinois. His commander issued Madison the pass, and the following day, accompanied by his mother and Stephen Douglas's personal physician, he left for Chicago. They arrived on May 20 to find the senator in a deteriorating condition.

Senator Douglas, at the suggestion of Adele and several of his friends, had taken up residence at the Tremont House in Chicago to rest and regain his strength following a speech. Unfortunately, his condition had worsened and doctors were unable to determine the cause. He passed in and out of consciousness as those closest to him looked on in silent dismay. Adele, knowing how close the senator and Madison were, knew that it would be important for them to be together. On May 31 it appeared that Douglas was recovering and out of danger, but this condition didn't last long. On June 2, Adele called for a priest. Bishop James Duggan responded, asking Douglas if he desired to be baptized. Douglas said no. The priest left the room but stayed close by at the request of Adele. Early on the morning of June 3, Senator Douglas woke, saying, "Death, death, death." It seemed his time was near. When Douglas's eyes opened and he spoke to Madison his voice of strength and confidence was gone. With great labor he requested that Madison take an oath to fight for the glory of both of them. Repeating after the dying man, Madison gladly pledged, "I, J. Madison Cutts, son of James Madison Cutts, nephew of President Madison, do most solemnly swear that I will support the constitution and laws of the land and maintain the interests of my family."[5]

Douglas soon fell asleep and woke only once again to mumble a message to his sons. It was impossible to completely understand what he had said, but Adele and Madison both knew that he spoke of honor and the Constitution, as he did with Madison earlier in the morning. Several hours later, he journeyed into the other world. The "Little Giant" was gone, but even on his deathbed he had proclaimed his support for the Union and Lincoln. More important, besides his children and wife, he left behind his legacy in Madison Cutts. From that time forward, Madison would fight for and forever strive to make glorious the name of Stephen A. Douglas.[6]

Madison remained in Chicago for the burial services, then returned to Washington to attend memorial services. He had the opportunity to once again meet briefly with President Lincoln, who paid his respects to his longtime friend and political adversary. The president spoke kindly of the senator and offered Adele his services should she ever need them. Adele thanked the president and reaffirmed her support for him and the Union. She was well aware that the president had lost a friend in her late husband.

The opportunity to fight seemed imminent in the days following the death of Senator Douglas. Madison rejoined his unit to learn from his commander, Capt. William Brown, that they soon would move on the Confederates.

As the Union army began to build in Washington and in the states throughout the North, a general strategy for war was being developed on both sides. Once Virginia seceded, the Confederates had moved quickly to seize Union armament depots throughout the South, including the strategic position of Harpers Ferry, Virginia. One of the first plans of the Union was to retake the depot at Harpers Ferry and to hold in check the Confederate army commanded by Gen. Joseph E. Johnston. With the Confederate forces there neutralized, the main Union army would march through Virginia to Richmond. Gen. Irvin McDowell had taken command of the Army of the Potomac and was under considerable pressure to attack.

In early June a large force that included the 1st Rhode Island Regiment, under the command of Maj. Gen. Robert Patterson, a veteran of the Mexican War, marched to Harpers Ferry to capture that city and to push Johnston and the Confederates into Virginia. The high-spirited Union force moved out to Harpers Ferry itching for a fight. It must have been strange, yet incredibly exciting, for Madison to be among his friends as they walked through the Maryland countryside en route to the enemy position. It was a grand march and a time of great anticipation. As they approached, the Confederate forces in Harpers Ferry began to withdraw, and by June 14 most of the Confederate forces had pulled back to Winchester, Virginia. General Patterson occupied the city until around June 19 when he returned to Washington. The whole affair was bloodless except for the blisters encountered from all of the marching. On one occasion, the army marched 35 miles in one day.[7] Unfortunately, this was a side of war that the new soldiers had not expected.

On June 23 and back in Washington, Madison received his commission as a captain in the newly formed 11th United States Infantry Regiment. It was a day of celebration in the Cutts family. He wished that he could tell his mentor, Senator Douglas, that he had been commissioned a captain but it was too late for that. He did, however, request, in honor of Douglas, that the state of Illinois be given credit for his commission.

Ironically, and unknown to Madison at the time, June was also the month that Basil Duke married his sweetheart, Henrietta Morgan, the sister of the Confederate Capt. John Morgan, and joined the Confederacy as a lieutenant. The two law partners from St. Louis were officers on different sides.

After a few days, Madison was ordered to report to Fort Independence in Boston Harbor for training. Not long after his arrival in Boston, he learned of the Union defeat and panic at Bull Run. Following his training and drill, he traveled to Providence, Rhode Island, where he supported recruiting efforts under the Volunteer Ready Service Act. After arriving in Providence, he obtained more information regarding the Battle of Bull Run. He was surprised by the loss and the confusion that followed the battle but learned that the Rhode Island boys had performed admirably during the fight.

On August 11 he learned more bad news, as reports came in from Missouri about the defeat of the Union army at Wilson's Creek the day before. His friend, Gen. Nathaniel Lyon, had been killed in the battle as he helped repel the rebel attacks at Bloody Ridge. With these two defeats, it became obvious that it was not going to be a simple matter to defeat the Confederacy. Later in August more bad news arrived: he received word that his Aunt Rose was being held under arrest at her home in Washington for spying. Although he had hoped it was a mistake, in his heart he knew that Aunt Rose's Southern sympathy was strong and that it was probably true. The family stood by her despite the fact of her undying support for the South.

In November 1861, Madison found himself the mustering and disbursement officer in Rhode Island. He embarked on this assignment as he would any other with discipline and determination, even though he really wanted to be with his friends fighting for the Union. He helped to organize the recruiting efforts for the state of Rhode Island and the 11th U.S. Infantry Regiment. Through his efforts Rhode Island would send many regiments of volunteers and quite a number of regulars to the support of the Union. At this same time, his sister had received word that if Stephen Douglas's two sons did not return immediately to their mother's home in Mississippi, the Confederacy was going to confiscate their property. Adele was lost and didn't know what to do. Finally, she wrote to the president for his advice. The confident Lincoln wrote back to Adele indicating the boys should stay with her, and the issue of ownership would not be a matter of question after the war was over.[8]

Madison longed to join the fight. He had missed the Battle of Bull Run in July and the skirmishes that followed. His only hope was to have someone help him get into a fighting unit. The only good news to come out of the war in 1861 consisted of the promotion of Colonel Burnside to the rank of general and his successful campaign into North Carolina.

In late August 1861, General Burnside began to execute a plan to attack the Cape Hatteras area of North Carolina in order to stop the Confederate blockade-runners and cut the supply lines running north to Virginia. He mounted an armada from Annapolis sailing for North Carolina, easily taking control of the Hatteras Inlet with the capture of Fort Clark and Fort Hatteras. These victories lead to a great deal of talk throughout the country, especially in Rhode Island, about the success of the general.

Gen. Ambrose E. Burnside, born in Indiana in 1824, was a member of the West Point Class of 1847. He served in the army during the Mexican War and later in the Indian Wars. He retired from the service in 1853 and entered private business. He had invented a new pistol and attempted, unsuccessfully, to sell it to the cavalry. Eventually the company he had worked for went out of business. He reentered the army as a volunteer at the request of Gov. William Sprague of Rhode Island immediately after Fort Sumter fell and took the first regiment from Rhode Island to Washington at the end of April 1861. He was viewed as an outstanding leader—decisive, commanding, and known as a good judge of character. Burnside was a fighting general and Madison wanted to be with him. Madison began to petition his friends and his father in Washington early in 1862 to see whether he could be reassigned to General Burnside's Department of North Carolina. His father spoke with General Burnside during one of the general's trips to Washington about the possibility of having his son on his staff, but it came to no immediate consequence. Initially, Burnside told Madison's father he had been informed that regulations forbade regular army officers from being assigned to the staffs of volunteer generals. Burnside indicated that he would gladly have Madison on his staff if this obstacle could be overcome.

With the suspension of the Volunteer Ready Service Act, Madison found himself reassigned to the staff of General Burnside, Commander of the Department of North Carolina, as aide-de-camp.

He returned to Washington on his way to his new assignment. During his stopover, he learned that his Aunt Rose had recently been sent, by order of the president, to Richmond and the Confederacy. She had spent months in the Capital Prison, which happened to be the former boarding house where she grew up, while the military and the president tried to figure out what to do with her. They knew that she had been spying and they knew she had led a large ring of Confederate sympathizers in Washington, but they found only small amounts of evidence to convict her of spying. The biggest problem for the administration was that she knew too much and had received much of her information from top government officials. Rose had connections with almost everyone of political and military importance in Washington. Even from her jail cell, Rose continued as an outspoken supporter of the South and an embarrassment to most of the politicians in the city. During this time, she broke off all communications with her sister and niece. Finally, after a hurried military trial, Rose was convicted of spying. In April, still refusing to talk to her sister, Rose was transferred to the Confederacy. On June 4, 1862, she arrived in Richmond, where she received recognition as the heroine of the Battle of Manassas Junction.[9]

Madison was ordered to report to the staff of General Burnside in North Carolina as soon as possible. During the spring of 1862, Burnside's army continued to make headway and after several battles had captured the key railroad center at New Bern. The general had succeeded in his plan. A bold move with a great deal of merit, it had seriously disrupted the railroad supply lines from the Deep South into Virginia. Although the plan was not without delays and faults, it was successful; and by the early part of April, the Union army commanded the heart of North Carolina. Madison Cutts had finally made it to the war.

Chapter III

Fighting with Burnside

In late April 1862, Madison traveled up the Neuse River to New Bern, North Carolina, where the church bells welcomed the arrival of his vessel. He reported to General Burnside for staff duty. Initially, he was assigned to the position of aide-de-camp; but after learning of his training as a lawyer, General Burnside made him his judge advocate. Madison quickly approached his new position and eagerly set to work.

General Burnside commanded the Army of North Carolina, which consisted of three brigades commanded by Brig. Gen. John G. Foster, Brig. Gen. John G. Parke, and Maj. Gen. Jesse Lee Reno. General Foster was a veteran of the Mexican War and—just before the outbreak of hostilities—an assistant professor of engineering at West Point. General Reno had been graduated from West Point in 1846 and also served in the Mexican War, where he had distinguished himself as an outstanding ordinance officer. Shortly before Madison's arrival, General Parke's brigade had accepted the surrender of Fort Macon, several miles southeast at Beaufort, North Carolina. With the capture of Fort Macon and New Bern, the action in North Carolina had been completed except for expeditions into the interior.

The expedition to North Carolina of some 15,000 troops in what some had called a folly had been a great success. General Burnside's troops never lost an engagement and with the captured Fort Macon on April 25, 1862, the Union army began its occupation of northeastern North Carolina.

After putting in several long days of legal work in early May, Madison and Capt. Duncan Pell, who was an original member of Company A, 1st Rhode Island Volunteer Regiment, made the rounds to check on the units in the field. On May 18 the two of them, under a white flag of truce, commanded a company of cavalry taking Confederate prisoners to be exchanged and some young women wanting to cross the lines.[1] Madison had his first chance to be near the front, but the exhange proved un-eventful and the detachment returned to New Bern.[2]

In June, Madison completed his work in preparation for a military commission to hear the cases of pending courts-martial. During the month, he brought before the commission of New Bern, the courts-martials of 11 men.[3]

Madison took advantage of the lull in the command activities to get to know his commander better. They talked at great length about battle tactics, and Burnside became impressed with Madison's ability to quickly grasp military strategy and tactics. He also spoke with the other generals and listened attentively when they discussed military matters. From Reno and Burnside, Madison borrowed many military academy textbooks and read through them with a passion. By the end of June, he had clearly added to his already vast knowledge of military strategy, and he showed signs of being a talented officer. However, everyone knew it was one thing to be versed in the art of war but something entirely different to apply it in front of the enemy or in battle. Still, Burnside developed a liking for the enthusiastic and determined captain. They admired and trusted each other's judgment.

Madison's obvious self-confidence and ease with all of the generals caused concern for all the other junior members of the staff. Unknow-ingly, Madison had started a competition among the small group, and he became the object of jealousy.

During this same time, Aunt Rose passed through North Carolina on her grand tour of the South. Acclaimed in Richmond as a heroine for her service to the South and the victory at the Battle of Manassas, she had been officially received by Pres. Jefferson Davis. Rose was assigned the task of inspecting the troops throughout the South. When her assign-ment was completed, she was sent to England to raise money for the cause.

On June 26, Maj. Gen. George B. McClellan began his Peninsular Campaign in an attempt to capture the rebel capital of Richmond. Upon hearing the news, Madison and the others thought that this time the Union army would be successful. The Army of the Potomac had come within seven miles from its objective. However, on June 28, after several set-backs, General McClellan decided to turn back, for he feared going for-ward might cause him to fall prey to a superior Confederate force and to risk destruction of the army.

With General McClellan's failure to capture Richmond, Lincoln had no choice but to replace him. The president named Maj. Gen. Henry Halleck as general in chief of all Union forces. Shortly after taking command,

General Halleck appointed Col. Richard D. Cutts, Madison's uncle, as his aide-de-camp.

On July 3, General Burnside met with his old friend General McClellan at Harrison's Landing, Virginia. At the close of their discussions, they agreed that Burnside would leave the Department of North Carolina and bring some of his troops in support of McClellan's battle-weary forces.[4] To help with his retreat, General Burnside ordered his newly designated IX Corps to Fort Monroe. His 14,000 troops were positioned to either support McClellan or, in the event of an attack on Washington, move there in support of Gen. Irvin McDowell. Shortly after making this move, Burnside decided on a more strategic position and established his headquarters in Falmouth, Virginia.

Madison and others quickly organized and effected the movement of troops to Falmouth, and the task was completed by August 1. Falmouth, on the north bank of the Rappahannock River across from Fredericksburg, was not new ground for Madison. He had been there several times in his youth to visit his relatives. Nearby was the familiar home of Martha Washington, a place where Madison had played with his cousin William.

General Burnside established his headquarters at Chatham, a large estate on top of a ridge overlooking the city of Fredericksburg. The native Virginians, although resentful of the Union army, well understood the severity of the situation and remained civil. During that time, Madison found himself heavily involved in the duties of judge advocate for Burnside's IX Corps. Whenever possible, he rode out to be with the officers and men of the corps. The focus of the conflict in the east shifted to the north where Union Maj. Gen. John Pope, commander of the Army of Virginia, searched for Lee's Army of Northern Virginia.

During much of July and August, General Pope maneuvered throughout the area west of Washington, D.C., in an effort to bring Lee's forces into a general engagement. General McClellan maintained his position at Harrison's Landing, still licking his wounds from the failed Peninsular Campaign. By the end of August, the Union had lost sight of Lee but knew Lt. Gen. Thomas Jackson had entered the town of Manassas on August 27.[5] General Pope, knowing that Lee's army was divided, began to move on Jackson at Stony Ridge about five miles north of Manassas. This was almost the exact point of the main fighting of the First Battle of Bull Run. As the two armies came together, their positions were exactly reversed from the first battle. On August 29, General Pope ordered an attack on Jackson's position. The Second Battle of Bull Run had begun. Jackson and his rebel fighters struggled all day to hold the Union forces at

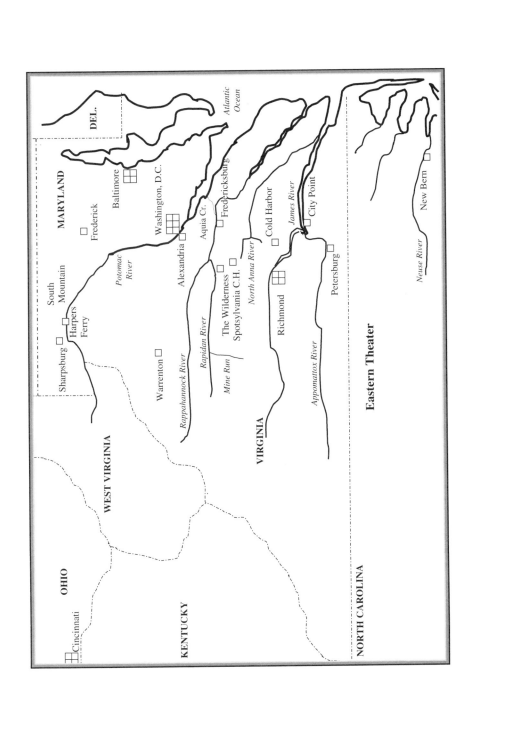

bay. In the evening, General Lee and Lt. Gen. James Longstreet's Corps arrived on the field. Lee requested Longstreet to attack the southern flank of the Union army, but Longstreet wanted more time to prepare. Lee reluctantly granted him the time, but in doing so lost a great opportunity to severely damage Pope's forces. On August 30, General Pope again struck at Jackson's right flank and thought the Confederates were withdrawing, but at 4 P.M. Longstreet's Corps hit his left flank at Bald Hill with all he had. The tired Yankees were not able to handle this attack and were forced to retreat. General Pope ordered a withdrawal and by midnight most of the army reached Centreville, Virginia, and safety. On September 1, smaller units of the opposing armies met in a driving thunderstorm at Chantilly, Virginia. General Jackson fought two brigades from the IX Corps while General Pope withdrew his forces to Washington. The Second Battle of Bull Run was over, with the Confederates again being the victors and standing only a short distance from the capital. On September 2, Lincoln removed General Pope from command and gave the army back to General McClellan. The Union army was suffering from low morale, and many in Washington were afraid that the army could not defend the city. When General McClellan arrived in Washington, he quickly combined the Army of Virginia with the Army of the Potomac and brought order and confidence to the men.

Dark clouds fell over Washington as the Confederate generals considered their next move. So imminent was the anticipated Confederate attack on the capital that the remaining units of the IX Corps and the troops stationed at Harrison's Landing were ordered to return to Washington with all possible haste.

Time was of the essence, and Madison committed himself to the success of the operation. Not only was the city in peril, so was his mother and sister. For five days and nights he tirelessly managed the immense details involved in the rapid movement and deployment of the corps. He slept little and ate on the run as he moved from unit to unit and commander to commander, helping to orchestrate the evacuation of Falmouth and the reinforcement of Washington.[6]

The IX Corps began arriving in Washington on September 4. All of the men were ready to take their place in the army and to have a chance at the rebels. They wouldn't have long to wait.

General Lee was charting a course of his own. Following Chantilly, he quickly moved his army north to Harpers Ferry and Frederick City, Maryland.

On September 7, General McClellan began to move the Army of the Potomac to the northwest to meet General Lee's challenge. The IX Corps, with Hooker's I Corps, making up the right flank as the Army of the Potomac, moved forward in pursuit of the rebel forces.

On September 11, General Burnside established his headquarters at Kempton's Crossroads near Damascus, Maryland. Madison and the rest of the staff had congregated in an upstairs room following dinner to talk about issues of the day. Major William Cutting had asked General Burnside whether a Charles Hutton could join his staff. Apparently, Hutton had been promised a position on Brig. Gen. Philip Kearny's staff but with the general's death at Chantilly, Hutton found himself without a sponsor. Madison listened to Cutting's request with almost indifference until something that Major Cutting said lead Madison to believe that Hutton lacked character and may even be considered a coward. This had been the second time Major Cutting had brought Mr. Hutton's name before the general and when the discussion concluded, Madison didn't hold the man in very high regard, but General Reno agreed to put him on his staff.[7] Although the two only communicated in official capacities, a tension existed between Madison and Charles Hutton from that day forward.

The army reached the area in front of Frederick City on September 13, 1862. As the IX Corps approached town, it appeared the vanguard of the huge Union force was waiting for the Confederate rear guard to vacate the town. Hearing of the delays at the front, the impatient Madison jumped on his horse and immediately rode down the National Highway for the advance unit. At the front, he found Col. Augustus Moor observing an artillery duel between a battery next to him and rebel gunners on the edge of the town. Madison told the colonel that General Burnside wished him to clear the town immediately. During their discussion, a rebel cannonball exploded killing a Union soldier standing next to them. After some discussion and prodding, Colonel Moor agreed to attack the town and drive the rebels out.[8]

As soon as Madison left the area, Colonel Moor ordered his regiment to charge the city. The road leading into the town made a sharp bend, making it impossible to see around the corners of the buildings until the entrance to the town was actually made. As Colonel Moor and his men made the turn, they were met with a number of rebels and a cannon. The cannon fired and caused some confusion within the Union troops. Colonel Moor and seven others were captured and taken out of town by the retreating rebels. The rest of the army soon took Frederick Town; and, once it was in Union hands, many residents came out to cheer and support the Federals. It was a great start to the campaign and would soon become even better. In the abandoned camp of Confederate Gen.

Daniel H. Hill, two Union soldiers found a copy of Lee's Order 191, containing the entire Confederate plan of operation.[9] This stroke of luck provided General McClellan with information needed to destroy Lee's entire army. He had discovered that General Lee's forces were divided with Longstreet's Corps moving northwest to Hagerstown and with Jackson and Maj. Gen. Lafayette McLaw laying a siege at Harpers Ferry. According to the maps, a ridge, known as South Mountain, separated the two opposing armies. If McClellan could get his troops over the mountains quickly and get between the two rebel forces, he stood a good chance of destroying each rebel corps, one at a time.

South Mountain, several miles west of Frederick City rises to about eleven hundred feet, with two gaps running through it. The main routes across the mountain were through Turner's Gap, located on the northern portion of the mountain, and Crampton's Gap, several miles to the south. McClellan's plan was simple and direct. On September 14, he ordered Burnside's IX Corps into Turner's Gap and Brig. Gen. William B. Franklin's VI Corps into Crampton's Gap. Acting as an aide-de-camp, Madison moved from one unit to another, providing direction and support in order to keep the IX Corps moving in the right direction. As the army moved forward, Madison began to feel the excitement of battle. General Reno's division attacked first at a smaller, less-used route called Fox's Gap, located about a mile south of Turner's Gap. After fierce fighting, his division succeeded in reaching the summit. By noon the fighting had died down, and Madison returned to headquarters. The rebels in front of them were part of Maj. Gen. D. H. Hill's division, and they took advantage of the terrain to slow the advance of the Union right flank. During the lull in the fighting, Maj. Gen. Joseph Hooker staged his troops at the bottom of the road leading through Turner's Gap. When the order to attack was delivered, the Federals moved up the right side of the road toward the highest point on the mountain. The Union troops proved too strong for the Confederates and, after a mad rush, the summit fell in their hands. Hill was reinforced just in the nick of time by the vanguard of Longstreet's Corps, but the narrowness of the gap made it difficult to do more than slow the movement of General Hooker's men. Still, the rebels had the advantage of the terrain and held on until after dark. Madison rode back and forth from headquarters all day long supplying information about the battle. When necessary, he found himself at the front line obtaining vital information about the progress of the battle and position of the Union and the enemy regiments. He also assisted in the placement of units and artillery. He made repeated trips to General Reno to confirm his position, then to

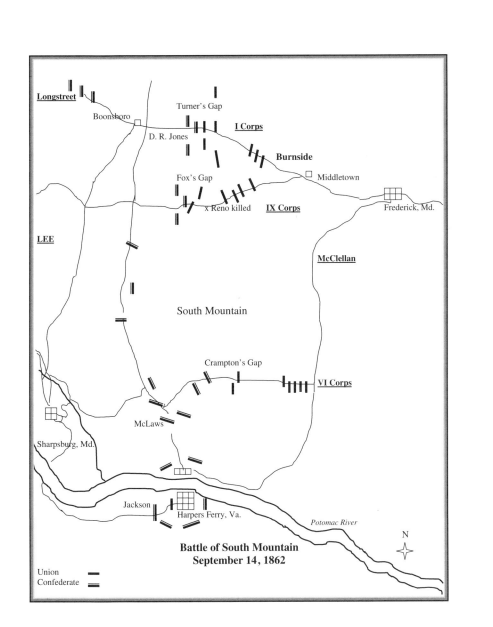

Longstreet

Boonsboro

Turner's Gap

D. R. Jones

I Corps

Burnside

Fox's Gap

Middletown

x Reno killed

IX Corps

Frederick, Md.

LEE

McClellan

South Mountain

Crampton's Gap

VI Corps

McLaws

Sharpsburg, Md.

Jackson

Harpers Ferry, Va.

Potomac River

N

**Battle of South Mountain
September 14, 1862**

Union
Confederate

General Hooker to exchange information. Late in the afternoon, General Reno was shot and killed by one of his own soldiers, a new man with the 35th Massachusetts Regiment.[10] This was a terrible loss to the army because of Reno's fighting spirit and his abilities as a commander. Brig. Gen. Jacob D. Cox, aware of Reno's death, immediately took command of his division. Madison went back to the front with orders for General Cox to continue to press the attack. Madison took part in the fighting with the 23rd and 30th Ohio Regiments on the left side of the line on the road that ran through Fox's Gap. He distinguished himself in this fight by remaining cool under fire and exposing himself to extreme danger in order to provide sound intelligence regarding troop positions. Lt. Col. Rutherford B. Hayes had watched Madison as he supported his command and thought highly of the courage he exhibited.

The battle raged well into the night, but in the end the Union forces were too much for Hill's troops. The rebels were badly used up and had no choice but to abandon Turner's Gap. The day was over, and Madison had fought in his first major engagement with distinction. It had been a good day's work, but the fighting wasn't over. Beyond South Mountain Lee's army withdrew and searched for a defensive position. The Confederate army was now vulnerable.

On the following day, September 15, at approximately noon, the IX Corps of the Union army poured men through Turner's and Fox's Gaps and into the valley beyond in pursuit of rebels. Several miles to the south, General Franklin had breached Crampton's Gap and continued to advance on the Confederate position at Harpers Ferry.

During this time, General Lee withdrew to the village of Sharpsburg, Maryland, where he attempted to consolidate his army to defend against an impending assault. Longstreet's Corps formed a line just east of Sharpsburg on the high ground waiting for the arrival of the Federals. Although his position was strong, his 19,000 troops were no match for the gathering Union army. The only bright spot of the day for the rebels was the fall of Harpers Ferry, which meant that General Jackson's troops were free to move to Sharpsburg. General McClellan elected, in his normal fashion, to take another day to develop his plan of attack, thereby giving Lee more time to strengthen his position.

At about 3 P.M. General Cox, the new commander of the IX Corps, joined General Burnside and General McClellan on a ridge that overlooked the impending battlefield. McClellan discussed his intended strategy, which required Hooker's Corps to move to the north. General Cox and the IX Corps were ordered to move south through farmlands to an area behind a few small hills and directly across from a bridge over Antietam Creek.[11] This area included the fields and home of H. Rohrbach. It was a beautiful farm with a large two-story farmhouse and several other buildings, including a large barn with brick sides and the initials *H* and *R* left open in the brickwork. General Burnside and General Cox established headquarters near the house, and Madison found himself rapidly moving between the commanders and the regiments as they came forward. Between the farmhouse and the lower bridge there was a small hill that had a clear view of the bridge and the enemy on the other side. Farther south on the Union side was a gap in the hill, which opened just south of the bridge. Madison had an opportunity to survey the area before the generals appeared on the scene. He moved rapidly to help deploy the troops of the IX Corps along the hills on the east side of Antietam Creek. At one point he rode to Brig. Gen. George W. Getty and offered his suggestions regarding the placement of the batteries. The general agreed and directed Madison to see to their movement.

He rode to a small rise to the north of the bridge and ordered the cannons to be directed to the area across the creek. He rode back to the headquarters of Brig. Gen. Samuel D. Sturgis, which was located behind the ridge at the Rohrbach Farm and found several more units of artillery coming up which he ordered to the appropriate locations.

Elsewhere that night, Gen. Lafayette McLaws and troops from Brig. Gen. Richard H. Anderson's division had reinforced General Lee, bringing his total number of troops to around 36,000. This hard-pressed group was facing the whole of the Army of the Potomac, which numbered in excess of 70,000 men. General McClellan's strategy was to hit both flanks of the enemy at the same time. When both of the flanks were turned, he would order an attack in the center.

At daylight on September 17, General Hooker attacked the Confederate left with all he had. Emerging from the North Woods, Hooker's men were instructed to advance toward the white Dunkard Church to their front. They did as instructed and moved under heavy fire through a cornfield toward the church and the center of Jackson's line. Although the Confederate line fell back, it didn't break. At about eight o'clock, Hooker called up Mansfield's Corps to finish off the rebels. Maj. Gen. Joseph King Mansfield came up to support but was killed almost immediately and replaced by Brig. Gen. Alpheus S. Williams. The fighting continued to rage and the rebels were pushed back farther. Hooker reached the high ground and saw the rebels retreating in disarray. Suddenly, his confidence swelled as he could see victory before him. He telegraphed McClellan that he had won a great victory and requested Maj. Gen. Edwin V. Sumner's forces to the field to support his now tiring corps. But victory, so close at hand, withered when Hooker was shot and his advance halted and pushed back by a strong counterattack. Maj. Gen. George G. Meade was able to rally the I Corps and, with Brig. Gen. George S. Green and Brig. Gen. Alpheus Williams, the VII Corps division commanders soon regained the lost ground. With Williams's men having to leave the field to get more ammunition and to rest, Green made a gallant effort to hold on to the ground around the Dunkard Church. After some delay, McClellan finally authorized General Sumner to move forward with his First Division under Maj. Gen. John Sedgwick. Sedgwick, with General Sumner at the front, attacked on the right side of Green at the West Woods but was soon surrounded on three sides by the Confederate units from Brig. Gen. Jubal Early's, Maj. Gen. Lafayette McLaws' and Brig. Gen. J. R. Jones' divisions. Sedgwick was forced to withdraw with staggering losses. At about the same time, Brig. Gen. William H. French, commander of Sumner's Second Division, moved in on Green's left. He was supposed to have followed Sedgwick but apparently took a wrong road. Maj. Gen. Israel B. Richardson, the commander of Sumner's Third Division, followed him and came up on the left. They both engaged in severe fighting around a sunken road that the soldiers quickly named the Bloody Lane. Repeated attempts to dislodge the rebels from their position caused the Federals to suffer great losses. Lee thought this was the main focus of McClellan's attack and began to pull troops from everywhere to support that area of his line. The rebels were so confident in their position at the sunken road that they taunted the Federals to come get them. The Union soldiers did just that and as they did, the rebel losses were enormous. The Yankees finally took the road in some of the most furious fighting of the day. The battle, which had lasted for three hours, was devastating to the left side of Lee's army.[12]

With the sunrise on the seventeenth, Madison found himself near General Cox and General Burnside awaiting orders. The generals were positioned on the ridge, looking down on the lower bridge of the Antietam and awaiting orders from McClellan to attack. According to McClellan's plan, Burnside would attack at the same time as Hooker and establish a diversion for the main attack on the right. He deployed his troops early but still had not received orders from McClellan. All morning General Burnside waited for orders that never came. Everyone's attention was drawn to the north since first light, when Hooker made his attack. They watched as units of the army's right wing made gallant attacks on the rebel position. General Burnside's plan was to send troops across Antietam

Creek near the bridge and then push the rebels back to Sharpsburg. In preparation for the attack, Madison moved forward to be with the troops.

Madison went to the front to encourage the men. The rebels began to fire across the creek in an effort to make things nasty for the Union troops. As Madison stood at the battle line, he maintained a calm as cannon shells and Minié balls flew around him. Close by were the brave souls of the 11th Connecticut Volunteer Regiment. He wouldn't make the charge with them, but he knew the work was about to begin.

At 10 A.M., as the main assault on the right was subsiding, the orders finally arrived instructing General Burnside's left wing to attack the rebel right flank. Immediately, the 11th Connecticut Infantry of Brig. Gen. Isaac P. Rodman's division, supported by troops from Brig. Gen. George Crook's brigade and Brig. Gen. Eliakim P. Scammon's division, advanced to the lower Antietam Bridge. As they entered the clearing on the east side of the bridge, a strong volley hit them from the small but well-positioned force of rebels on the other side of the creek. Two Georgian regiments of about four hundred men, with orders to hold off the onslaught of the IX Corps, bravely stood their ground on the west side of the bridge. The terrain was in the Confederates' favor. They were on the high ground overlooking the bridge with a commanding vantage point from which to hold off the attack. The 11th Connecticut made a brave effort; but within 15 minutes, the intense fire from rebels forced them to retire. A second attempt was initiated an hour and a half later by the 2nd Maryland and the 6th New Hampshire over the same open ground, but that, too, was repulsed in a matter of only 15 minutes. At about 1 P.M., a third attempt was ordered. The new plan of attack was for Brig. Gen. Edward Ferrero's brigade of Sturgis's division to come at the bridge from the easterly direction. As the brigade moved toward the bridge, they were met with a tremendous fire from the rebels. The men raced for the protection of a stone wall extending along the bank to the north of the entrance to the bridge. Some reached it, but men were falling all around. Madison was given orders to take to Col. John F. Hartranft, which instructed the colonel not to wait but to proceed immediately across the bridge. Madison braved a hail of bullets to reach the wall and Hartranft.

He delivered the orders to the colonel, then moved closer to the entrance to the bridge. He wanted to be with the first ones to cross. When Capt. William Allenbaugh ordered his men forward, Madison rose with them as they made their gallant charge.[13] The men raced across the bridge in a storm of rifle fire and within minutes had succeeded in reaching the other side of the river. Soon the bridge and the hillside, where the rebels had held them off for so long, were in Union hands. After crossing the bridge, Madison assisted in taking the hill on the west side and then reported back to the general. Before them was a large, open area of a little over a mile that ran up an incline to a ridge located on the south side of the town of Sharpsburg. The rebels were moving back to a position about halfway up the slope while artillery on the ridge continued to pound the Union position. The rifle and cannon fire continued as the rebels tried to hold off the blue tide that was building in front of them. The bridge had been crossed, but at a heavy cost. It took General Burnside three hours and five hundred men either killed or wounded to make the crossing. As the Confederates retreated, a heavy rain of Confederate artillery fell on the men of the IX Corps.

By 3 P.M., over 10,000 men were located in the staging area on the west side of Antietam Creek, ready to move on the Confederate right wing. Soon the order to attack was once again given and a surge of blue moved westward. It was magnificent to see the mass of Union soldiers moving over the open and rolling ground. The Union troops were too much for the rebels as they continued to fall back. Brig. Gen. Orlando B. Willcox's division on the right began to push the enemy back to Sharpsburg, and it appeared that the rebels were about to be routed. Everyone could feel that a victory was in sight.

Madison had been all over the field during the fighting, carrying orders and moving from one unit and commander to another. As the Union forces fought their way to the edge of Sharpsburg, the line began to concentrate into a group west of Otto's Lane and the Lower Bridge Road. Seeing the danger of a possible flanking action by the Confederates, General Rodman ordered several units to be brought up to protect his left flank. Soon after issuing his order, Rodman was hit in the chest with a fatal wound. The 9th New York moved up on the left, west of Otto's Lane, with the 16th Ohio protecting their left flank. Madison with the 9th New York pushed toward a field ripe with Indian corn on the left of the Union line. The firing from the rebels was terrific, and most of the 9th New York dropped to the prone position in an effort to find as much protection as possible. With the strength of the rebel regiments in front of them, it became imperative that someone would go for reinforcements. But with the galling fire from the rebels, just standing up was an invitation to death. A Union officer jumped to his horse and began to ride for help, but both rider and horse were shot down. Madison saw what had happened and without thought ran to his horse, jumped on, and headed for reinforcements. A rush of bullets flew as he rode, but none found their mark. As he left

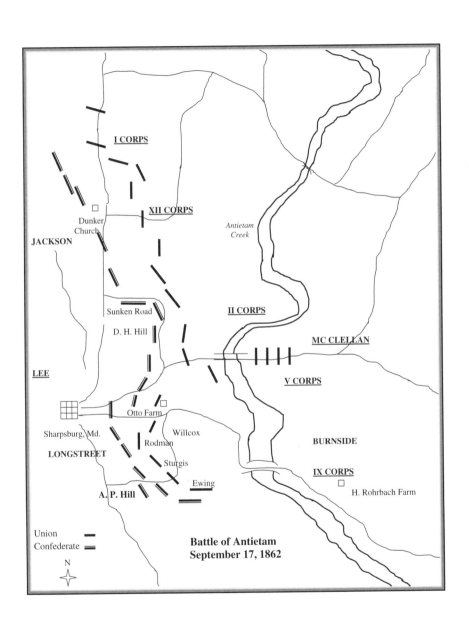

I CORPS

XII CORPS

Antietam
Creek

JACKSON

Dunker
Church

II CORPS

Sunken Road

D. H. Hill

MC CLELLAN

LEE

V CORPS

Otto Farm

Sharpsburg, Md.

Willcox

BURNSIDE

Rodman

LONGSTREET

Sturgis

IX CORPS

Ewing

A. P. Hill

H. Rohrbach Farm

Union
Confederate

N

**Battle of Antietam
September 17, 1862**

the 9th New York, the 103rd New York and the 89th New York arrived on the field on the left side of the 9th and continued to push toward Sharpsburg. In the meantime, Madison located Col. Hugh Ewing's brigade, consisting of the 23rd and the 30th Ohio, in a depression in the land behind the far left flank of the Union line. Madison told Colonel Ewing that the 9th New York was in dire need of support. Ewing agreed telling Madison to position his brigade wherever necessary. As the brigade moved forward, it appeared that the 16th Connecticut needed support, so the 23rd and the 30th Ohio were brought up on their right. With a determined enemy and a rising slope to their front, the Buckeyes were reluctant to move beyond the protection of Otto's Lane. All of the officers present kept ordering the men forward but they resisted.

Lt. Gen. A. P. Hill who force-marched his men 17 miles from Harpers Ferry to support Lee's beleaguered army arrived on the field just in time. Around 4:30 P.M., Confederate Brig. Gen. Maxcy Gregg of A. P. Hill's division turned his South Carolinians loose on the left flank of the IX Corps. The first Union unit they hit, the inexperienced 16th Connecticut Volunteer Regiment, recoiled from the surprise and deadly shot. The green troops on the far left of the IX Corps quickly broke.

The Confederates increased their deadly fire. Those who didn't run for the rear lay down and looked for protection from Mother Earth. The Confederate riflemen were hitting the Yankees with such a deadly fire that anything moving on the Union side suddenly became a target. Being outflanked on the left, the entire Union line was in jeopardy of being routed. As the Minié balls flew around them, the men and officers finally organized themselves into a fighting force as they moved forward into the guns of Gen. Henry L. Benning's Georgians. Unfortunately, the 23rd Ohio became immediately surrounded on three sides in the cornfield. Madison continued to remain strong as he walked among the 23rd Ohio, demonstrating to them by his own example the meaning of bravery. They regained their composure under hellish circumstances and fought their way out. The 30th Ohio did not fare much better, and eventually the entire left flank of the Union army retired to the protection of Otto's Lane. The Union advance collapsed altogether, and by nightfall the IX Corps had retired back to the bridge. The Confederates succeeded in preventing the capture of Sharpsburg; and with the fighting finished, the IX Corps was roughly in the same position as it had been at the start of the day.

The battle lasted 12 hours with nearly 26,000 men—Union and Confederate—killed, wounded, or missing. No one was sure who had won, but everyone knew that the struggle had been monumental. In the dark of night, the battlefield was strewn with bodies of men and horses. For those who were able to sleep in the cold night air, the plan for the following day was a lifetime away.

Madison had been under heavy fire while he rode back and forth between Burnside's headquarters and unit commanders for the entire day. He helped place the artillery, which led to the crossing of the bridge, and lined up troops for the final assault on Confederate lines. The whole time, Madison continously exposed himself to rifle shot and artillery shell. With a devotion to duty and incredible bravery, he made it through the day unharmed. In a letter written many years after the battle, General Willcox, wrote to Madison,

> *I may safely say that no staff officer habitually exposed himself to danger in carrying orders and gaining intelligence more than yourself.*[14]

Madison had served well, and all of the officers and men of the IX Corps knew and respected him as a brave officer. General Getty wrote of him,

> *During the Maryland Campaign, which resulted in the battles of South Mountain and Antietam, I was the chief of artillery of the right wing of the Army of the Potomac. You rendered most efficient aid to me in selecting position for the artillery, and subsequently in conducting the batteries to the positions selected.*[15]

In his report on the battle, General Burnside wrote,

> *The Battery commanders deserving special mention for the efficient service rendered by them during the day. I beg to call attention of the general commanding to the valuable services rendered by Lieutenant-Colonel Getty, chief of artillery, who posted the batteries.*
>
> *To my personal staff I am under renewed obligations for their constant and unwearied efforts and their faithfulness and courage exhibited in the various duties required of them. They are as follows: Captain J. M. Cutts, Aide-de-camp.*[16]

There was no question about Madison's bravery. The most remarkable comment he had ever received about his services in the face of battle came years later from Col. Hugh Ewing who had observed Madison during the placement of his troops in the afternoon of the battle.

> *The troops which I commanded were led to their position in line of battle by Colonel (Captain) Cutts, and the soldierly skill,*

coolness, and bright courage displayed by him that day won from me the highest admiration.

He displayed on that field the noble qualities that go to makeup the brilliant soldier, and I do not recall a single other officer during the entire course of the war that so quickly and profoundly impressed me. What more can I say? He was a bright light on the field of battle, cheering up the duller of spirits, and by such service long continued as few rendered or could render, he secured the gratitude of the soldier and earned the lasting gratitude of the Republic.[17]

The following day, both armies stood opposing each other licking their wounds, but with neither willing to make an attack on the other. They carried their wounded from the field and prepared for whatever else the other side had to offer. The rebel army had been mauled and was unable to mount an attack, while the Army of the Potomac with a significant number of fresh troops prepared to advance. During the night of September 19, the rebels retired to the south, back across the Potomac River to the safety of Opequon Creek.

General McClellan settled in to savoring his victory and to reinforce his army. To McClellan, the victory of forcing Lee back across the Potomac was of great value to the country and to himself. He had succeeded in defeating the Confederate army, and as soon as he could rebuild the Army of the Potomac, he planned to strike at Lee in Virginia.

McClellan's troops had marched for several weeks and fought in two general actions, one of which was the bloodiest of the war. Although the soldiers were ready to finish off the rebels, McClellan resisted. The Army of the Potomac remained at Sharpsburg for six weeks. Madison celebrated his birthday on October 20. Six days later, the army moved south in pursuit of the Army of Northern Virginia. By November 6, the IX Corps had moved to a position near Waterloo, Virginia, just a few miles southwest of Warrenton. McClellan's plan was to move further south to Gordonsville and cut between Lee's army and Richmond. From Gordonsville, he could destroy Lee's line of communication and either move on Richmond or Lee as he wished. But on November 7, the command of the Army of the Potomac was given to General Burnside. At the age of 25, Madison found himself on the staff that commanded the most powerful army in North America.

General Burnside twice refused to take command of the Army of the Potomac, claiming that he was not qualified to manage such a large force. He had seen Generals McClellan, McDowell, and Pope fail in their attempt to achieve victory. If the best generals in the Union couldn't do it, how could he? He was a classmate at West Point and longtime friend of George McClellan, and he didn't want to be the one to replace him. But on orders from General Halleck and the president, Burnside reluctantly accepted. Once in command, he immediately set out to design a plan for destroying Lee's army. He had four options: first, continue with McClellan's plan and attack Gordonsville or Culpeper; second, return to Washington; third, wait for General Lee to come to him or; fourth, move to Fredericksburg, secure his supply lines, and then move on to Richmond. He submitted his plan to General Halleck on November 9, 1862, recommending the fourth choice. On the following day, the Army of the Potomac lined up for miles to cheer the beloved General McClellan as he departed camp for the last time. General Burnside had a heavy load on his shoulders as he began to reorganize the army.

With General Burnside's promotion to commanding general, Madison found himself technically, but not officially, in the position of judge advocate of the Army of the Potomac. His work was never ending, and he found that by the grace of God he had been positioned to fulfill Douglas's dream of glory and victory.

On November 14, President Lincoln accepted Burnside's plan to move the army to Fredericksburg and start the attack on Richmond. The president believed the plan was workable, but only if he acted quickly. The following day the Army of the Potomac moved out for Fredericksburg, following the roads along the Rappahannock River to the site of the old headquarters of the IX Corps, in Falmouth, Virginia.

To improve his ability to command, General Burnside segmented his army into three main bodies. Each of the "Grand Divisions," as he called them, included two corps. Generals Sumner, Franklin, and Hooker commanded them. On November 17, General Sumner's Grand Division was the first to reach Falmouth. Sumner immediately requested permission to cross the river and to occupy the high ground south of the city, but General Burnside declined the request. Since he hoped to soon be receiving equipment to cross the river, Burnside had no reason to risk allowing part of his army to be cut off from the rest. He requested pontoon bridges to be sent to Fredericksburg prior to leaving Warrenton; but because the orders were sent through the mail, the execution was delayed. Any opportunity to get across the river unmolested had been lost on November 21 when Longstreet's Corps arrived and took control of Marye's Heights south of the city. Burnside missed an opportunity several days later to cross the Rappahannock River upstream and to catch Lee's divided army, again. At this point, for Burnside's plan to work, he had to cross the river in front of Longstreet and take the high ground. This option became even harder when on November 30 part of Jackson's Corps took its place on the right flank of the Confederate line east of Fredericksburg.

As the two armies gathered, Madison traveled to Washington with Burnside in order to confer with General Halleck. On the return trip, Madison asked General Burnside if he had any intentions to promote him to major and officially name him judge advocate of the Army of the Potomac, a position he currently held. The general had come to like Madison whose bravery in battle and military judgment were outstanding and the young captain impressed him. He had made sure that Madison received his richly deserved recognition in his report on the Battles of South Mountain and Antietam. He told Madison to be patient, that he had bigger things in mind for him and that he should not be concerned with the future. Madison, pleased with the general's remarks, let the matter rest.[18]

The delays at Fredericksburg cost Burnside dearly. It was 11 more days before the assault began. Lincoln's fear and those of the other soldiers had come true. The Army of the Potomac faced the entire Army of Northern Virginia, fixed in a superior position. With all of the delays, Burnside had not been able to move fast enough to effect his plan, but he felt that success was still possible if Lee had not had enough time to consolidate his entire army. Unfortunately, Lee had already taken care of that.

On the morning of December 11, the order was given to begin laying three pontoon bridges across the Rappahannock River and to cross the troops. The most difficult area to construct a bridge was directly across from Fredericksburg. Some Mississippi sharpshooters under the command of Brig. Gen. William Barksdale started shooting at the bridge builders from the buildings and entrenchments in the city. The Union officers responded to the shooting by directing a squad of volunteers to stand on the extended portion of the pontoon bridge and fire back at the rebels. Despite a valiant effort by the Union soldiers standing in the open, they were not successful. With the failure to protect the engineers, the construction of the bridge was delayed until the sharpshooters could be dealt with. The next attempt to solve the problem involved having Brig. Gen. Henry J. Hunt's cannons destroy the enemy. Union cannons fired on Fredericksburg for two hours. When the smoke lifted, the buildings closest to the river had not been touched by the fire, and the cannons could not be deflected enough to destroy them. After eight hours of attempting to construct the bridge, the order was given to have volunteers cross the river and dislodge the rebels. Madison jumped at the chance to make the crossing, and at about 4:30 P.M. he joined the 7th Michigan and the 19th and 20th Massachusetts Regiments and paddled across the river. Once across, the 7th Michigan led the way by marching up Farquhar Street to engage the enemy. Barksdale's determined Confederates poured on such a severe fire that it stopped the 7th and made it necessary for the 19th Massachusetts to rapidly come forward. The fighting was intense as the Union troops pushed forward to Carolina Street. The rebels, shooting from behind barricades on the south side of the street, intensified their fire, forcing the left side of the Union line to fall back. Madison, seeing the desperate situation, returned to the brigade commander with a request for more support. The 20th Massachusetts responded with Madison showing them the way up Farquhar Street to Carolina Street. While forming up and coming under heavy fire, the suffering 20th Regiment quickly executed a wheeling movement pouring deadly fire on Barksdale's sharpshooters. This action secured the left flank, which led to the capture of the town for the safe crossing of the army. By nightfall, the pontoon bridge was completed and Maj. Gen. Darius N. Couch's division started across the river. The rebels wisely left the city under the cover of darkness, having successfully delayed the crossing of the entire Union army by a day. Madison returned to Phillip's House to report to General Burnside. He was proud of the day's work.[19]

With the pontoon bridges in place, the troops began to cross and take up positions inside Fredericksburg. Since it was necessary to maintain a level of surprise, no fires were permitted the night of December 11. It wasn't until the night of December 12 that all of General Sumner's and General Franklin's Grand Divisions were across the river and in position. General Burnside's plan was to have General Franklin attack the Confederate right flank near the small town of Hamilton's Crossing while General Sumner attacked the center of the Confederate line around Telegraph Road. If both attacks were successful, or if even one was successful, it was thought that the Union could capture the heights. As Madison quickly surveyed the situation, he came to the conclusion that it would take everything they had to capture the high ground, but even that might not be enough. The rebels were well entrenched on a six-mile front, which they had days to prepare. Still, Madison was determined to do all he could do to help secure a victory.

December 13 began with a low fog over the Union ground. General Burnside delayed sending his orders to the field commanders, and some of his staff stopped along the way to eat breakfast, causing more delays. When the orders finally arrived, General Franklin and other commanders on the Union left were shocked to learn that Burnside had ordered Franklin to protect his line of retreat and only send a division to assault the Confederate lines to their front. Out of more than 40,000 men at his disposal, General Franklin sent about 10,000 into battle. Most of the generals and men on staff felt this was insane, but they obeyed orders. The attack started with Gen. George Meade's division of Pennsylvanians marching toward a marshy position in the center of Stonewall Jackson's line on the Confederate right. Meade's attack was initially successful as his men fought with a vengeance and drove the rebels back. As the Confederate line gave way, Meade requested more support from Brig. Gen. Daniel E. Sickles and Maj. Gen. David B. Birney from Hooker's Grand Division. Their response was slow resulting in a counterattack, which forced the Federals to fall back to their original position.

Madison was in constant motion. Once again he repeatedly exposed himself to rebel fire and artillery as he rode back and forth on the battlefield, gathering intelligence and carrying orders and information to and from the battlefield. He spent most of his time with General Franklin's units. Franklin's headquarters were located in a grove of trees near the mansion called "Mansfield." It was a beautiful stone structure looking down on the Rappahannock River. Madison stood nearby as a cannonball crashed into the headquarters area, landing less than 10 feet from General Franklin and striking Brig. Gen. George D. Bayard, a gallant cavalry officer, who was taken into the house for treatment of his wounds that proved mortal.[20] Soon after another cannonball struck the mansion totally destroying it.

By 1 P.M., the Union attack on the left had stalled. General Franklin had the largest force on the field; but by following General Burnside's order, Franklin found himself unable to take advantage of his strength.

General Sumner commenced his attack on the Confederate center at 11 A.M. by ordering a charge by French's division followed by Hancock, Howard, and Sturgis. The advance appeared like waves on the shore as they crossed the cleared ground south of Fredericksburg. They were met with a fury of shot from the rebels on Marye's Heights and Marye's Hill. The Confederates, under the command of Brig. Gen. Thomas Cobb, secured a position in a sunken road behind a stone wall at the bottom of Marye's Hill. This protected position offered them a tremendous advantage. Behind the wall, they poured a devastating fire on the attacking Union soldiers. All of General Sumner's attempts to take the heights were beaten back with heavy losses. All during the morning, Madison continued to ride between the corps and division commanders. He had made contact with just about all of the field officers of Franklin's Grand Division in an effort to communicate orders and achieve success from what had become an impossible task. By 1:30 P.M., General Burnside's initial attempt to gain the high ground failed.

Efforts were made to find another way to take the heights. An advance was made on the Union right, but this route was found to be impassable because of the swampy terrain. General Hooker's men took a terrific beating in front of Marye's Heights and along the sunken road. Madison after spending some time at General Burnside's headquarters returned to General Franklin's front in the early afternoon to survey the situation. The firing of cannons and rifles erupted to his north as the Union attempted to break the rebel hold at the heights. Some firing that came from the rebel lines to his front didn't seem to be as strong. Madison questioned the aides to Franklin about their immediate plans and found that the general was not intending to move forward and wouldn't do so unless given orders. Franklin came to the conclusion that his primary orders were to protect the line of retreat. Madison knew that the only way to take the pressure off the advancing troops at Marye's Heights was to cause damage and concern on enemy lines in front of Franklin's force.

In his typical fashion, he decided to see what was out in front of the line and to report it to General Burnside. Madison jumped on his horse, determined to ride the length of the Union left flank and to provide a map of the units for his commander. As he rode along the line, Madison again came under constant fire from enemy guns, but continued to press on. He knew the intelligence he was gathering would be of great value and must get to the generals. As he passed through the gallant Pennsylvanians—who had almost broken through the rebel lines that morning— he noticed that they were still in a good state of mind. He spoke briefly to the commander about the enemy strength in front of him and learned that they would have routed the rebels earlier in the day if they had been given more support. Madison continued to move toward the front and soon found himself beyond Union lines. He periodically brought his horse to a stop to make notes on his small map of the line. The rebels watched him move along the line and began to take aim. Whenever rider and horse came to a stop, the Minié balls flew past him; Madison calmly focused his attention on the map of the enemy position as he took to his

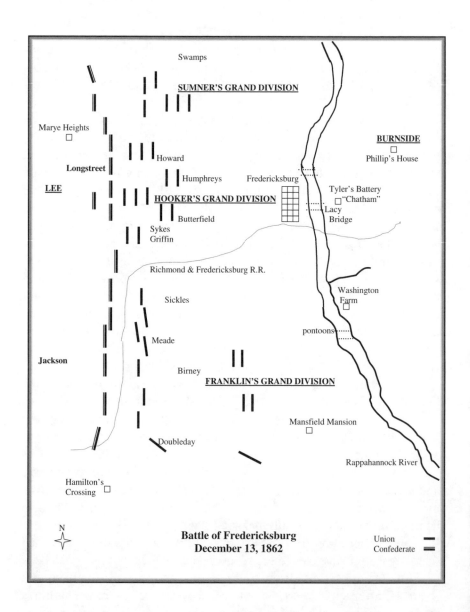

Battle of Fredericksburg
December 13, 1862

work as if it were a Sunday outing. To Madison's amazement, the position appeared to be lightly manned. After a portion of the line was observed, he would move behind the Union line to continue his reconnaissance.

Once his map was completed, he anxiously returned to headquarters. Along the way he passed by the artillery placement of Col. Robert O. Tyler's Battery stopping momentarily to learn of their situation. The battery was firing rapidly and taking a shelling from the rebels in a bloody duel. He spoke with a friend from Washington and a member of the staff, Capt. Ulric Dahlgren, who gave him a full account of the situation. Dahlgren then took him to a shelter where Capt. Charles G. Hutton and Capt. G. R. Fearing from the staff had taken cover from the shelling. Dahlgren told his friend that neither had shown any signs of venturing out onto the field all day.[21] The sight of Captain Hutton displaying such cowardice only confirmed Madison's assumptions made from comments earlier by Major Cutting. Madison yelled to both of the officers to do their duty, but they stayed where they were. Madison had no time to deal with them. He had gained a great deal of information and had to get to the general. He returned to his horse and rapidly continued toward the army's headquarters at the Phillip's House. Upon arrival at the headquarters, Madison immediately went upstairs and reported to General Burnside and the council of war. He presented his map to the generals and offered his thoughts about the condition of the left flank of the Union army. It seemed clear to each of the officers present that not only was Madison's information extremely valuable, it had been obtained at great risk to his life. After reviewing the information, Madison was dismissed but before he left the room, Burnside said to him with warmth and sincerity, "Thank you. Thank you. Thank you."[22]

Following his meeting with General Burnside, he walked downstairs to report on the behavior of Captain Hutton.[23] He could not allow the general's staff officers to behave in such a way without paying the consequences. He reported his observations at Tyler's Battery and then returned to his duty.

Madison left the headquarters to look for a new horse when he ran into an old friend of the family and the quartermaster general of the Army of the Potomac, Brig. Gen. Rufus Ingalls, who had kept an eye on Madison and was well aware of his bravery and valor. He also knew of the personal struggle the Cutts family had endured because of Rose Greenhow and other family members' support of the Confederacy. Ingalls respected him and admired his spirit.

Madison returned to the headquarters of General Franklin to advise his staff to make ready for another attack while waiting on orders from General Burnside. Burnside eventually ordered General Hooker to make another attempt to break the Confederate line at Marye's Hill and ordered Franklin to renew his attack on the Confederate right. Hooker protested that the enemy was too well entrenched; but he reluctantly ordered Brig. Gen. Charles Griffin's division, followed by Brig. Gen. A. A. Humphreys' and General Getty's divisions, to attack.

After the orders for General Franklin to attack had arrived and Madison learned that Franklin was not going to make an attack, he left Franklin's command to ride toward the part of the field commanded by Hooker. He arrived at Maj. Gen. David Butterfield's command just about the time that the Regulars went into battle. The fighting was severe, with bullets and cannon shot all around, but Madison worked as though the enemy fire meant nothing and remained focused on his duties. Each advance had been cut down as the heavily reinforced rebel regiments held on at the stone wall. As Humphreys' division moved toward the wall, they were halted and ordered to the prone position. They remained there until withdrawn late the following day.

By nightfall the battle came to a close, and the results to the Army of the Potomac were devastating. The slaughter at Fredericksburg was evident in the 10,000 Union casualties. That night, as snow fell, General Burnside called a council of war to urge that they renew the attack the following day; but Generals Sumner, Hooker, and Franklin voted against it. As part of his report on the battle and the behavior of his soldiers, Burnside cited only Madison for exemplary behavior during the battle.

He was proud of the way he had done his job, but was ashamed of the way the battle had been conducted. As at Antietam, the entire army moved in sluggish fits and starts, which never achieved the coordinated attack that the commander originally intended. As he looked at the cold night sky and watched the unusual northern lights, Madison contemplated the terrible losses and nothing to show for it.

On the 14th, the fighting was sporadic. The most advanced units of the army had to remain where they were in order to keep from being shot as they withdrew. Lee expected that Burnside would make another attack but it never came. In the late afternoon of the following day, Madison found himself riding along the Union line near Bowling Green Road. There had been fierce fighting in that area during the morning, but all appeared calm as he road forward. He was surprised to see the troops yelling and cheering as two soldiers boxed each other in the middle of the battlefield.

Apparently, the fighting earlier in the morning had been started by some of the 24th Michigan troops who relieved the 2nd Wisconsin that night and not knowing that a mutually agreed upon truce had been in effect. With the morning light the Michigan boys mistakenly opened fire on the rebel position. Once the shooting stopped, the two sides began to exchange verbal assaults on one another. Later in the day the 6th Wisconsin, replacing the 24th Michigan, took offense at being put down by the rebels for breaking the truce. Finally, two lads decided to meet in the middle of the lines to settle the matter with their fists.

Madison watched the two men, thinking it strange that such a duel would occur in the middle of a battlefield with so many soldiers cheering the participants. As he watched them fight his eyes swept the rebel's lines. He made a mental note of the troop strength in case it would be necessary to renew the fighting. It had been a good, if not unusual, exercise in reconnaissance.

In the late hours of December 15, the Union army effected a brilliant withdrawal across the Rappahannock without leaving a soldier or gun behind. The Battle of Fredericksburg was over.

Madison felt disappointed at the outcome of the battle. General Burnside had developed a good plan that would have worked had he been a stronger commander. Madison believed the general to be weak and vacillating. Burnside had the opportunity to order a full attack on the Confederate right, but failed to do so. There was plenty of blame to go around for the defeat. Madison thought Burnside bore the responsibility for most of it. The casualties were unfortunate, many of those lives could have been saved if General Burnside had ordered General Franklin to make an all-out attack either in the early morning or later in the afternoon. In any case, it probably would have resulted in rolling up the Confederate right. Madison wasn't the only one who was feeling remorseful about the results of the battle. Everyone from the lowliest private to the Grand Division commanders were sitting around the campfires reliving the battle in conversations and in their minds. Gallantry in action was well recognized, and so was incompetence. The commanding general was the major object of this blame, and the whispers of discontent grew louder as the days passed. Still, Madison remained loyal.

Years later General Franklin wrote about Madison:

> *The service that you rendered was brave, able, and efficient and deserved honorable recognition by the authorities, although I have never heard that you received.*[24]

Several days after the battle, burial details ventured out on the battle-field to collect and bury the dead. It wasn't a pleasant sight, as most of the dead had been stripped of all of their possessions and were grotesque in the configuration of death. In those same days following the battle, General Burnside tried to answer many of the questions running through his mind. He had doubts about the enthusiasm with which his key command-ers took their troops into the fight. He learned of members of his staff who showed a lack of bravery and reprimanded them for it. The focus of the reprimand was Captain Hutton. Madison brought this action on in order to rid the general's staff of those who lacked the courage to provide support to the general in times of battle. Madison asked Captain Dahlgren to stand outside of the commanding general's tent during this confronta-tion in case he needed a collaborating witness. The day after the general delivered his reprimand, two members of Brig. Gen. John Buford's staff, Capt. Joseph O'Keeffe and Capt. Myles Keogh, told Madison that they had heard Captain Hutton making comments that indicated he would get even. They warned him to beware of Hutton.[25]

The Battle of Fredericksburg was over, and Burnside had met a ter-rible defeat in the same manner as his predecessors. His only hope for any success was to initiate another attack. After five weeks of beautiful and calm weather, the general initiated a plan of redemption to send the Grand Divisions of General Franklin and General Hooker to the north along the Rappahannock River, cross, and effect a flanking action on the rebel left. To be successful, the movement required an abnormally large degree of coordination between all of the units involved and cooperation from the weather. Unfortunately, in the afternoon of January 20, after the Grand Divisions had begun to move, a fierce storm fell upon the area, bringing with it a torrential downpour of rain and sleet. Within hours, the roads turned into pools of mud. The storm continued to rage all that night and the following day, to the misery of the soldiers. The men spent two days in a grueling march through knee-deep mud and cold rain to reach a ford, only to find a large force of the Confederate army waiting for them on the other side. Seeing no advantage in forcing a crossing, General Burnside called off the movement and ordered the Grand Divisions back to their original starting point at Falmouth. Madison participated in the move-ment by transferring orders to and from the commanders. He endured the hardships of what the soldiers called the "Mud March." By January 23, the troops, now terribly demoralized and lacking in confidence, were back in Falmouth. On that day, Madison was ordered to report to Wash-ington, D.C., to serve as judge advocate for an important court-martial.[26]

He left Falmouth as soon as he could relishing the idea of being able to spend a few days at home away from the mud, the cold, and the misery of war.

Upon arrival in Washington, he learned that he was to be the judge advocate in the court-martial of Maj. Delancey Floyd-Jones. Major Jones, the commander of the 11th Infantry Regiment, was charged for "Misbehavior in the presence of the enemy." Madison had known and respected Major Jones from his days of training at Fort Independence. He quickly learned that the military commission he was to report to was made up of men who were of good reputation; and Madison felt that, whatever the outcome, the major would be given a fair trial.[27]

On the night of January 23, Madison visited his parents. He had recently received news that his father was ill. He sat and talked with his father for some time, encouraging him to take care of himself, but he refused to slow down because of the great need the army had for war materiel. He continued to work long hours to ensure that the war effort continued unimpeded by bureaucratic red tape. They talked of war and of the women in the family. They were close, and both men knew that they could rely upon one another for strength.

It was during this time that Madison had the opportunity to speak with his Uncle Richard, providing him with intimate details of the most recent battle and the inner workings of General Burnside's command. Madison remained loyal to his commander as much as he could but did not hesitate to express his opinion regarding the Battle of Fredericksburg. He indicated his relationship with the other officers of the general's staff was not close and although he maintained respect for the higher commanders of the staff, he expressed few favorable thoughts about the other aide-de-camps. The incident at Tyler's Battery was shared with his uncle, father, mother, and sister. In the end, Madison was confident he would remain with General Burnside no matter where they were assigned.

While Madison and his uncle were having their discussion, General Burnside was planning a meeting with President Lincoln. After the defeat at Fredericksburg and the Mud March, the general found himself feeling bitter about the performance of his Grand Division commanders. He believed they did not support him in the battle and felt they should be dismissed from the service or relieved of command. While at headquarters in Falmouth, Burnside penned his Special Order 8, in which he called for the dismissal of Generals Hooker, Brooks, Newton, and Cochrane, and the relief of Generals Smith, Sturgis, Ferrero, Franklin, and Franklin's assistant adjutant general, Col. J. H. Taylor. With his special order in hand

and only a couple of aides, he traveled to Washington early in the morning of January 24 for a meeting with the president. Presenting his Special Order 8 to the president, they discussed the situation of the army for some time. Lincoln indicated that General Halleck should hear of his proposal and that they would get back together the following day.

General Burnside went to the Willard Hotel for a much-needed rest. He returned to the executive mansion at ten o'clock in the morning to meet with the president and General Halleck. The meeting didn't last long. Burnside was relieved of command; and not only was his Special Order 8 not accepted by the president, but Lincoln advised him that Gen. Joseph Hooker, whom he had recommended for dismissal, would take command. Burnside immediately offered his resignation from the service, even though both General Halleck and the president asked that he stay. General Burnside returned to Falmouth, and on January 26 turned over the command of the Army of the Potomac to General Hooker. Later that day, Burnside and the balance of his staff boarded the steamship *Carrie Martin* for Washington. Madison, who was working on the prosecution of Major Floyd-Jones, found himself on the outside as the demotion of his commander swirled around him. The trial of Major Floyd-Jones began on January 26, in a room above Butler's Restaurant on Fourteenth Street near Pennsylvania Avenue. Major Floyd-Jones's leadership had been called into question for a period between June 27 and September 20, 1862.[28]

When asked by the court how he pleaded on each specification, Major Floyd-Jones replied, "Not guilty," and with that, Madison began to call witnesses and build his case. It appeared that, although the major's actions were questionable, the burden of proof was very thin. Madison found it difficult to prosecute a man he deeply respected, but he did his duty. The court-martial lasted only a few days and Major Floyd-Jones was found guilty only on leaving his unit on September 17 at a time when they were expecting an attack. On February 14, 1863, he was sentenced to a reprimand. With the trial over, Madison returned to General Burnside and his staff duties.

Madison soon learned more of the details of Burnside's removal as commander of the army. The president had suggested that General Burnside take command of the Department of North and South Carolina, but Burnside wouldn't have it, claiming this would displace his old friend Gen. John G. Foster. The general decided to take a leave of absence in order to think about his next course of action and wasted no time in returning home to Rhode Island. While there, his staff maintained offices in Washington to await his return. They didn't have long to wait. Around this same time, Congress convened hearings on the conduct of the war and was bringing generals in to testify regarding their role in key battles and actions. General Burnside returned to Washington to testify in early February.

Burnside claimed the Battle of Fredericksburg was lost due to General Hooker's reluctance to attack late in the afternoon of December 13. General Burnside said that one of his staff told him a general was doing all he could to make the attack a failure.[29] The hearings continued through February and into March. In one of the congressional meetings, General Burnside contradicted his former commander and good friend, George McClellan, when he indicated that his troops were in good spirits at the end of the battle at Antietam and were ready to continue the attack on the Confederate line the following day. But the order to attack never came. This caused quite a stir which resulted in ending the lifelong friendship between Burnside and McClellan.

At a secret meeting on March 16, Burnside met with Halleck who ordered him to take two divisions of the IX Corps to Cincinnati where he would take command of the Department of the Ohio. The Department of the Ohio consisted of the states of Michigan, Ohio, Indiana, Illinois, and Kentucky. The current commander, Brig. Gen. Horatio G. Wright, reported that an attack on three positions in Kentucky was imminent. Wright was calling for 20,000 more troops to meet this attack and to maintain order within the department. Antiwar feelings were growing in Indiana, where it was said that a large store of guns and ammunition were under the control of Southern sympathizers. Col. Henry B. Carrington in command in Indiana was also concerned and called for more troops.

General Burnside immediately ordered General Getty's division to Newport News, Virginia, in order to keep it out of the hands of the Army of the Potomac and General Hooker. Generals Sturgis and Willcox were ordered to take their divisions to Baltimore, and Generals Cox and Parke moved their divisions to Ohio. On Sunday, March 22, General Burnside and his staff departed Baltimore for Cincinnati with only short stops in Altoona and Pittsburgh. They arrived tired and worn in Cincinnati at 5:30 on the following morning. On March 24, General Burnside formally took command of the Department of the Ohio from General Wright.

Madison considered staying behind to serve as judge advocate for the Army of the Potomac under General Hooker, and it was said by some that the position was his for the asking; but he elected to remain loyal to his general and move on with Burnside to Cincinnati. He respected General

Burnside's ability as a military strategist and, with the unrest in the states, he found good reason to believe there was a great deal to do in that part of the country.

Effective March 23, Madison was pleased to be named acting judge advocate for the Department of the Ohio knowing that this appointment would be a great opportunity to improve his rank and status. He remembered the ride with Burnside coming back from Washington several months before and thought that possibly now Burnside's plan for him would unfold. Having served gallantly in the actions at South Mountain, Antietam, and Fredericksburg, he was sure that General Burnside would give him more responsibility and a promotion. Everyone on the staff knew of his gallantry and of his abilities as an officer. Still, there were several members of the staff who didn't like Madison and were jealous of his accomplishments. Captain Hutton, in particular, had not forgotten being chastised by him at Fredericksburg and knew that Madison had him called before the general for behaving improperly during the battle. As Madison focused his attention on the tremendous backlog of legal cases before him, Hutton looked for ways to get his revenge.

Chapter IV

Cincinnati, Ohio

Upon arriving in Cincinnati, Burnside's entire staff moved into the Burnet House, a large, elegant six-story hotel in the heart of town that provided warm accommodations for both military and civilian travelers. The staff worked in a small office space in a building on Fourth Street, just down the street from the hotel. The headquarters for the Department of the Ohio comprised of two large rooms on the first floor for staff and rooms on the upper floor for General Burnside and the other generals. When Madison reported for duty, he found the judge advocate's office in a mess with many cases still pending and requiring a great deal of attention. Burnside ordered that all future actives for the judge advocate be assigned to Madison, who quickly accepted the challenge and set down to business. The work, which was long, hard, and tedious, was what Madison enjoyed most. He immediately set out to get the legal affairs of the department in order. He hadn't had a legal workload like this since his days at Harvard, so he worked during the day and well into the night reviewing warrants and planning his cases for prosecution. Although he enjoyed the work, it made him tired and often impatient with others. Madison's desk was placed in the front room of the building along with Lt. Col. Lewis Richmond and Maj. Nathaniel H. McLean.[1] As a general practice it was well understood that other members of the staff were to use the desks in the back room. A matter of concern to Madison and the field officers was that someone would move or mix up the files on their desks, which would cause them extra work. It wasn't considered an unreasonable practice and, for the most part, the other junior officers obeyed. Only Captain Hutton, still feeling the pain of the reprimand at Fredericksburg, felt compelled to use the desks in the front room. He and Madison had words regarding this issue once when Madison caught him sitting at his desk writing a letter. After some sarcastic words, Hutton moved.

Madison had lost all respect for Captain Hutton, and both he and Hutton knew where they stood with each other. Madison felt that Hutton was unworthy—to say the least—but generally not worth the trouble of thought. Hutton thought of Madison as arrogant and self-righteous. Jealous of Madison and looking for opportunities to embarrass him, Hutton resigned himself to wait for the proper time.

Cincinnati was a lively center of commerce and travel. Travelers came throughout the southwestern part of Ohio and northern Kentucky to trade and make travel connections on the railroad. Among the many travelers at this time were Ginnie Moon and her mother, both suspected of treachery and of supplying information and supplies to the Confederacy. General Burnside ordered them to be held under house arrest at the Burnet House, where they stayed for several months. During their stay, Burnside attempted without success to convince them to give up their support of the South. Later in their confinement, Ginnie's sister Lottie, who held the same Southern sympathies, joined them. Lottie, also a spy, had performed valuable services to the South. General Burnside knew Lottie Moon well. She had left him standing at the altar in their younger days. With the attractive and lively Moon sisters under house arrest, the evenings at the Burnet House were quite interesting. Many Union officers made efforts to court the young women, and in doing so provided them with a great deal of information that eventually found its way into Confederate hands. Madison did not approve of the activities of the Moon sisters or the way they were treated by the general. He knew all too well the fervent heart of the Confederate loyalists from his Aunt Rose, and in his opinion the women posed a threat to every man on the field of battle and should have been treated more harshly.

On Friday, April 10, Madison found himself in his hotel room, reading and writing briefs for a military commission to be formed in the coming days. The work was hard and tiring, and he occasionally stood up to let his mind wander. Earlier in the day, he had been captivated by a woman living in the room across the hall. Somewhat out of character, he took the liberty to look through the keyhole of the door to see if she was there. Not seeing anything and hearing someone coming down the hall, he returned to his room.

Later that evening while working in his room, Madison realized that the woman and her husband had returned to their quarters. As his attention was drawn to them he heard that the woman was going to retire for the evening and her husband was going out. Overcome with the thought of seeing her, he moved quickly to satisfy his irrational impulse and soon found himself in the hall. Seeing no one coming, he quickly looked through the keyhole of her door. She was there in the room, walking back and forth before him. Like a moth being drawn to the light, he had to get a better look. He quietly placed a suitcase near the door and stepped onto it. As his head raised above the opening in the transom, his eyes beheld the woman in all of her natural splendor. Suddenly from down the hall a man came running, and Madison quickly realized that it was the woman's husband. He had been caught in the act. After a short period of embarrassment the matter was put to rest and the incident forgotten. Knowing it was wrong for a gentleman to do such a thing, Madison took responsibility for his actions. He resolved that should the incident in the hotel materialize into something more serious he would admit his error, make amends, and face the consequences like a man. The woman and her husband remained in the city for three days but never pressed charges.[2]

Several days later, General Burnside had filled the staffing assignments and began to restore order to the department. For Madison, the work was never ending. It was important that records were brought up to date and that a military commission be created to take care of legal matters. And legal matters of the Department of the Ohio were forming as rapidly as the clouds before a storm. The resistance to the Union in Kentucky, Indiana, and Ohio, and the strong antiwar rhetoric of the newly formed Peace Democrats, or "Copperheads" as they were known, caused great concern for Burnside. He felt it was necessary to take immediate action, and on April 13 he issued General Order 38. This order stated that anyone within the Department of the Ohio found aiding or comforting the enemy would be tried as a traitor and, if convicted, sentenced to death. Its provisions included the idea that anyone who declared support for the enemy was also to be considered a traitor and therefore would be tried as a spy. General Order 38 provided a much-needed guide for the people in Kentucky who lived in the borderland between the Confederacy and the Union; however, for those further north the general order represented despotism and hard military rule. Madison, directed by his legal and political training, spoke against the order from the beginning and recommended that the general rescind it without delay. Treason was a serious offense, still there remained a great difference between what people said in speeches and acts of treason. Madison believed that the use of inflammatory language regarding the conduct of the war was not reason to arrest and try individuals on the grounds of spying. In his opinion the general had ventured on to tenuous ground. Madison knew the general order was potentially dangerous because it would permit the arrest of individuals on hearsay and rumor, clog the jails and legal system within the department, and usurp the legal rights of the citizens. He believed that the conservative and constitutionally minded citizens of the Department of the Ohio would resist the harsh language of the order, thereby causing increased civil unrest. In addition, there was the question of jurisdiction, civil or military and whether the Constitution provided for such action. It was Madison's opinion that General Burnside's order played into the hands of the Copperheads. This order would force normal, law-abiding people into action because of the apparent threat to their constitutional rights. The president's declaration of martial law in 1862 and the suspension of habeas corpus justified a crackdown on dissidents; yet, it was untested in areas removed from the fighting where civil courts were properly functioning. In the long run, the general order tended to be on questionable legal grounds and very bad politically. Madison strongly protested to General Burnside; nevertheless, the general stated that the president's declaration of martial law gave him the authority to make such an order and it was Madison's responsibility to see that it was carried out. Burnside dismissed Madison's concerns saying that once the radicals and the Copperheads were in jail, the department would calm down.

In making his protest to Burnside in such a vehement way, Madison knew his loyalty to the general would be called into question. Nevertheless, he did not back away from the issue. The two had strained their relationship over the general order and the treatment of the Moon sisters, which he continued to question. Being a man of strong principle, Madison held his ground.

On April 28, while riding to Indianapolis with Burnside, Capt. Duncan Pell mentioned to the general that he had heard about an incident in which Captain Cutts was caught looking upon a woman at the Burnet House. Outwardly, Burnside admonished Pell for speaking in such a way about a fellow officer and questioned him about where he had learned of this incident. Hearing enough to warrant further investigation, Burnside charged Pell with the responsibility to either prove or disprove it and report back to him. Captain Pell now had the authority to investigate the incident and, if proven, bring disgrace upon the always perfect and high-minded Captain Cutts. It was a great opportunity to help his friend, Captain Hutton, and repay Madison for his remarks about Hutton at Fredericksburg. When Pell returned to Cincinnati, he set to work investigating the Burnet House incident.[3]

Soon after, Francis Haseltine, the husband of the woman in the Burnet House, responded to Captain Pell's inquiry. Haseltine indicated that a person, undoubtedly Madison, was caught looking over the transom of his hotel room at his wife. He also indicated it would serve no purpose to make this incident public because the dishonor of having the members of General Burnside's staff knowing of the incident was enough punishment. As a gentleman and a former soldier, he understood the nature of a "lusting of the eyes" and didn't want this indiscretion to adversely impact Madison's career.[4] Despite his comments on the matter, Haseltine had provided Captain Pell with the necessary information to destroy Madison's reputation.

On May 1, Clement L. Vallandigham, a former member of Congress and the state leader of the Copperheads, made an inflammatory speech at Mount Vernon, Ohio. In the crowd that listened to his remarks that day were members of Burnside's staff. The speech was claimed to contain comments sympathetic to the enemy and questioned the power of the government to put down the rebellion. If Burnside wanted to make an example of the general order, Vallandigham was the perfect opportunity.

On May 4, with all of the information collected regarding his speeches, General Burnside ordered Captain Hutton to arrest Clement Vallandigham. Hutton immediately set out for Dayton, located and arrested Vallandigham at his home, and took him to Cincinnati where he was charged for violation of General Order 38. Madison, upon learning of Vallandigham's arrest, suggested to General Burnside that the general withdraw the prosecution of the case. After a heated discussion between the two, Burnside firmly ordered Madison to prosecute Vallandigham without delay. The discord between Madison and the general was obvious, and the bond between them had come unraveled. Instantly, the staff learned of the situation between the two and began to look unfavorably on Madison's behavior. Suddenly, Captain Hutton began to feel more confident.

Madison immediately set to work on preparing for the prosecution of the famous Copperhead. Although he found himself heavily immersed in his preparations, his life was taking a different course. He had received word his father's health was failing. He wanted to return to Washington but was unable to do so because of the upcoming trial of Vallandigham. As the days passed, Captain Hutton and other staff members seemed more distant towards Madison, but he didn't see the treachery about to surround him.

A military commission was established to hear the case against Vallandigham, and the trial began soon after his arrest. As expected, there was a great deal of excitement generated by the press, and the entire nation soon became interested in the outcome of the trial.

Madison continued to be concerned about the use of General Order 38. He didn't like Vallandigham's statements but felt his prosecution was a political mistake. Still, he did his duty and prosecuted him to the fullest extent. Early in the proceedings, Madison requested that the trial continue around the clock in order to get it completed before too much attention could be drawn to it. In the end, the trial lasted two days with the defendant's attorneys protesting that since he was not in the military, he should be tried in a civil court and that a military commission had no jurisdiction. The commission overruled the objection, convicted Vallandigham, and sentenced him to confinement at the military installation at Fort Warren, Massachusetts, for the duration of the war. The public instantly became outraged. Ironically, some people supported the former congressman, while others supported the Union and complained that the commission was too easy on the Copperhead.

Madison couldn't be bothered with the publicity once the trail ended. He requested a leave and immediately left Cincinnati for Washington to attend to his father. Unfortunately, there was little time, and on May 11 his father, James Madison Cutts, died. Madison and Adele mourned the loss of their father, whom they considered a kind and loving father. Despite the controversy between President Buchanan and Congress over his appointment, James Cutts performed his duties in a most admirable fashion. Madison's father was paid full respect by the Federal government and those who knew him. The family received expressions of sympathy from many in government and the military. The elder Cutts had lived a long, noble life and was admired as a dedicated public servant that, in time of great civil strife, put the welfare of the country in front of his own personal health.

Madison rode with his mother and sister to the beautiful Oak Hill Cemetery in Georgetown. His father and uncle had purchased the family plot in 1857 upon the closing of the cemetery at St. Joseph's Church across from Lafayette Park in Washington, D.C. The family had gathered there for the internment of Madison's grandfather, grandmother, and other family members. The family plot was located north of the Remwick Chapel in the woods away from the noise and the war, where his father would find eternal peace beside the marble monument marking the remains of his proud family. With his father's internment, the strong relationship between a father and a son had come to an end. Madison stayed in Washington long enough to manage the family affairs for his mother and then returned to Cincinnati.

On the same day as his father's death, attorneys for Vallandigham applied for a writ of habeas corpus, which was later denied by the United

States Circuit Court in Cincinnati. The affair caused quite a stir in Washington and elsewhere around the country. In Albany, New York, a group of Peace Democrats called for Vallandigham's release in a letter of resolution dated May 19, 1863. In an attempt to lessen the impact of General Burnside's actions, the president responded to the Albany Democrats, indicating he believed that the president of the United States, in fact, had the power and the constitutional support to arrest Vallandigham because the Founding Fathers had not considered the First Amendment's application in time of war or civil strife. However, Lincoln admitted that he would most likely not have arrested and tried Vallandigham. Later in the month he ordered Vallandigham to be sent out of the Union and to be given over to the rebels. Upon hearing the president's remarks, General Burnside offered his resignation in view of the fact that Lincoln rescinded the general's imprisonment orders, but the president refused to accept it. Although the circuit court had denied the writ of habeas corpus, there remained a question as to whether the Supreme Court would follow suit. In addition, while Madison was away, someone had started a rumor that he had said General Burnside had demonstrated cowardice at the Battle of Bull Run. The false rumor in no time at all reached the general feeding his resentment. Madison was clearly out of favor.[5]

Upon returning to Cincinnati from Washington, Madison called on the general to ask the disposition of his request for promotion to major and to officially be assigned as judge advocate for the Department of the Ohio. General Burnside indicated a promotion was out of the question, thus Madison would remain as acting judge advocate. In addition, he announced that he intended to go after the traitorous newspapers. In fact, he sanctioned the break-in and destruction of the *Jeffersonian* newspaper in Richmond, Indiana, for publishing radical and inflammatory articles. Burnside also indicated that the army was suppressing the Chicago *Times* and would not allow the New York *World* to be distributed in the department. Expectedly, Madison again vehemently questioned the judgment of the general for stifling the press. He indicated that the general had stepped way beyond the bounds of good sense and was making decisions that held great legal and political implications. General Burnside lost his patience with the young soldier and turned against him. As if to lash back at him, he changed the subject and asked Madison about the incident of April 10 at the Burnet House. Madison, stunned that the issue was even known, admitted that it was true and that he made a terrible mistake. The general told him that his position would remain as it was and that he was to turn his attention now to the Chicago *Times* for writing "repeated expressions of disloyal and incendiary statements."[6] The dauntless Madison advised the general of the trouble one could run into when attempting to control the press. The general blew up again at Madison's continued resistance, but Madison continued to press his point, telling the general that to take a newspaper to court for what it writes is madness and will cause more harm than good. The First Amendment was designed for the express purpose of preventing the government from restricting the press, and the action would be considered the act of a tyrant. Burnside countered by reminding Madison that while a war was going on, the survival of the Union required extraordinary action. Burnside was confident that the president would give him permission to shut down the papers. Madison knew better. Still, Burnside, with his temper almost to the point of losing control, commanded Madison to prepare the charges.[7] Madison stood fearlessly before the general as he had several weeks before. He knew how politicians thought; therefore, it was his duty to help his general. As he had stated in his commencement address at Brown University, "Truth was his shield." Unfortunately, any chance of reasoning with Burnside was gone, along with their relationship. Madison concluded the meeting by agreeing to do his duty. The meeting had not gone well. Not only did he not get confirmation of a promotion; he again had lost the argument with his commander. There is a rule in the military that states there is no higher power than a general in time of war. Try as he might, this was a battle that he could not possibly win.

Madison followed orders, yet he longed for a commander with better insight and leadership. If Burnside wasn't careful, he would turn the whole North against the war and the Union cause. As for the general, he had had enough of the outspoken Captain Cutts.

At the end of May the country received the news of the disaster at Chancellorsville. Although Burnside expressed displeasure with the defeat, he gloated in knowing that Lee had taken the brash, outspoken Hooker to the woodshed. It was the end of Hooker as the commander of the Army of the Potomac.

On the morning of June 18, as Madison walked into the front room office at the headquarters offices he found Captain Hutton sitting at his desk. There were two other vacant desks in the room and Hutton knew better than to be using his desk. Madison, in his normal hurried manner, told Hutton to move.

Captain Hutton had reached a new level of inner strength, knowing that Madison was in great disfavor with the general. With Hutton's arrest of Vallandigham in early May, he had become the bright star in the staff. After gathering his papers and moving, Hutton began to question Madison's right to the desk. Their discussion centered on whom had authority in the office and eventually deteriorated into name-calling. Captain Hutton took offense in Madison's remarks and later sent a note demanding an apology. Madison received the letter from Captain Hutton with disgust and refused to give him the satisfaction of retracting his words. He knew what he had said to Hutton could be interpreted as inflammatory, but as long as he didn't allow it to go further, there could be no further issue. To respond to Hutton or even to suggest an apology, which he had no intention of doing, would lead him into a greater conflict. He had never liked the man, especially since the time he had seen him in action at Fredericksburg. After reviewing the letter, Madison quickly scribbled his reply.

> *Headquarters of the Ohio*
> *June 18th 1863*
>
> *Returned with the information that I do not propose to enter into any consideration of the subject matter of this letter.*
>
> > *J. M. Cutts*
> > *Capt. 11th Infantry*
> > *Judge Advt*
> > *Dept of the Ohio*[8]

Madison hoped that the insolent Hutton would not attempt to make more out of this conversation and would simply let the matter rest. Hutton had acted the same way once before in front of Lieutenant Colonel Richmond, making inappropriate remarks to Madison in a similar situation. Although Madison heard his comment, he chose not to make an issue of it, especially since Lieutenant Colonel Richmond remained in the room. This time, however, it was different. Hutton demanded an apology.

The following morning Maj. William Cutting came to Madison with another note from Captain Hutton.

> *Cincinnati*
> *June 19th '63*
> *Burnet House*
>
> *Capt. J. M. Cutts*
> *U.S.A.*
> *Sir,*
>
> *My note of last evening requesting an apology for and retraction of the insulting expression made use of by you in our discussion of yesterday having been returned with the endorsement "That you did not propose to enter into any consideration of the subject," I presume that you are willing to afford*

*me the satisfaction to which I am entitled and which I now
personally demand.*

*This will be handed to you by my friend Major Cutting,
who is authorized to receive any communication from you,
and to make all necessary arrangements for a meeting.*

> *I am Sir,*
> *Yr. Obt. Sert.*
> *Charles Gordon Hutton*
> *Capt & A. D. C.*[9]

Captain Hutton had challenged Madison to a duel. Madison knew that to
accept the challenge was against military law, but also not worth the effort for such a lowly individual as Captain Hutton, so he quickly endorsed
the letter.

> *Head Qtrs. Dept. of the Ohio*
> *June 19th 1863*

*Respectfully refused with a copy of the communication to
which it relates to Major General Burnside, through Lt. Col.
Richmond, with a request that he will direct some capable officer in whom he has confidence as a brave man and a gentleman to investigate the entire subject and report therein to him.*

> *I am General*
> *Yr. Obt. Sert.*
> *J. M. Cutts*
> *Capt. 11th Infantry*
> *Judge Advocate*
> *Dept. of the Ohio*[10]

It was Madison's hope that General Burnside would take control of the
situation by ordering an investigation of the incident. He had no real
quarrel with Hutton and felt that an inquiry would settle the matter.
Madison quickly wrote another note to Captain Hutton.

> *Head Qtrs. Dept. of the Ohio*
> *Cincinnati, O June 19th '63*

Capt. Hutton
A. D. C.
Sir,

*In answer to your note of same date herewith, delivered
into my hands by your friend Major Cutting, I have to refer
you to Articles 25, 26, 27, 28 of the Rules and Articles for the
Government of the Armies of the United States. I have further*

to inform you that communications of today and yesterday have both been respectfully forwarded to Maj. Gen. Burnside through Lt. Col. Richmond with a request that he appoint a capable officer in whose character as a brave man and a gentleman he may have entire confidence to investigate the entire subject, and report therein to him. The only kind of personal bravery I know anything about or care to exhibit to the world, is the bravery of an officer who always tries to do his duty. This is bravery above and higher than any known to the "Dueling Code." That call—being simple, absolute, and unqualified "Cowardice."

> *I am Sir*
> *Yr. Obt. Sert.*
> *J. M. Cutts*
> *Capt. 11th Infantry*
> *Judge Adv. Dept. of the Ohio*

(NS) Not choosing to submit myself to any formalities in this matter, I send this by an orderly. It is therefore sealed. You are not to suppose that I have any desire of secrecy in the matter. You are at perfect liberty to show it to your friend Major Cutting.[11]

Matters did not improve. General Burnside elected not to call for an investigation. He indicated to Lieutenant Colonel Richmond that the members of his staff should work their differences out in an honorable fashion and get on with their work. Unfortunately, Captain Hutton chose to share the contents of Madison's second note to others, with the result being interpreted that Madison had started the whole affair by calling Captain Hutton a coward. The other staff officers immediately began to talk among themselves, and Madison became the focus of their contempt. He felt it was necessary to provide Major Cutting with an out from this rapidly deteriorating situation, so he wrote a note to the major.

> *Head-quarters. Dept. of the Ohio*
> *June 21st, 1863*

> *Major Cutting, A. D. C.*
> *Sir,*
>
> *In recommending your friend Captain Hutton to a staff appointment you will remember that you described him as an accomplished rider, etc. etc., but a coward. You gave him this character in the presence of General Burnside, myself and other members of the staff. I heard you make this statement in regard*

to him more than once. This was about the time he appeared as a vol. Aide de Camp in General Reno's staff. I think you first spoke of him at Fredericksburg, Va., during the occupation of that place by the IX Army Corps. At all events, you thoroughly remember the facts, and it can be easily proved. In a recent transaction, you appeared as one willing to be his second in a duel, and yourself the bearer of a challenge, which I declined.

I ask you, sir, whether, if I had declined the challenge on the ground that your principle was a coward, your own position as witness to the fact would have been very creditable to yourself or honorable in the eyes of the world. I do not mean to make any offensive allusions to yourself or your principle but only make this statement to you to ask the additional question "Is it possible for Major Cutting to cast any blame upon Capt. Cutts, or find any fault with his conduct and bravery throughout the entire transaction?"

I am sir
Yr. Obt. Sert.
J. M. Cutts
Capt. 11th Infantry
Judge Adv. Dept. of the Ohio [12]

On the following day, Major Cutting sent a response to Madison by way of the surgeon Dr. Church denying that he ever made such a disparaging comment about his friend Captain Hutton. It surprised Madison that the major didn't remember his own comments regarding Hutton at Aquia Creek and in Maryland. He thought the major had to have been mistaken. The statement clearly expressed in front of the general and several other members of the staff on the two occasions could easily be proved. Another letter was sent to Major Cutting in order to help improve his memory, but the damage had been done and now Madison found himself at the center of treachery that threatened his career. In this final note, delivered to Major Cutting, Madison gave him an opportunity to remove himself from this situation and to step away from Captain Hutton. It was Madison's hope that, if he provided all of the information to Lieutenant Colonel Richmond and General Burnside, the commanding general would gather all of the officers together to settle this affair as a father would settle disputes within a family. General Burnside chose another course. Within minutes of sending his last note, Madison, Major Cutting, and Captain Hutton were placed under arrest. The general decided to let a court-martial settle the affair.

Chapter V

The Military Court

On the 29th day of June 1863, a military commission set the trials of Maj. William Cutting, Capt. Charles G. Hutton, and Capt. Madison Cutts. Madison's court-martial convened on June 30 and although it remained serious, Madison was hopeful of an acquittal.[1] Only five of the original members of the court showed for the first day's proceedings. Madison objected on the basis that a military court is required to consist of not fewer than five and not more than 13 members. During the opening session, Madison protested that he had the right to be tried by a full court. The court overruled his objection, and the trial continued. Madison was brought before the court for the charge of conduct unbecoming an officer and a gentleman and faced three specifications to the charges: (1) he exasperated and wounded the feeling of a brother officer by calling him names; (2) that he intentionally brought disgrace upon a brother officer by calling him a coward; and (3) he looked over the transom of a hotel room at the Burnet House at a lady undressing.

Madison's experience as a judge advocate taught him a great deal about how the military legal system worked. Courts-martial were used as a means of maintaining discipline and order within the military. It was a common practice to take the men to task and to penalize them for bad behavior even in the face of the horrors of war. He also knew that jealous or vengeful officers used courts-martial to discredit others or eliminate rivals. In many cases they used minor incidents or misbehavior, no matter how small or insignificant. Madison realized that he had, through his actions in the hotel and the comments to Hutton and Major Cutting, placed his future in their hands. He knew that a shred of truth, no matter how small, could be made to appear gigantic in the eyes of the military commission. In his typical way, he analyzed the situation and resolved that General Burnside had the power to court-martial him and make it stick.

Therefore, his only hope would be to build a case based on logic and let the appeal process overturn the court's judgment. He hoped the charges listed against him in the first two specifications would be thrown out along with the third charge, since the incident in the hotel had not seriously damaged his reputation or that of the United States Army. He was disheartened by allowing himself to get into such a position but confident the court would see its way to a just conclusion.

Court resumed on July 1 with a request for a plea from the accused. Madison pleaded "not guilty" to specifications 1 and 2, and "guilty" to specification 3 alleging no criminal intent. Madison then submitted a list of the individuals to serve as witnesses.[2] With the words from his witnesses, all of the questions regarding the comments made by Major Cutting could and would be made clear and true.

To start the trial, the judge advocate first called Capt. Charles Gordon Hutton to the stand and proceeded to examine the witness. Captain Hutton's testimony and cross-examination were a good description of the events of June 18. Madison drew out of him that the defendant was not excited during the exchange between the two and that a similar situation occurred earlier in front of Lieutenant Colonel Richmond with the same results. Captain Goddard, the second witness, indicated that only Captain Hutton raised his voice. When Major Cutting took the stand he testified that he had never used the term "coward" in describing Captain Hutton and confirmed he had carried Captain Hutton's challenge to a duel to Madison.

The next witness for the prosecution was Francis J. Haseltine who retold the story of the incident on the night of April 10. Madison did not object to the testimony of Mr. Haseltine and during cross-examination established that Haseltine had not pressed the issue at any time after April 10. It was only after Captain Pell wrote him requesting information about the incident that it became a matter of record. Although Madison had pleaded guilty to the charge of looking at Mrs. Haseltine, he claimed it wasn't necessarily a great scandal if no one elected to prosecute the matter.

During the first part of the trial, the attention of all the members of the court and of the nation became focused on the battle that had been raging around Gettysburg, Pennsylvania. Everyone was reading the announcements with a feeling of relief and joy at the news of the great Union victory and of Lee's retreat into Virginia. Madison heard the news of General Meade's victory, and longed to be back with the Army of the Potomac and the war. He could not stand the petty jealousy among the members of the staff or the circumstances he faced.

When court resumed on July 6, General Burnside was called to testify. The general indicated that he could not recall the remarks in question made by Major Cutting concerning the character of Captain Hutton; in fact, he remembered his staff being full at the time and indifferent about adding another officer. General Burnside spoke of the conversation he and Madison had had regarding the incident at the Burnet House and indicated that he thought Madison should have resigned. Madison pressed him to admit that the general had stated in their meeting that the incident at the Burnet House was of no consequence compared to the issues at hand and nothing further need come of it. General Burnside stated to the contrary that he would have relieved him from his staff. Finally, General Burnside stated that Captain Hutton was a good and brave officer who had served with General Reno at South Mountain by rendering service to General Burnside during the march through Virginia following the Battle of Antietam. He confirmed that during the Battle of Fredericksburg, Captain Hutton and Captain Fearing were sent to Tyler's Battery to report from time to time the progress of events.[3] General Burnside also stated that he was not familiar with the letters and endorsements that Madison had sent to him regarding Captain Hutton's challenge to a duel. Altogether, the general's testimony did not go well for Madison.

On the following day, July 8, Adele arrived from Washington to help in any way she could.[4] Madison submitted several motions regarding specification 3, in which he contended that Haseltine's remarks should be stricken from the record on the basis that none of them referred to the accused and that they represented only Haseltine's opinion. He also requested that the entire specification be thrown out along with his plea and that he be directed not to provide a defense to the specification. The court overruled both of his motions and ruled that in order to expedite the trial the judge advocate would read into the record a statement regarding the character of the accused.

It having been intimated by the Accused that he desired the attendance of witnesses and also that he desired to examine the witness now on the stand for the purpose of proving good character and bravery etc., etc., and now to avoid the necessity of the attendance of such witnesses and to facilitate the proceedings of this court to make the following admissions, as to the character of the accused, upon record.

First: that the character of Capt. Cutts as an Officer and Gentleman has been good;

*Second: That he was always recognized and bore the character
of a brave man;*
*Third: That the character of the accused for truth and veracity
is good.*[5]

With the reading of these general statements, Adele's testimony regarding Madison's character would not be necessary but she remained with him for the remainder of the trail for moral support.

The following day news reached Cincinnati that a large group of Confederate soldiers had crossed the Ohio River at Brandenburg, Kentucky, and had entered southern Indiana. The news created a stir in the city, for many feared a situation similar to Lee's campaign in Pennsylvania. Others thought that the rebels would solidify the Copperheads in the region and cause great destruction.

It became apparent that the staff of General Burnside paid Adele little respect, and they held Madison in contempt. There was no question that regardless of the outcome of the trial, he would no longer remain a part of the staff.[6] Remembering, *Don Quixote*, Madison maintained his courage even when others laughed. He was strengthened knowing that right would prevail.

On July 9, Madison called Lieutenant Colonel Richmond to the stand. Richmond confirmed that the officers in the front room of the headquarters building had their own desks, one of which was for Captain Cutts. He also confirmed Captain Hutton had taken that desk in the past and, when asked by Captain Cutts to move, did so with an insolent remark. The court would not allow Lieutenant Colonel Richmond to respond to any of Madison's questions regarding the relationship between Captain Cutts and Captain Pell. Madison's goal was to provide the court with information indicating the relationship between the two captains was very much strained, and Captain Pell and Captain Hutton were using their influence to turn the commanding general against him. The other witnesses permitted to testify indicated that Madison had been placed under a great deal of pressure by the large load of cases pending before his arrival and the large number of cases generated by General Order 38. Major McLean confirmed the arrangement of the desks at headquarters and that he too found papers on his desk misplaced because someone else had sat there. Dr. Church was called next, but he did not add much to the existing testimony. Madison then asked the court to secure a deposition from Captains O'Keeffe, Keogh, and Dahlgren in which they were to answer questions about the behavior of Captain Hutton at the Battle of Fredericksburg and the subsequent discussions after the reprimand by General Burnside.

The judge advocate objected on the grounds that the deposition and Captain Dahlgren's comments were irrelevant and immaterial, and the court upheld the objection. Madison then attempted to secure a deposition from his uncle, Col. R. D. Cutts, and from his mother, in order to collaborate his contention that he had previously heard Major Cutting refer to Captain Hutton as a coward. The court upheld the objection of the judge advocate on the same grounds. With that, the trial was near an end.

In his statement, Madison mentioned that treachery had necessitated his trial and he requested the court's good judgment in seeing through it. The court should either find him not guilty or guilty with no criminal intent to the first two specifications and to throw out the third specification. The court took several days to deliberate, in part, due to the need to protect the population from Morgan's Raiders.

On July 15 at 9 A.M., the court reconvened to render a verdict in the case. The court found the accused "guilty" on all three specifications, and Madison listened as the president of the court ordered him to be dismissed from the service—a terrible blow but not totally unexpected. Unable to obtain the important depositions to support his case, he knew that without that information it was his word against the others. To Madison, General Burnside demonstrated his lack of character in the whole affair, and for that he pledged then and there never to forgive the general for his actions. Still, he remained undaunted. Madison viewed the entire episode as a vendetta against him that would not hold up in the eyes of righteous people. Still, he knew that his reputation as an honorable soldier would be forever blemished. Following the conclusion of the trial, Madison had to undergo more embarrassment and ridicule as a result of the trials of Captain Hutton and Major Cutting. Madison instructed Adele to return to Washington. Adele was reluctant to leave, but assured Madison that she held greater influence in Washington and would use it to see that justice was served.

Since the start of the war, Adele had reached the very height of Washington society. After the death of Stephen Douglas, she became one of the most well-respected women in the city. She developed a strong relationship with President Lincoln, attending many of the receptions at the executive mansion. Her greatest mark of distinction was achieved when standing alone against all of Washington's aristocracy following the tragic death of the president's son, Willie. Many at that time looked upon the Lincolns with low regard and considered them bumpkins from the West. With Willie's death, most considered them unfit for the position they commanded. Knowing and respecting Lincoln as she did, Adele continued to accept invitations to attend social functions at the executive mansion and in doing so she helped to bring order and dignity to those social gatherings. Despite the jealousy of Mrs. Lincoln, not a word could be said against the lovely and most honorable Mrs. Douglas. Lincoln found her to be quite pleasant and often spoke to her during receptions and dinners. She had been a true friend to the president. Adele and her uncle would do everything in their power to see that Madison was treated fairly.

During the closing days of Madison's trial, it appeared that the Union army had Morgan's Raiders on the run. Union Brig. Gen. Henry M. Judah pursued Morgan by the river route, while Generals Edward H. Hobson and James M. Shackleford followed him on interior roads.[7] Their goal was to bring to bear as many troops as possible to force the raiders into a stand. To slow the raiders, the generals telegraphed ahead to the towns in the enemy's path, telling them to place barricades on the roads. To add to Morgan's troubles, Union gunboats patrolled the Ohio River to prevent his escape to the South. With the number of Union troops at hand, there was no doubt as to the result of a battle between the two armies. The raiders had crossed southern Ohio not so much to raid but to stay out in front of the ever-pursuing Union cavalry. Everyone was exhausted from the ride, particularly the rebels.

On July 19, news reached Cincinnati that Morgan's Raiders had been trapped near Chester, Ohio. All three Union commands attacked the rear guard of Morgan's forces and after some hard fighting captured the entire unit. Morgan took the rest of the force, about 1,400 strong, upriver to Belleville, where his attempt to cross over into Kentucky was stopped by gunboats. Eventually, only about four hundred men, including Morgan, made it across the Ohio River, while the rest were captured. Morgan himself was captured a few days later.

Within several days, the Union army returned to Cincinnati with more than 1,500 prisoners. The prisoners were taken from the boats and marched to the city jail where Madison was surprised to see among the group of officers his old law associate, Basil Duke. Madison made contact with his old friend at the jail where they briefly spoke of the old times. Although they fought on different sides, they still respected each other as honorable men.

Basil told Madison about going to Montgomery in April 1861, his return home after their parting in St. Louis, and his marriage to Henrietta Morgan. In October 1861, he had gone to Tennessee, joined up with his brother-in-law, and became an officer of the 2nd Kentucky Volunteers, the notorious Alligator Horsemen. Basil was shot at the Battle of Shiloh, and he eventually was promoted to the rank of colonel. He said that many of the boys captured in the raid were his men. He questioned Madison as to why they were incarcerated in a city prison. Colonel Duke expressed his opinion to Madison that as soldiers and gentlemen, he and his men should be treated as prisoners of war and imprisoned accordingly. Madison explained that Morgan's raid had caused a stir among the public, and politicians considered the raiders to be criminals. In reality, he explained that the jails were full due to a general order issued by General Burnside, which virtually filled all of the jails in the district. At the conclusion of their conversation, and despite the fact that he was also in trouble with his commander, Madison approached Burnside to request the soldiers be treated honorably and provided with the appropriate military courtesy. This did not sit well with the general, and Madison was soon dismissed from his presence. Eventually, all of the enlisted men among the rebels were sent to the military prison at Johnson's Island. Due to the demands of Governor Todd of Ohio and the press, the officers were sent to the Ohio State Prison in Columbus.

Madison was struck by the conditions of the Department of the Ohio more than ever and not surprised at the level of discontent rising among the citizenry with respect to General Order 38. Knowing General Burnside lacked the strength of leadership to maintain such an important command, Madison took it upon himself to call for his removal. In late July, he sent a series of telegrams to the president of the United States. In them, he indicated the poor state of affairs in the Department of the Ohio, and insisted on the urgent removal of General Burnside.

On July 30, the judge advocate general's office returned their finding in the proceedings of Madison's courts-martial. The opinion of the judge advocate general specified that the trial was conducted in a fair, equitable, and legal manner and that the sentence would stand as directed. Madison found it difficult to believe that the judge advocate general's office could render such a decision. His only hope rested with the president seeing things differently and reversing the decision.

For Madison, it was a lonely time. Although he maintained a strong image to everyone and continued to remain confident that honorable men would not let his conviction stand, he truly stood alone in the city and among the staff of General Burnside. Looked upon as a leper and set apart by the other members of the staff, even they would not talk to him or acknowledge his presence. Madison persevered, knowing in his heart that he was right and the victim of a sordid treachery from a commander who could no longer tolerate his voice of good conscience and the mean-spirited Captain Hutton. Through it all, Madison maintained his sense of dignity and honor. His predictions about civil unrest had come true. The Department of the Ohio remained in a turmoil with anti-war Democrats and Copperheads staging rallies, hard-line Republicans calling for the strictest of punishment for radicals, and moderate loyalists concerned about protecting their rights to freedom of speech.

Madison's faith in his ability and the strength of his convictions held his spirits high even under such adversity. The trials of Captain Hutton and Major Cutting did nothing to improve his situation. Hutton was charged for violation of the Article of War 25 for sending a challenge to duel. Hutton pleaded "guilty" to the charge, and after "mature" consideration by the court, he was found guilty and sentenced to be reprimanded by the president of the United States. Madison observed the court proceedings with a degree of contempt, knowing there was only one sentence fixed by the Article 25 for an officer issuing a challenge to duel and that meant being cashiered from the service. In the case of Major Cutting, charged with violation of the Article of War 26 for "carrying a challenge," he was found not guilty and freed.

The sentences from the courts-martial of Captain Hutton and Major Cutting were not in keeping with the articles of war. Clearly a miscarriage of justice had occurred when the instigator of a duel was given a reprimand, the carrier of the challenge set free, and the only person who had obeyed the law received a sentence to be dismissed. The verdict in the cases of Captain Hutton and Major Cutting only further proved the level of treachery involved in the whole affair.

On August 20, the judge advocate general's office rendered its opinion of the court proceedings involving Captain Hutton and Major Cutting. In the case of Captain Hutton, the reviewing officer restated the facts of the case, indicating the prosecution offered no testimony in addition to the guilty plea of the defendant and confirmed that the court found the defendant guilty of violating Article 25. What was found unusual in the case was the court's sentence of Captain Hutton. The court took it upon itself to forgo the required sentence of cashiering Captain Hutton out of the service for a simple reprimand. This was done over the expressed opinion of the judge advocate trying the case. In concluding his recommendation of the court proceedings, the judge advocate general said, "It is believed that this is the first instance on record in which a sentence other than cashiering has followed a conviction of having sent a challenge to fight a duel and if approved will probably establish a precedent whereby the purpose of the law may be defeated."[8] The judge advocate general then recommended that the records be sent back to the court for reconsideration.

In the case of Major Cutting, the judge advocate general's report indicated that Major Cutting, "carrying a challenge in violation of the 26th Article of War," knew the contents of the message. With that, the judge advocate general wrote,

> *The court would have been justified in convicting the accused upon the evidence, but they appear to have decided otherwise and found him not guilty. The record fails to show a final decision; and this is an irregularity, for it is a well-settled rule that following the findings upon the charge of which a person stands accused, an acquittal or sentence shall be pronounced.*[9]

In view of both the facts and of the irregularity referred to, the record might be returned to the court for reconsideration and completion if it had not been dissolved.[10]

In all of the cases in this incident, it appeared as though the court already knew what the outcome of the proceedings would be before the cases were even heard. In addition, the court rendered a harsh decision on the man who least deserved it and, for the most part let the true offenders go. With the judge advocate general's opinion on the cases complete, the records of all of those involved were sent to the president for his consideration and final approval.

Madison remained in Cincinnati throughout the rest of the summer, awaiting a final ruling on the cases from President Lincoln. During that period, both Adele and her uncle paid close attention to the results of the other cases and grew disheartened at the findings of the court. Finally, they made their personal appeals to the president on Madison's behalf.

At first glance, the president humorously remarked that Madison might be elevated to peerage and be accorded the title of "Count Peeper," noting the similarity to Count Piper of Sweden.[11] Yet, after further review, the president could see the inequity of the decision of the court and the treachery levied against Madison. He also concluded, through the court records and through Madison's telegrams, that the young captain had challenged the authority and wisdom of a general during a time of war. Although noble and right in his actions, it was not a wise thing to do to further one's military career. In the same sense, it appeared as though Madison had alienated himself from the junior officers on Burnside's staff, thereby opening the door to jealousy and resentment. Lincoln observed that Madison had made a common mistake of the young by being impatient and relying too much on being right as a savior. Lincoln knew that having right on your side isn't always enough when evil men wish to have their way. In Madison's case, surely the forces against him were too much to prevent his disgrace at the hands of the commander and his junior officers. Madison traveled to Washington in early September to await the president's review.

On September 26, the president made his decision regarding the courts-martial of Captain Hutton, Major Cutting, and Madison. The president found in the matter of issuing a challenge to a brother officer, the only prescribed sentence was dismissal from the service and therefore ordered Captain Hutton dismissed. In the case against Major Cutting, no further action need be taken. As for Madison, the sentences for specifications 1 and 2 were thrown out. Taking into account his previous demonstrations of bravery and gallantry in battle, the sentence regarding the third specification was changed to a reprimand, which the president would deliver himself.

It was a troubled time for the family, not yet fully recovered from the death of the patriarch and the humiliation of the court-martial. Madison attended services at St. Aloysius and prayed that he would be able to redeem himself from his disgrace and gain the strength necessary to achieve his destiny.

In the late afternoon of October 16, Madison was admitted to the executive mansion and shown into the office of the president. The young officer stood at attention and saluted the president as the secretary left the room to the privacy of the commander in chief and the captain. Mr. Lincoln understood the pain the court-martial had inflicted upon Madison. He provided some fatherly advice to his captain by recommending that he put this incident behind him and go forward with his life. At the conclusion of the meeting the president handed Madison his letter of reprimand and shared a personal moment when he said, "I have done worst things myself, but nobody was ever mean enough to tell about them."[12]

Madison left the executive mansion and walked across the street to Lafayette Park, where he had played as a young man. His vindication from the maliciousness of his brother officers in Cincinnati had not removed the tainted scar of being court-martialed. He walked to the bench that he remembered sitting on as a child and read the president's letter.

Executive Mansion

Capt. James M. Cutts   Washington, Oct. 26th, 1863

Although what I am now to say to you is to be, in form, a reprimand, it is not intended to add a pang to what you have already suffered upon the subject to which it relates. You have too much of life yet before you, and have shown too much of promise as an officer, for your future to be lightly surrendered. You were convicted of two offenses. One of them, not of great enormity, and yet greatly to be avoided, I feel sure you are in no danger of repeating. The other you are not so well assured against. The advice of a father to his son 'Beware of entrance to a quarrel, but being in, bear it that the opposed may beware of thee,' is good, and yet not the best. Quarrel not at all. No man resolved to make the most of himself, can spare time for personal contention. Still less can he afford to take all the consequences, including the vitiating of his temper, and the loss of self-control. Yield larger things to which you can show no more than equal right; and yield lesser ones, though clearly your own. Better give your path to a dog, than be bitten by him in contesting for the right. Even killing the dog would not cure the bite.

In the mood indicated deal henceforth with your fellow men, and especially with your brother officers; and even the unpleasant events you are passing from will not have been profitless to you.

A. Lincoln[13]

He was sorry for the pain he had inflicted on himself and his family. Despite his devotion to the Union, there would always be a scar on his personal character that would follow him forever. Returning to the 11th U.S. Infantry Regiment, he was sure to find himself once again in combat. Madison pledged to himself on the honor of Stephen Douglas, his father, and all of the members of his family that he would achieve redemption or die trying.

Chapter VI

The 11th United States Infantry Regiment

The United States Regular Army regiments had attained a high degree of respect and admiration from the volunteer regiments as a result of their discipline and fighting spirit. Under the leadership of Maj. Gen. George Sykes, the Regular Division, or "regs" as they were called, was as good as any to take the field. They proudly wore the white Maltese cross to distinguish themselves as the Second Division of the V Corps of the Army of the Potomac.

Prior to the outbreak of the Civil War, the U.S. Regular Army Infantry consisted of the 1st through the 10th Infantry Regiments, which were scattered throughout the West. These were the originals and commonly referred to as the "old army." It was a small army, relegated to the territories and backwoods of the growing country. Soon after war was declared, President Lincoln called for more soldiers, and the regular army was expanded. On July 29, 1861, Congress confirmed the establishment of the 11th through the 19th Infantry Regiments.[1] To build these forces, officers were quickly named and sent to various parts of the country for recruiting and training. The 11th U.S. Infantry Regiment was assigned to Fort Independence, Massachusetts. There, the newly designated officers, with Madison being one of the originals, learned the ways of war and began filling the ranks of the new regiment with recruits. Life for a soldier in the regular army was tough with heavy demands placed on officer and enlisted man alike. Regular officers were expected to lead their regiments from the front and to drill their troops to perfection. The enlisted men were treated harshly and were paid only $13 per month. The daily routine of attention to detail and endless drill was their stock and trade. They lived in barracks and were provided food, a uniform, and a musket. The soldiers, unique because they had little or no family and not very good prospects for a future, chose to make the army their life with the

82

length of enlistment lasting five years. They quickly learned that their lot was that of well-disciplined and hard-working soldiers. During the early days of the war, they set the standard of discipline for the thousands of volunteers that found themselves in the army.

In the darkest hours following the fall of Fort Sumter, many units came to the aid of the president in Washington, and the regulars quickly responded. In June, they were officially assigned the job of protecting the capital. In July, some of the original first 10 regiments of the old army marched with Gen. Irvin McDowell to Bull Run where they fought admirably under the command of then Maj. George Sykes. Following the battle, the regiments returned to Washington where they became well known for their discipline and drill. In March 1862, General McClellan reorganized the Army of the Potomac, in which, among other things, he formed the regulars into a separate brigade under the command of Sykes. On May 20, newer regular regiments or units were assigned to Sykes's command, and the brigade was designated the "Regular Division." With his new division, the hard-driving Sykes was promoted to brigadier general. The division won recognition for saving McClellan's army at the Battle of Gaines' Mills. They fought bravely in the Battles of Second Bull Run, Antietam, Fredericksburg, Chancellorsville, and Gettsyburg. Within the ranks of the Regular Division were the soldiers of the 11th U.S. Infantry Regiment.

After General Sykes took command the V Corps on June 27, 1863, Brig. Gen. Romeyn B. Ayres became commander of the regulars, a tough and disciplined unit skilled in military tactics and tested by the hardships of battle and military life. Even after marching for miles, the regulars would immediately set to putting bootblack on their shoes and straightening up their uniforms. Their matter-of-fact attitude prevailed when marching into battle and in setting up and tearing down camp. The regulars were not permitted to complain about the duty, the conditions, or to do anything but their duty. The unit approached their assignments with determination; their valor in combat had always been of the highest order. At Gaines' Mills and on the second day of Gettysburg in front of Little Round Top, the regulars saved the day. On the second day of the Battle of Gettysburg, hundreds of them sacrificed themselves in the Devil's Den and along Plum Run. Paying a terrible price for their victories, as professionals, they asked for no special tribute. Madison eagerly rejoined these brave men of war, which strengthened his resolve to be honorably respected by them. He truly belonged in a fighting unit. The war with all of its horrors had cast a spell on him, and he found energy and excitement knowing he would be at the very front of the hell of war.

Madison knew many of the officers of the division from previous actions but was closest to the officers of the 11th Infantry Regiment. He knew many of them from their training at Fort Independence on Castle Island in Boston Harbor in 1861. At that time, the unit was commanded by Lt. Col. Edmund Schriver, a hard taskmaster who forced the new officers to recite battle tactics and army regulations before allowing them to participate in recruiting activities. Madison remembered the training as detailed, rigorous, and redundant; consequently, he found it extremely good as a means of building discipline and leadership among the officers. This discipline and leadership separated them from the volunteer units on the battlefield. Following his training, Madison was sent to Providence, Rhode Island, to begin recruiting duty. Maj. Delancey Floyd-Jones eventually took command of the 11th U.S. Infantry Regiment until the days following the Battle of Gettysburg.

Still smarting from the terrible losses incurred at Gettysburg, the regulars were used to help quell the draft riots in New York City. Their actions in New York were noteworthy, for within a few weeks the New Yorkers had had all of the "regs" they could stand. Calm having been restored, the regulars returned to the Army of the Potomac.

The Union army had moved into Virginia in July in pursuit of Lee and the Army of Northern Virginia. Both armies continued to lick their wounds, while they skirmished throughout most of the summer of 1863. With the approach of fall and the prospect of good weather, General Meade hoped to maneuver the rebels into position for a general engagement.

By the time Madison caught up with the 11th, the regiment was involved in a series of moves designed to counter Confederate activities as Lee attempted to outflank the Union army and drive it from Confederate soil. Both armies sent large numbers to the western theater in preparation for a major engagement developing near Chattanooga, Tennessee. General Meade saw an opportunity to destroy Lee's weakened army, and with the coming of winter, Meade hoped for one final engagement that would draw Lee out into the open where he could again defeat him.

The new commander of the 11th, Capt. Francis M. Cooley, welcomed Madison. The regiment, on the march for the most part since September 14, had settled near Warrenton Junction. During the time when the troops were not marching, they continued to undergo tough training.

Captain Cooley was from Reading, Pennsylvania; and, like Madison, he received his commission as a captain when the new regular army regiments were formed. Cooley, a bright, enthusiastic, and fearless young man was not as well versed in military strategy and tactics. Both Captain Cooley and Madison had spent hours rehearsing and practicing military maneuvers under the direction of Lieutenant Colonel Schriver, Maj. Delancey Floyd-Jones, Capt. Henry L. Chipman, and the paternal Sgt. John Parr. The two officers recalled the times they immersed themselves in the manuals distributed to each officer by the War Department for their training: *Ordnance Manual;* Wayne's *Sword Exercise*, the *Army Regulations*, and Scott's *Tactics*. This information was necessary for the building of strong, knowledgeable officers who would have to lead the regiment. Cooley spent much of his time recruiting at Fort Independence prior to joining the main body of the 11th Infantry in Virginia. Soon after arriving, he was involved in minor actions with the rebels at Leetum and Snicker's Gap. He was aware of Madison's reputation of being a brave soldier and respected him despite the events that had occurred in Cincinnati.

Captain Cooley commanded the 11th, but rank didn't seem important to Madison. He only wanted to fight. On the battlefield, Minié balls made no distinction between commanders and subordinates. He was given command of Company F and second in command of the regiment. Both Cooley and Madison took their positions seriously, working hard to maintain the strict discipline of their troops.

On November 7, the regiment marched toward Rappahannock Station, where they fought on the left side of the line successfully taking the critical high ground overlooking the Confederate position. Later, a large force of Union infantry stormed the center of the Confederate line in one of the war's most successful assaults of an enemy entrenchment. That day, the Union army captured or killed more than 1,700 rebels, forcing Lee to withdraw his army south of the Rapidan River. In the fighting, the 11th U.S. Infantry lost one man with another one wounded. The following day, the regiment moved south of the Rappahannock Station until they set up camp about three miles from Kelly's Ford. On the morning of November 26, the V Corps and the 11th U.S. Infantry crossed the Rapidan River at Culpeper Mine Ford and moved through the forest to the New Hope Church, located near a small creek called Mine Run. If General Meade's plan was successful, his army would crush Lt. Gen. Richard S. Ewell's Confederate force before Lee could come to the rescue. Once Ewell's forces were defeated, Meade would then turn on the rest of Lee's army to defeat it in part. The plan required a great deal of planning and timing, but if successful it would result in a stunning victory and a severe defeat for the rebels.

Mine Run, which ran down the middle of a small valley filled with thick underbrush and swamps, made its way to the Rapidan River. The ground sloped upward on both sides away from the creek presenting a formidable obstacle for each side, North and South. The rebels, although smaller in number, had the advantage of a crude entrenchment and the knowledge of the surrounding terrain.

The 11th U.S. Infantry marched forward on the 27th crossing the Rapidan River unopposed as they continued their march through the Wilderness. Eventually, the 11th reached their assigned position, the New Hope Church. When the soldiers finally came in sight of the church, they found it in the hands of cavalry from Confederate Maj. Gen. Henry Heth's division. They immediately drove the cavalry away and began to scout the Confederate right for signs of weakness. Not finding any, the regulars set to work on digging entrenchments and preparing for action. The rebels counterattacked the V Corps' position without success. Unfortunately, the remaining Union army was slow—the other units, General French's Corps in the center and General Sedgewick's on the right, were not in position until the late afternoon of November 27. Early the next day it rained, delaying any Union movement except for skirmishers sent to determine the enemy's size and strength. Under the cover of darkness, the V Corps moved farther to the left in order to prepare for an assault on the Confederate right in the morning. The following morning the two armies sat facing each other for the entire day while engaged in a waiting game with neither general wishing to attack the strongly held position of the other. In the end, General Meade ordered an attack on the left, right, and center of the Confederate position the morning of November 30. The assault began with artillery; however, when the time came to attack, the enemy was considered too strong, so Meade reluctantly agreed to call off the attack. That night, no fires were ordered and as luck would have it, the weather became bitterly cold. The officers and men had not prepared to stay out in the open and brave the cold. Madison stayed with his men while they endured their hardships. That night several men died from exposure.

Finally, Meade ordered the troops to withdraw back across the Rapidan, and with that came the conclusion of the campaign. Madison and the 11th U.S. Infantry crossed the Rapidan River the night of December 2 marching to camp at Catlett's Station. After several days, they marched again and

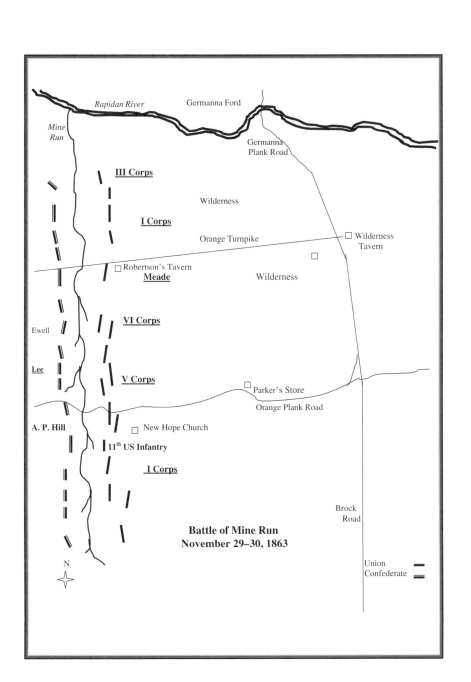

Battle of Mine Run
November 29–30, 1863

halted at Bealeton Station, where they set up camp. On December 27 they moved north to Bristoe Station, Virginia.

After campaigning with the regiment for two months, Madison became comfortable with his new surroundings and the men. As is customary, he took the opportunity to get better acquainted with the officers of the regiment, brigade, division, and corps. On one occasion, he met Col. Joshua Chamberlain whose reputation Madison had known from stories about the Battle of Gettysburg and about how Chamberlain's 20th Maine anchored the left side of the Union line on the second day of fighting. When Madison finally spoke with Chamberlain, they talked of the war, home, and their college days. Remarkably, Madison learned that Chamberlain was also a member of Alpha Delta Phi Fraternity. From then on, they maintained that eternal friendship found only among the members of fraternal organizations.

In their leisure time, the men and officers would often engage in competitive sports. Boxing was popular and on occasion there was an opportunity to see loosely organized fights among the troops. Madison, a great enthusiast as a result of his boxing days at Brown University, carried with him a constant reminder of a punch that landed squarely on his nose. Still, he always enjoyed watching a good fight and even encouraged it to keep the men in good spirits.

The quiet duty of the winter continued. The 11th U.S. Infantry maintained its winter quarters at Bristoe Station throughout most of January 1864. On January 30, Madison's regiment had been detached from the V Corps and assigned the task of guarding the Orange and Alexandria Railroad trains as they traveled between Bristoe Station and Alexandria, Virginia. As part of that overall order, the 11th U.S. Infantry was to move north by rail to establish a new camp at Alexandria.[2] Madison enjoyed being closer to home where he could visit his mother and sister more frequently. He enjoyed Sundays with his mother attending St. Aloysius Church. Occasionally, he commanded a small group assigned to guard a train to and from Bristoe Station. When they weren't guarding the trains, the regiment continued to drill.

Madison remembered the untried Ohio units on the left side at the cornfield at Antietam, and made it his goal to make sure that everyone in the 11th maintained discipline and performed his duty. When making an assault, it was important that the front line not fire until after the enemy had fired and then only when the proper command was given. Once the front line fired, the next line would move forward through the first and double-quick to the enemy position. This classic maneuver was often difficult to do in the face of a determined enemy. Through continuous practice and training, the tactic became imbedded in the minds of both officers and men. When it came time to fight again, Madison knew the regiment would perform well. Both he and Captain Cooley worked hard to ensure that the 11th earned the honored position of the right side of the battle line.

There was a great deal of talk in their spare time of the previous battles. Occasionally, a veteran who had received wounds at Gettysburg or in a previous engagement would return to the unit from convalescent leave. The regiment performed gallantly at Gettysburg on July 2 in the woods around the Devil's Den, the Wheatfield, and Plum Run by protecting the left flank of the army. They successfully helped to save the strategic Little Round Top hill from falling into rebel hands. The rebels attacked in force in an attempt to carry the high ground, which included the two hills rising out of a ridge south of Gettysburg. The strategic importance of the hills provided a complete view of the entire Union line extending to the north. Had that position been lost, the outcome of the battle may have been quite different. The fighting was fierce and deadly, but the regulars met the challenge. At the end of the day, 120 men were killed, wounded, or missing out of the 286 men of the 11th who went into battle.[3] This was the legacy of the 11th U.S. Infantry—the tradition of doing its duty. Although regularly used as the brunt of many jokes from the volunteer regiments, everyone in the Army of the Potomac knew of the bravery of the 11th and the other regular regiments. Each of the "regs" was professionally bound to see that they never disappointed the army. As the weather began to warm in late February, the men knew a spring campaign would begin and they were ready to fight.

Madison was glad to be in a regiment away from the pettiness of a general's staff. The officers and men of a regiment maintained a mutual respect for each other as a result of battle. Nevertheless, the incident in Cincinnati had blemished his record. The officers gave him a mild welcome upon his arrival showing him respect for his rank only. Madison felt no compulsion to set the record straight, for he knew his mission. No one could fault him for that, and futhermore it would only be a matter of time until a rebel bullet would settle the matter once and for all. Still, he looked forward to the opportunity to prove himself again.

The commander of the V Corps, General Sykes, also shared his men's feelings towards Madison. Sykes knew of the court-martial in Cincinnati and of the presidential pardon. If it had been up to him, the unmilitary behavior would have meant his immediate dismissal from the service.

On March 2 the news arrived in camp that Lt. Gen. Ulysses S. Grant had been made lieutenant general and was named commander of all of the Union armies. General Grant traveled to Washington to accept his new commission and assignment in a simple ceremony. He immediately returned to the West to meet with Maj. Gen. William T. Sherman to formulate a plan for conducting the war. Grant then returned to Washington to see the famous Army of the Potomac and to set his plans in motion.

The army showed excitement about Grant's taking command, because it was believed that he had the ability and determination to win the war. Madison, encouraged by Grant's reputation, knew he was what the army had been looking for.

On March 10, General Grant traveled to Brandy Station to meet with General Meade. From the meeting, Grant concluded that Meade should stay in command of the army although he required that some changes be made in the commanders and corps. Following his brief meeting, Grant returned to the West, where he turned over his command to Gen. William T. Sherman. After they agreed upon a final strategy for the new campaign, Grant returned to Washington.

When Grant reached Washington on March 23, he made only a few contacts before proceeding to Culpeper, Virginia, where he established his headquarters in the field. Upon his arrival, Grant shared his plans with General Meade, which set in motion the changes necessary for the spring offensive. Great optimism swelled within the Army of the Potomac; victory was in the minds of everyone.

One of the results of General Meade's reorganization of the army combined the III Corps commanded by Maj. Gen. Gouverneur K. Warren with the V Corps. Because of his poor health, General Sykes relinquished command to General Warren. On March 23, 1864, Sykes left Bristoe Station without fanfare. He did, however, make a brief statement regarding the valor of the regulars he commanded through much of the war.[4] Immediately after taking command, General Warren ordered Gen. Charles Griffin to command the First Division. Under his command the First Brigade commanded by Brig. Gen. Romeyn B. Ayres consisted of the 2nd U.S., 11th U.S., 12th U.S., 14th U.S., and the 17th U.S. Regiments, the 146th New York, the Zouaves of the 140th New York, the 91st Pennsylvania, and the 155th Pennsylvania Volunteer Regiment. Both hard fighters, Griffin and Ayres were well respected by the infantrymen. Upon learning of their transfer to the First Division, the regulars retired their white Maltese cross for the red. In addition, the division consisted of Col. Jacob B. Sweitzer's Second Brigade, made up of the 9th Massachusetts, 22nd

Medal of Honor

Presented to J. Madison Cutts, Jr.,
May 2, 1891.

Courtesy of Harriet Cutts Lundquist

Medal of Honor (Reverse Side)

Presented by the Congress to Capt. James
M. Cutts, U.S. 11th Infantry, for gallantry
at the Wilderness, Spotsylvania, and
Petersburg, 1864.

Courtesy of Harriet Cutts Lundquist

Front row, left to right: Capt. Charles G. Hutton, Maj. William Cutting, and Maj. Gen. Ambrose Burnside; second row, left to right: Capt. J. Madison Cutts, Lt. Col. E. R. Goodrich, and unknown officer.

11th United States Infantry Regiment

The 11th U.S. Infantry Regiment camp, Alexandria, Virginia, April 3, 1864.

Massachusetts, 32nd Massachusetts, 4th Michigan, the 62nd Pennsylvania Regiments, and the Third Brigade commanded by Brig. Gen. Joseph J. Bartlett. This brigade consisted of the 20th Maine, the 18th Massachusetts, the 1st Michigan and the 16th Michigan, the 4th New York, and the 83rd and 118th Pennsylvania Regiments.

In mid-April, the 11th U.S. Infantry joined the army at its winter quarters. Madison prepared his mother and Adele, knowing that his unit was joining the army for the spring campaign. Each of them knew that the coming weeks would be consumed in Grant's efforts to meet and destroy the Army of Northern Virginia and that Madison was about to return to battle.

Madison eagerly returned to the army with a clear sense of purpose—a quality he learned well under the guidance of his great-aunt Dolly. She had told him about the many great men who set aside their fortunes and gave their lives to make the great American experiment work. He had no lofty plans to achieve a place alongside the other great people in American history. His only goal was to do his duty for his beloved country as an honorable man, and the only way to perform honorable service to his country was to consider himself a dead man, living only to fight.

Madison and the 11th U.S. Infantry joined the rest of Ayres's brigade camped at Bealeton Station on April 29, 1864 with a full complement of veterans and new men ready to destroy the rebel army.[5]

Chapter VII

The Battle of the Wilderness

The night sky filled with smoke and fire as the Union soldiers burned their winter lodgings in the early spring of 1864. It was a strange event when the piles of wood and scrap that had housed the men for so many months filled the night with light and warmth. The men quietly continued to watch the fires of the army and eventually walked back to their tents. The next day the army would move south.

On May 1 in the early morning hours the troops began to prepare themselves for the march. Being of strong constitution and always an early riser, Madison had disciplined himself to make do with small amounts of sleep. Generally, the orders of the day, which were made during the late night, passed down through the chain of command in the early morning hours. He had learned to sleep well when given the chance and to come alive when duty called.

After a few hours, the great Army of the Potomac was to be set in motion—a spectacle of more than 150,000 men, artillery, and the supporting trains moving south to confront the Army of Northern Virginia. The army moved out from different locations, all headed for one key area, the Rapidan River near the Wilderness where the next campaign against Lee would begin. As the sun rose on May 1, the men fell in and prepared to march. Lined up four abreast in their new uniforms everything about them signaled that the two thousand regulars were ready to fight.[1] With the calls of "Forward march!" echoing down the line, the First Brigade left camp near Rappahannock Station, crossed the Rappahannock River, and joined the rest of the V Corps near Brandy Station.

On May 3 at approximately 11:00 p.m., the 11th U.S. Infantry Regiment crossed the Rapidan River at Germanna Ford as part of the lead regiments of the V Corps. They marched to the crossroads at the Wilderness Tavern several miles to the south and bivouacked. During the following day they waited and watched as the Army of the Potomac poured across the Rapidan. The spring campaign had begun.

Cooley and Madison led their men across the pontoon bridge into the Wilderness that lay beyond. The spirits of the troops were high as they moved south on the Germanna Road. Since Madison was designated second in command of the regiment, Lt. David Hazzard took command of Company F. Later in the day the lead elements of the V Corps had reached the junction of Germanna Ford Road and the Orange Turnpike in the middle of the Wilderness. It had been a long march, and the men were tired. The march stopped early in the afternoon to give the men a chance to make camp before nightfall. The First Division encamped on the side of the Orange Turnpike about half a mile west of the junction. The men recognized the Wilderness because they had marched through it several months earlier en route to Mine Run.[2] The soldiers set up camp, strung telegraph wires to the Lacy House, General Warren's headquarters, and watched as the rest of the corps passed behind them. To everyone's relief, General Lee had not come up to challenge the crossing of the Rapidan. They still were in the middle of the Wilderness, the place of bad memories for many of the veterans. The Wilderness, an area about 10 miles-square, had received its name because of the thick growth of trees and underbrush that filled just about the entire area. A land of marshes, streams, and knolls made travel almost impossible. Grant couldn't have picked a more dangerous place to stop; however, with the Confederate army so far away, there didn't appear to be any real threat from the enemy. The area contained the memories of the previous spring when Stonewall Jackson had pushed through the Wilderness to surprise the right flank of the Union army, which led to the terrible disaster at Chancellorsville. The soldiers soon found the remnants of that battle in the form of the bones of the dead. The older veterans made jokes about the bones; however, the new recruits were not laughing. In a forest, command of troops and artillery support proved difficult because no one could see the movements of their own or the opposing troops. When forced to fight in a forest, there was no telling who would be victorious.

Pickets were sent forward to guard the road as the rest of the corps came forward to make camp along a narrow trail leading southwest to a place called Parker's Store. As darkness fell, the men settled into an uneasy rest. As the soldiers talked about the bones of their comrades scattered in the woods around them, they wondered if their remains would be there tomorrow. The new men, who had never seen or smelled battle, were nervous. The other soldiers continued to make light of camping in the Wilderness, although each of them knew that it was a dangerous place to be, and they couldn't wait until the forest was well behind them. Some of the newer men, tired from the day's hot weather and the march, turned in knowing that in the morning more marching and maybe some fighting would be required. It was a strange mixture of men. Some at the campfires continued to make light of the impending conflict while others slept. Madison knew this area well, not only from the Mine Run Campaign the preceding fall but he had been through there in his youth when his family visited Montpelier.

The Union army had positioned itself in such a way as to make a powerful assault on the Confederate army. Maj. Gen. Winfield S. Hancock's II Corps had crossed the Rapidan at Ely's Ford and was camped near the old Chancellorsville battleground. General Sedgwick's VI Corps, which followed the V Corps, remained at the Rapidan River ready to cross at Germanna Ford the next day. General Burnside's IX Corps stayed to the north at Bealeton Station, moving south to cross the Rapidan sometime later on the following day.

The plan of action for the V Corps called for Maj. Gen. Samuel W. Crawford's Third Division to move south on the road to Parker's Store, followed by Brig. Gen. James S. Wadsworth's Fourth Division, Brig. Gen. John Robinson's Second Division, and then Ayres's First Division. The V Corps would begin its movement at sunrise.

The 11th U.S. Infantry Regiment, which comprised the 1st Battalion of the First Division, was considered the strongest of all the regular units. The company commanders of the 11th consisted of Capt. William Lowe, Company B; Lt. Edward Ellsworth, Company C; Lt. George Head, Company D; Capt. Joshua Fletcher, Company E; Lt. David Hazzard, Company F; and Capt. William Edgerton, Company H. Each had proven to be a capable leader in battle. Madison served at the battalion level as a temporary field commander.

On May 5, the morning dawned as a clear, warm spring day. The men had slept in the area along the Orange Turnpike, which was a narrow road carved out of the dense forest. Before dawn, the V Corps began to move out toward Parker's Store, with Crawford's division in the lead followed by Wadsworth's division. The men of the 11th U.S. Infantry watched their brothers of the Third and Fourth Divisions march to the west.

Approximately an hour after the lead of Crawford's division moved out, a captain from the 1st Michigan reported the rebels were coming down the turnpike in force. Brig. Gen. Joseph J. Bartlett's Third Brigade, the lead unit of the V Corps, was located where the road cut off for Parker's Store. While the 1st Michigan Regiment held the picket line on the turn-pike just beyond Saunders Field, the regiment quickly extended its line across the turnpike with support from the 18th Massachusetts. The rebels already had begun to fan out on both sides of the turnpike in front of the Union line making a clash imminent. The rest of Griffin's division began to stir as the sound of gunfire erupted from the skirmish between the rebels and the units of Bartlett's brigade. At first sighting of the enemy, General Griffin sent word to General Warren of the enemy's position. Surprised by the report, Warren calmly handled the situation by inform-ing Meade of the enemy's approach and telling him he believed Lee's main force was miles away. Griffin received intelligence from along his entire front, which indicated the enemy had to be infantry and, accord-ing to the dust in the west, they were rapidly being reinforced.

Brigadier General Bartlett, who advised the rebels had formed a line of battle on the west side of Saunders Field about a mile from the Union position, provided early reconnaissance of the area. If Lee wanted to fight, Grant would give it to him, so he ordered an immediate attack. At 7:50 A.M., General Warren ordered Griffin's division to mount an attack. Prior to receiving this message, General Griffin ordered General Ayres to move along the eastside of the field north of the turnpike and to form a line of battle. The orders went out, and word quickly came that the 11th U.S. Infantry was to command the vital right side of the line. The movement of troops on the south side of the turnpike became extremely difficult and slow because of the overgrowth of dense vegetation. General War-ren had recalled Crawford's and Wadsworth's divisions and ordered them to link up with Griffin to form the left side of the line. This presented a difficult task, as the forest in the Wilderness on the south side of the turnpike proved to be as thick and overgrown as on the north side. The low, tangled growth made it almost impossible for troops to move; and, even when movement occurred, they soon became lost or disconnected from each other. The situation became a nasty affair, with both lines form-ing yet neither knowing the location or strength of the other. At Saunders Field, the Union soldiers observed the enemy movements; and once the rebels reached the west end of the field, they likewise could see the Yankees to the east. General Griffin immediately understanding the situation came to the conclusion that an advance would be extremely dangerous, espe-cially if his flanks remained unprotected. By 9 A.M. General Grant arrived at Meade's new headquarters, located at a point near the old Wilderness Tavern. Upon arrival, Grant directed Meade to attack the Confederates immediately. In a flurry, the word went out to advance on the rebels. At 10:30 A.M., the V Corps was ordered forward, but it did not move.

On the far right of the line, the United States Regulars searched for the VI Corps, which should have been providing support on their flank. They were not there. As Ayres received information that the VI Corps was not on their right, he passed the information on to Griffin who indicated to General Warren that the VI Corps was not on his right and that Wadsworth's division had still not reached the Orange Turnpike on his left, which meant that his flanks were exposed. General Warren, under continued pressure from General Meade, again ordered an immediate advance. As Grant became more impatient, he pressured Meade and the other generals to move forward as quickly as possible. Griffin continued to delay the order, knowing the potential for disaster. By noon, he could delay no longer, so he gave the order, and the troops in two lines of battle prepared to move across Saunders Field. Crawford and Wadsworth finally linked up on the south side of the turnpike with the left of Ayres's brigade.

General Ayres positioned his brigade in two lines, with the 140th New York in the front on the left, next to the Orange Turnpike, and the United States Regulars with the 11th U.S. Infantry on the far right to the north. Captain Cooley designated the Color Guard and Company F to march in reserve on the right side behind the first line of battle. Madison took his position behind the right of the line as field commander. In the second line were the 14th U.S. and 12th U.S. Regulars followed by the 2nd U.S. and 17th U.S. Regulars with the 146th New York Regiment, the 155th Pennsylvania, and the 91st Pennsylvania to their right.[3] As the front line of Ayres's brigade emerged from the woods, the rebels began to fire. The shots from the rebel sharpshooters fell into the dirt in front of the regulars. As the bullets hit the ground, small puffs of dust kicked up like drops of rain at the start of a July thunderstorm. The rebels were sending a message to the men in blue. The regulars stood shoulder to shoulder staring at the gully and ridge to their front, ready to move.

At one o'clock, the order was given. Ayres's brigade on the right and General Crawford's and General Wadsworth's divisions on the left started their advance on the rebel positions. The long lines of the brigade, about five thousand men, advanced through the woods and open field. The officers knew the challenge before them when it became evident that the VI Corps had not come up on their right. Their only hope was that they could push the rebels back and hold them until they received support from the VI Corps. The same problem existed on the left, which meant that the V Corps found themselves attacking with both of its flanks in the air.

Saunders Field, an abandoned cornfield about eight hundred yards long and approximately four hundred yards wide, reached north and south extending on both sides of the turnpike with a gully running down the center for most of the field. The field, now dry and dusty, had been planted with corn the year before.[4] The troops maintained beautiful order as they marched down into the gully in the middle of the field and back up the other side. The brigade moved forward and did not waver or fire their weapons in the face of the rebel fire. Opposite the attacking Union soldiers were the men of Brig. Gen. Edward Johnson's division from General Ewell's Second Corps. The men in the trees in front of Ayres's brigade belonged to Brig. Gen. George Steuart's brigade. Further to Steuart's right were the brigades of Brig. Gens. James Walker and Leroy Stafford.[5] As Ayres's brigade approached the west side of the field, the rebels discharged a volley of fire from behind the tree line. The rebels fired in a line from the right side of Ayres' brigade down the line to its left—classic military strategy: fire in a line from left to right or vice versa.

The strategy was to control the fire, to cause as much damage on the enemy as possible. In addition, the noise and impact of the massive fire caused many men to retreat from fear of the next volley. Ayres's brigade having seen rebel volleys before did not hesitate. The brigade kept moving forward as if on a parade ground. Miraculously, the rebel fire from the first volley went high resulting in little damage. A short time later, the rebels fired again down the line. This time, it was effective and the Federal front line fell as if cut by a scythe. With this second firing, the 11th Regulars, veering off to the right, continued to make their way forward. As the brigade closed with rebels they moved at the double-quick to the edge of the tree line, stopped, took aim, and fired with deadly accuracy. The 14th U.S. Infantry on their left and the 12th U.S. on their right joined the 11th U.S. The 146th New York came in behind the 11th while the 155th and the 91st Pennsylvania Volunteers slowly made their way through the woods on the far right. The 2nd and 17th U.S. Infantry Regiments maintained support positions at the gully in Saunders Field.[6] With a steady level of fire, the Union troops continued to push the rebels back through the woods. Both armies kept sending in more units to the fight in order to either break through or stem the tide. The combined regular units were able to push the rebels back to a third row of entrenchment, where the resistance stiffened. As the firing continued, the rebels began to circle around in search of the Union's flank. With Madison maintaining command of the regiment, Captain Cooley elected to take command of the reserve units, the Color Guard, and Company F by ordering them to advance to the right to fill a gap between the 11th and 12th U.S. Infantry Regiments. Madison continued to command the battle line encouraging his men to pour on the fire.

Because the forest was thick with trees and underbrush, it was hard to tell the enemy's position. The brigade kept the pressure on forcing the Confederates back almost three-quarters of a mile. As the fighting intensified, the branches of trees and the underbrush began to thin out. The assault on the rebels in front of Madison was successful; at the same time the rest of the main line of attack had stalled, putting the regulars out in front. The woods came alive with the buzzing of bullets, as the firing on both sides of the line became intense. If the bullets weren't hitting bodies, they tore into the trees. Men lay on the ground either dead or wounded from the terrifying battle. In the thick woods and the smoke, lost soldiers formed into small units for collective preservation. Often these units fired on their own men out of mistaken identity or poor visibility. The brigade was fighting against a growing number of rebels as General Ewell kept throwing his forces at the Union line. The sound of the battle was incredible; the fighting remained fierce, with terrible loss of life on both sides. The rebels had been routed and pushed back; unfortunately, all was not well on the Union side. The rebels quickly began to exploit the flanks of the regulars. Ewell's Corps of about 17,000 was immediately thrown against Warren's 15,000 Federals. Soon, a new menace appeared in the woods. Aside from all of the bullets and the blinding smoke from the muskets, the men began to smell the smoke from the burning pines. The dense forest suddenly began to erupt in flames. The 14th U.S. could no longer remain, thus the men began to retreat. The same was true for the 12th U.S. who had been mauled by the rebels on their flank. Men on the skirmish line of the 11th U.S. began to fall back, as men on the ground screamed for help in hopes that those moving for the rear would take them with them. Many of the men stopped to help their comrades, as their worst nightmare came true. Soon, the woods filled with the smell of burning flesh and the screams of those being consumed by the flames. The intensity of the shooting and the fire made it difficult for anyone to think beyond his own safety. The Confederates continued to take advantage of the exposed flanks of Ayres's brigade at both ends, by mounting counterattacks that struck the Federals from the front and sides. Suddenly, the great Union line began to fall back. Madison called to his men to steady themselves and remain calm. He took command of the entire

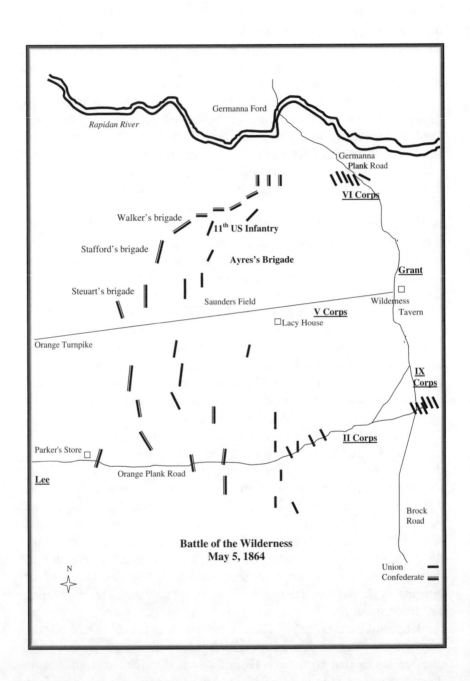

Battle of the Wilderness
May 5, 1864

skirmish line. As the line moved back, Madison sent a runner to Captain Cooley, informing him that the line could not hold its present position and that he must bring the reserve back to the rest of the line. No sooner had this been done than Madison began to see large gaps in his line with gray uniforms pouring through.

The firing up and down the line was as intense as at any point in the war. Far off to the left, the members of the 140th New York also pushed forward attempting to hold the ground it had captured from the rebels; but they were in dire straits from being flanked on their left. As the fighting continued, the rebels continued to move forward.

The 140th New York and the regulars did all they could to keep from being rolled up. It became evident that much of the entire brigade had to be recalled or it faced the possibility of being completely destroyed. General Griffin's worst fear had become reality. Ayres had been outflanked by the Confederates on both sides, and the brigade was falling back.

With their lines stretched out and little support on their left, the 140th New York Regiment found themselves faced with the same situation as the regulars. The intense flanking fire and the forest fire only added to their problems. The New Yorkers, after about an hour of fighting, began to withdraw from the field. As they retreated across Saunders Field in the face of heavy enemy fire, few believed that troops in reserve would have much effect on the outcome of the battle.

The rebels continued to pour in on them and the regulars faced the greatest of peril. The chaotic scene was indescribable, as the rebels concentrated their fire on the gallant men at the north end of Saunders Field. Some of the Union soldiers lay prone on the ground and others moved forward, while still others were retreating. Everywhere were bullets, shells, the dead, and the dying. The Union line was breaking down.

Company F and the Color Guard rejoined the rest of the regiment as they reached the tree line where they had encountered the rebels less than an hour before. Brig. Gen. James Walker's and Brig. Gen. Leroy Stafford's Confederate brigades began to press the 11th U.S. on the right, and rebels began to open fire on them from the left. Madison saw that the rebel fire was coming from the front, the right, and even from the rear. As the front line began to retreat from the burning forest, the 2nd U.S. and 12th U.S. Infantry Regiments became pinned down by rebel fire from the woods on the right. Not only had the Union advance become outflanked, the enemy prevented reinforcements from reaching the 11th. It was just a matter of time before they would envelop the units still on the field and take the Federal colors as a trophy of the battle. Madison refused to let his regiment be taken. He would not allow them to show anything less than total gallantry on the field. If victory could not be achieved, they would die with honor. He ordered the men to go prone and form a line, which allowed them to lay down fire to their front and sides. The colors were placed in the center of the line to serve as a rallying point for anyone who made it to their position. Madison remained calm as he walked back and forth behind the line encouraging his men to stand firm. He had become the commander of the entire right side of the brigade. He forced his men to stubbornly stand their ground.

At the eastern edge of Saunders Field, near the Orange Pike, Generals Griffin and Ayres watched as the Union troops of Ayres's brigade began to filter back across the field. The only spark of life remained with the regulars still fighting it out in the northwest corner. General Griffin could only look on as the finest division in the army was being decimated. He knew all along that it would happen.

General Warren read the reports from the field with justifiable concern. The reports from General Griffin and those from Crawford's and Wadsworth's divisions were not encouraging. Tangled in the thickets of the Wilderness and beaten by fire and rebels, the entire Union line had stalled.

Madison ordered his men to fight on. To fight was what they were there to do and they did it with honor. He stood at the front of the line in order to encourage his men. Then he moved on to another point on the line. He ordered Lieutenant Hazzard on several occasions to do the same. Hazzard, one of Madison's favorite officers, knew no fear. Madison stood as a giant among the men as he refused to give ground. It had become a matter of determination and pride that he would not allow the rebels to force him from the field. Other regular officers and units joined in as the rebels made their move to clear Saunders Field, but clearly Madison commanded the line. After about two hours of fighting, the regulars had been decimated, yet they would not withdraw.

At 3 P.M., the VI Corps arrived on the field to secure the flanks of Ayres's brigade. With the VI Corps coming in fresh some of the regulars were withdrawn from the field. Griffin's division consolidated to the south of the turnpike, and what was left of Ayres's brigade was moved behind the lines, where they slowly began to regroup.

The battle on the Federal right continued with an advance by Col. Emory Upton's brigade of the VI Corps. As they moved into position on Saunders Field, they joined Madison's beleaguered men. Madison, refusing to leave the field, stayed on the battle line while Upton continued his attack. The battle on the right side of the Union line continued to rage until approximately 4:30 P.M., when both sides finally had had enough. The two sides had fought hard for three and one-half hours, only to find themselves holding the same ground as when they started. Madison, who continued to lead the units on the right side, had stayed in the battle the entire day. As the troops of the VI Corps withdrew from the field, Madison slowly returned to his unit. Not since the battle at Antietam had he seen such death and destruction. Through his determination, the 11th U.S. Infantry had held off almost certain destruction and despite being driven back maintained their honor. He was exhausted but still alive.

General Ayres had watched the spectacle with apprehension. He had seen his brigade face circumstances in which no unit could have succeeded. It had been the same at Gettysburg, and the results were the same. The brigade had been practically destroyed trying to do the impossible. He did, however, note one bright light on the field in the person of Madison Cutts. Following the battle, General Ayres sent his aide Capt. Frederick Winthrop to Madison with his compliments. Recognition in battle by one's commander was the finest reward a soldier could receive. He was momentarily proud of himself until he looked out over Saunders Field at the dead and wounded. He could not think of glory only the pain of his comrades, who had bravely marched forward and met with death.

The regulars were placed in reserve behind the Union defenses, with Denison's brigade on their right, and Bartlett's on the left. By evening, the Union line stretched six miles along the Brock Road, running north and south through the east side of the Wilderness.

It had been a hard day's work. The 11th U.S. had performed well by maintaining a disciplined and organized advance on the enemy position. They did what they had to do and held the right of the line. The power and strength of Madison to hold the officers and men together while being flanked became a testament to his character and discipline.

The men of the regiment had been beaten pretty badly; nonetheless, they quickly built campfires and attempted to eat anything they could. Most sat exhausted from the battle with a distant look of contemplation about what they had experienced. Groups of soldiers sat discussing the attack and events leading up to the fires and their withdrawal from the field as the roar of the battle continued to their south. For many of the new men who had just recently joined the V Corps, theirs had truly been a baptism by fire.

Madison had performed well during the battle and demonstrated strong leadership in the face of personal danger. He never showed fear and managed to keep the right side of the line together. All who saw him that day were truly struck by his bravery. Unfortunately, some of the other brave officers who fought gallantly were not so lucky. Col. David T. Jenkins was lost, as was the gregarious Lt. Col. Henry H. Curran, both from the 146th New York Regiment. Of the 2,061 regulars who fought in the battle, 302 were killed, wounded, or missing. When the count was over, the 11th U.S. Infantry had taken the greatest loss of the regulars, with one-third of their original two hundred troops either killed, wounded, or missing. During the day the rebel and Union forces had thrown more men into the woods along Orange Plank Road to the south, and the fighting all along the line was fierce. Hancock's Corps arrived on the V Corps left; later in the day and with the help of Burnside's Corps, who filled a gap that developed between the II and V Corps, they fought the rebels to a standstill. General Lee had brilliantly used the terrain to help equalize the strength of the Army of the Potomac by striking them in the godforsaken Wilderness.

General Grant not pleased with the results of the day's fighting had hoped the army could make it through the Wilderness unmolested and engage the enemy in the open. When the fighting began, he saw it as an opportunity to damage Lee's army. Unfortunately, the results were not what he had expected. Lee clearly had held off his superior forces and prevented him from obtaining a victory. Defeating General Lee was not going to be easy; however, Grant was confident an attack by the II Corps on the Union left the following day would turn the tide.

In order to keep the pressure on, both sides dueled with cannons entire night. The men built bunkers of large timber to protect themselves from the cannonballs. None of the soldiers were able to sleep a great deal anticipating heavy fighting the next day.

The morning of May 6 was again clear and beautiful. The forest between the two armies had taken on a new look from the cannons, troop movements, and fires. Both sides had constructed entrenchments of one type or another during the night in preparation for another day's work. At 5 A.M. the left side of the Union line exploded with the thunder of Hancock's II Corps hitting the right side of Lee's line. The impact of the charge drove the rebels back in fierce fighting. At the same time, the entire Union line moved forward. The 11th U.S. Infantry along with everyone else advanced into Saunders Field, yet the enemy was too strongly entrenched. The regiments on the right returned to their line to once again experience a heavy rain of Confederate artillery shells. The V and VI Corps remained in position as the heavy fighting roared to their south.

The fighting on the far left of the Union line soon became as vicious as the first day's fighting. The guns continued to fire during fierce fighting that lasted all day. The tide swung toward Hancock's II Corps in the morning with their tremendous surge at daybreak. It was stopped only by the timely arrival of Longstreet's Corps.

In the late afternoon, the sounds of heavy fighting even farther to the left and behind Madison's regulars signaled the II Corps was being flanked. Longstreet had successfully outmaneuvered Hancock. The tide shifted to the rebels until near dark when the lines stabilized not far from where it had been at first light.

In the early evening, the far right side of the line erupted as the Confederates, under the command of Brig. Gen. John B. Gordon, attacked the VI Corps flank with a sudden fury. The right side of the Union line soon regained itself and repulsed the attack. As night came, the two armies settled into an artillery duel and name-calling across the lines. A clear night again meant there was little rest for anyone along the line.

On the following morning, May 7, at about 10 A.M., with the 11th U.S. in reserve, the 2nd U.S., 12th U.S., and 14th U.S. Infantry Regiments moved forward on reconnaissance. Skirmishes and heavy cannon fire occurred up and down the line, as the two opposing forces stubbornly faced each other without any movement. Both Lee and Grant knew that the lines of defense on both sides were too strong to achieve a successful frontal assault. The men, who were tired and dirty from two days of unmerciful fighting, rested most of the day as the generals planned their next move. Late in the afternoon, the word spread that the Union army was moving out. On hearing the orders, many of the soldiers became disgruntled fearing this meant they would withdraw from the field, as always, and return north to the safety of the Rapidan River. They still wanted to fight.

At 7 P.M. General Ayres's brigade, along with most of the V Corps, moved back to the Wilderness Tavern to prepare for a night march. Later in the night the troops began to move to the south immediately signaling Grant was not giving up. The tired soldiers had to stop frequently and when they did it gave them time to sleep. Every step on the dry, dusty, and dark road moved them farther away from the Wilderness. Following the Battle of the Wilderness, Madison's position as a field commander for the 1st Battalion became official. With this promotion, his dream came true. He had achieved the equivalent of a field grade officer.

Chapter VIII

The Battle of Spotsylvania

The men of the V Corps marched south on the Brock Road all night long to arrive in the early morning hours at Alsop's Tavern. The march was slow and as they reached the tavern, they heard gunfire further to the south. Word spread that the Union cavalry down the road had run into some dismounted rebel cavalry trying to delay the movement of the army. Trees had been laid across the road at the top of Laurel Hill, making it good cover for the rebs. Shortly after their arrival at Alsop's, orders were given to the commanders of the V Corps to move forward with the infantry to dislodge the enemy. Robinson's division, first in line of the march, were first to arrive at a clearing about three miles south of Alsop's. They advanced only to find the enemy stubbornly entrenched. Robinson informed General Warren that taking the hill would require more troops and the rebels were not Confederate cavalry, but infantry. General Warren ordered Griffin's First Division to take up a position on the west side of Brock Road in support of Robinson's right flank. As the new troops arrived, they immediately formed a line of attack. Before them was an open field that rose at a slight angle to the top of a hill. In the center of the hilltop stood a lone house that belonged to Sarah Spindle, and beyond the house was a hundred yards of cleared field. At the far end of the field there were woods that provided excellent cover for the rebels. At stake was not only the farm at the top of the hill, but Lee's entire flank. Laurel Hill was located just north of the small Virginia town of Spotsylvania Court House, which had quickly become the focal point of the two opposing armies.

Officers and sergeants down the line called their men to quickly form up; however, the men were exhausted from the night march. It became readily apparent they were tired and not in any mood to do battle. The rebels had secured the high ground directly in front of Ayres's brigade.

The officers continued to bark orders to get the men into position. Madison assisted in the staging of the troops.

At 8:30 A.M., the order came down to attack, yet the men responded slowly. Quickly, Madison stepped from the rear of the ranks. Out in front of the line he began to encourage the men to move forward. In a single wave, Robinson's division on the left and Griffin's division on the right moved forward in perfect order. The Battle of Spotsylvania had begun.

On a hill behind the Union lines, the commanders observed the assault with admiration and confidence. The Union line advanced in a handsome formation. In front of the Federals a determined line of Confederate infantry stood their ground. The line continued to advance until they reached a point at which they would direct the first volley of fire. Then at the command of "Fire," the brigade unleashed a deadly rain of bullets. The command of "Charge" was given, and the line continued to move forward in a textbook assault. The rebels quickly retired to the tree line beyond the farmhouse while the Federals regrouped along a line with the ridge and house. On the left, Robinson's men began firing too soon, which slowed their advance. As the Union advanced, the rebels placed a cannon on Brock Road and began to fire canister on Robinson's Maryland regiments with devastating effectiveness. The fighting became furious as Griffin's division continued to give it to the rebs. The Minié balls flew as thick as ever, and cannon fire continued to cut large holes in the Union line. As Ayres's brigade approached the wood line, the rebel cannon on Brock Road opened enfilading fire, bringing down large numbers of men with every shot.

General Aryes moved with his brigade toward the wood line where the fighting soon became desperate. The rebels, who fought gallantly, quickly received reinforcements. Some in the Union soldiers began to fall back, and Ayres had to rally them in order to get them back to the fight. The men responded for a short time until the situation became more desperate. Madison kept the regulars in place as they continued to press the attack, but a familiar tactic was again employed against the Union attackers. On the far right, Brig. Gen. Joseph B. Kershaw's South Carolinians struck hard at Gen. Joseph J. Bartlett's division, which had just arrived to support the right of the Union advance. At nearly the same time, Brig. Gen. Benjamin G. Humphreys's Mississippians outflanked Robinson's division forcing it to withdraw on the left. Ayres's entire brigade was again being flanked. Simultaneously, the commander of the 140th New York Regiment was shot, along with a large number of men and officers. The Confederate action proved too much for the center of the Union line; as a

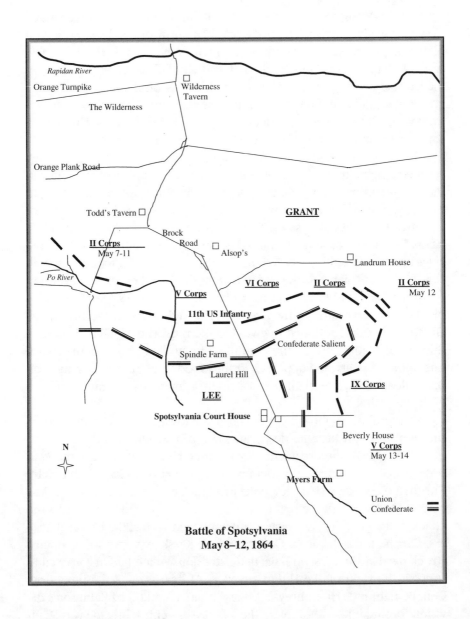

Battle of Spotsylvania
May 8–12, 1864

result General Ayres's brigade was forced to withdraw. But in doing so, Madison had his men hold the right side of the line in an honorable fashion. They remained in place until ordered to withdraw. General Ayres had watched Madison during the battle with great respect and admiration.

By 9:45 A.M. the attack ended, and the Union soldiers began to build entrenchments on the north side of the field at Spindle's Farm, from which they had started earlier. The rebels maintained their position at the tree line on the south side of the field, while the artillery on both sides continued to pound away at the exhausted troops. Looking back on the battlefield, Madison saw the Spindle farmhouse burning and many of his comrades on the field.

At about 10 A.M. more Union troops began to arrive on the field. Crawford's Third Division arrived to take the position previously held by Robinson's division. Another advance was quickly made but was met with stiff resistance from the rebels. The two armies then regrouped as cannon fire continued to roar around them. Everyone knew it would require more men to take that hill.

Approximately 1:30 P.M., General Meade ordered the II Corps to support the V Corps in another attack. The II Corps began to come in line west of Brock Road, but the men were exhausted, and by 2 P.M. the advance had stalled. During the engagement, the rebels began to fire on the right flank of Griffin's line. To prevent this, the Fourth Division of the V Corps, commanded by Brig. Gen. Lysander Cutler, drove the rebels out of an orchard on the northwest corner of Spindle's Farm.[1] As Cutler attempted to strengthen his right flank, the line suddenly gave way sending the division retreating in confusion. The regulars without support on their flank were ordered from the field once again.

Around 6 P.M. the II Corps began to attack the rebels on the west side of Brock Road, but without the support of the V Corps the success of the II Corps advance was limited. At nightfall, the Union line remained in the same position as when it arrived earlier in the day. Later that evening, the regulars erected a defense at the burned-out Spindle farmhouse. After a day of marching and fighting, both armies settled in for the night. The day had been tough, with heavy and desperate fighting by both sides. What was thought to have been a relatively easy move down Brock Road to Spotsylvania Court House turned into something far different.

In the darkness near the ruins of Spindle's house, Madison's exhausted troops maintained a skirmish line. The men went up Laurel Hill earlier in the day, from their all-night march, to face the unmerciful enemy fire. All who were involved in the attack did so with the highest degree of honor and bravery. The regulars performed well, maintaining their strong discipline once more in the face of a stubborn enemy. Madison had again gained the respect of those he commanded by his total lack of concern for his own safety. He had conspicuously distinguished himself throughout the battle. When other units within the brigade broke to the rear, Madison and the 11th U.S. Infantry held the line. At the close of the day, Capt. Frederick Winthrop visited Madison again. The captain proudly extended the compliments of General Ayres to Madison for his bravery on the day's fighting. This was the second time in four days that Madison had been given such an honor. In the volunteer regiments such gallantry most likely would have led to a promotion, yet in the regulars there was no such thing, and anyone fortunate enough to be so recognized took pleasure only in knowing that they had conducted themselves honorably.

The morning of May 9 opened as a clear day with the V Corps again facing the rebels on Laurel Hill. The regulars who had spent the night on the ridge were ordered to return to the main Union line. During the previous day's fighting the Union had lost almost 1,400 men.

Griffin's division and the regulars remained west of Brock Road. Bartlett's brigade was next to Brock Road with Sweitzer's brigade to his front on a slight rise. Ayres's brigade, with Madison and the rest of the regulars, extended their line to the west. On their right flank was Cutler's Division with Crawford's further to the west. The line extended almost three-quarters of a mile from Brock Road to the Po River. The morning was spent strengthening their position. Capt. Charles E. Mink set up his batteries behind Griffin's line and fired at the Confederates on the hill. Their firing kept the rebels from advancing their sharpshooters.[2]

At approximately 10 A.M., the news came of the death of General Sedgewick. Madison knew Maj. Gen. John Sedgewick, the VI Corps commander, as a most capable commander whose men warmly regarded him with honor and admiration. Madison could only hope that he could meet such an honorable fate. He paid his respects to the general then returned to his duties.

Madison reviewed his men as he walked along their improved fortifications. Despite the day being hot and dry, the two sides were not ready to fully engage each other. The rebels dug in on the high ground, prepared to meet anything the Yankees could throw at them. Cannon fire continued all day as more Union artillery began to arrive on the field. The skirmishers fired along the line as they tested their positions and maintained their ground. It became apparent that there would be no battle this day; but it was certain that, as soon as everything was in order, Grant and Meade would strike out at Lee. The First Battalion of Ayres's brigade with strong discipline and leadership proved their value in battle. To be effective, the officers treated the soldiers harshly while at the same time helping them build pride in themselves as individuals and as a unit. They had performed well marching up the slopes of Saunders Field and Laurel Hill.

All of the soldiers worked hard during the day in fortifying their positions. Late in the afternoon, Griffin's division was given the assignment to make an immediate advance on the rebel skirmishers to his front. On the far left, Sweitzer's brigade moved forward taking the ground around the burned-out Spindle farmhouse, while Ayres's brigade moved up on the right. Madison moved the men of the 11th U.S. to the brow of the hill where they took a defensive position. The successful assault, however, was short-lived. Cutler's brigade, positioned to the right of Ayres, moved forward at the same time as the other units. Heavy fighting again drove Cutler's men back thereby exposing the right flank of Ayres's brigade. The rebels, recognizing their advantage, attacked around midnight with a brigade of South Carolinians under the command of Col. John Bratton. The South Carolinians pressed their attack until it became necessary for the brigade to withdraw. As they had done in the Wilderness several days before, the right wing under Madison's command protected the rest of the division as they returned to their original entrenchment. The fighting had been a frustrating chain of events with success followed by failure.

On May 10, Generals Grant and Meade, not knowing the full extent of the army before them, determined it was necessary to attack in force. The order of the day was to attack all along the line.

The action began early in the morning on the right of the V Corps, with the advance of Crawford's division. As his division moved forward, General Griffin ordered the left of his division to again regain the rifle pits at the rise of the hill at the Spindle house in preparation of further action later in the day. As Sweitzer's brigade moved forward, so did Ayres; and by 11:30 A.M., Ayres had moved beyond the rifle pits to the orchard. The goal of the advance was to attack the rebel position in the tree line beyond the Spindle house. Sweitzer's brigade on the left of the V Corps almost made it to the woods as did Ayres's brigade. Unfortunately, Cutler's Fourth Division was thrown back leaving Ayres's flank in the air.[3]

In front of the 11th U.S. Infantry beyond the clearing was the junction of Brock Road and Block House Road. On top of Laurel Hill, the

Confederates of Kershaw's division consisting of Humphreys's, Henagan's, Bryan's, and Wofford's brigades held a strong defensive position. Behind Wofford's brigade near the intersection of Brock and Block House Roads, Parker's battery stood guard. To Kershaw's left, Bratton's brigade and Field's division extended southwest to the Po River. They presented a formidable force in front of the Union V Corps. The 11th Infantry Regiment knew this area well because it was the same ground they had charged across for two days.

At about 4 P.M., Warren ordered a full-scale assault on the Confederate line. The whole division moved out except for Griffin's First Division, which maintained its position at the Spindle farmhouse. The rest of the corps moved against Field's heavily armed and entrenched division. The Confederate guns from Parker's battery fired down the Union line as the Union troops struggled to reach the Confederate breastworks but were forced to withdraw. Later that night, General Warren's V Corps with Hancock's II Corps on his right was ordered to again assault Laurel Hill. In the end, the 86th New York and the 3rd Maine from Gen. David B. Birney's Third Division of the II Corps were able to break through the Confederate lines if only for a short while. The fighting for the day was finished with little results. It had been a tough day for the regulars, who were sent into action when it became apparent that the lines were being flanked. With their support, the rest of the Union troops were able to safely withdraw.

On the 11th of May, Grant and Meade made several adjustments to their position. Burnside's IX Corps was ordered to the left side of the Union line, while at the same time Hancock's Corps scouted the right.

In the evening, during a lull in the fighting, Madison was approached by the officers of the regiment who had been so impressed by his conspicuous bravery in the previous fighting that they came to him to express their gratitude for upholding the honor of the regiment. This single act of his peers was the most valuable form of recognition Madison had ever had. With it came redemption. The trial in Cincinnati and the stigma of the court-martial were now gone. He had succeeded in winning the acclaim of his commanding general on two occasions and the respect of his brother officers.[4] He felt relieved knowing he had brought honor to his family. While he enjoyed the company of his fellow officers, General Grant and General Meade were planning the next day's attack.

During the period of time that the two armies skirmished back and forth at Laurel Hill, the positions of the two forces began to take shape. General Lee had made use of the terrain, resulting in an unusual configuration of the Confederate line that extended almost five miles in length. The center, a salient appearing like the corner of a castle, became the crowning piece of Lee's defenses. It amazed the Union officers as they questioned how best to attack it.

General Grant, impressed with the success of Upton's concentrated attack on May 10, drew a plan in which General Hancock's Corps would make a concentrated assault at the point of the Confederate salient. The attack was set for dawn on the following day.

At around midnight, while the troops of the II Corps moved to get into position for the main attack, the rains came. A heavy downpour continued for the entire night. At 4:30 A.M., the II Corps advanced on the Confederate line with such a sudden surprise that within minutes four thousand rebels were captured. With the rupture of the rebel line in the center of the salient, Hancock's men continued their rapid forward movement.

At the sound of the attack on the salient, the V, VI, and IX Corps moved forward from their positions in a demonstration against the well-fortified rebel line. Griffin's division joined in the attack that again focused on Laurel Hill. The 11th U.S. Infantry with the rest of Ayres's brigade was held in reserve just west of Brock Road. With the severity and duration of the fighting, the regulars would soon see action before the end of the day. Everyone's spirits soared when they heard the initial success of the II Corps.

It rained heavily all morning, and the noise of thunder, cannon fire, and muskets were never ending. Like two great titans locked in battle, both sides refused to back away. For the men in the middle, it was a slaughter.

The V Corps held its own in front of the well-entrenched rebels on Laurel Hill without breaching the defenses. It became necessary to call up the regulars and Ayres's brigade to join the division on the hill. As the regulars neared the enemy's position, they came to a halt, aimed, and fired a deadly volley. Madison remained out in front of his men to guide their movements. As in the past he continued to expose himself to certain death as he pressed the attack. Exhausted and bloody, the regulars and rebels continued to trade shots with each other until they were sent back to the Union line to await further orders. The men with their uniforms covered with mud and blood searched for any type of shelter they could find. Some of the men stood in the rain by the fires while others quietly walked off. All contemplated their good fortune in surviving the morning. Others sat with fixed stares as though they were a thousand miles away. Madison's old unit, Company F, had sustained the loss of Sgt. Edward Britt, Pvts. Gideon Germain, Timothy Lowery, and Albert Eagle in the fighting.[5] The regiment as a whole had taken a severe beating, losing a total of 83 men and officers. After four days of hard, bloody fighting, this was the regular's last trip up Laurel Hill.

Around this point in time the officers and men of Ayres's brigade began to refer to Madison as the "Hero of the Republic." He had continuously and conspicuously demonstrated courage in the face of the enemy that astonished even the toughest of the veterans. For all who saw him standing before them in the heat of battle he was truly the bravest of the brave.

Although the attacks along the line were well executed, the rebels kept the Yankees at bay. Late in the morning, the attacks on the left and right sides of the Union line were called off with the IX and V Corps returning to their fortifications. In the center where Hancock and Wright's Corps were positioned, the fighting grew more intense.

Hancock's men reached a quarter of a mile into the rebel line until they met a second line of defense. Rebels rapidly came forward fighting savagely for the survival of the Confederate army. Hancock's momentum stalled, and after several flanking movements he was forced to fall back. The fighting continued to concentrate on the center of the line at the salient. Units on both sides began to pour more men into this abyss in order to gain an advantage over the other side. The struggle intensified as one unit after another was fed into the salient.

As the fighting raged on, General Hancock and General Wright called for more support. Around 2:30 P.M. Ayres's brigade, including the 11th U.S. Infantry, was ordered to form up and move to the Landrum House directly across from the Confederate salient. Ayres's men moved by way of Gordon Road arriving at their objective as ordered. Upon arrival, Ayres maintained his position awaiting further orders.[6] Cannons continued to roar as they had done since the start of the battle. As the hard rains continued to fall, the confrontation grew to be one of the most intense battles of the war. On the field were the dead, the dying, and those who knew that their time for death had most likely arrived. Once in position, the Federals fired volley after volley into the Confederate entrenchment of logs and branches. Some of the Union troops leaning against the fortifications fired aimlessly into the other side.

With no sign of weakness in the Union army or the Confederates, the men continued to join in the battle. For those fascinated by the sight and sounds of war, it was intoxicating.

The detachment from Griffin's division stayed in their position behind the Landrum House until later that evening. General Wright requested the use of Griffin's and Crawford's divisions to strengthen his position. Meade denied the request and ordered Ayres's detachment back to their former position. Madison and the battalion had been to the abyss and offered their lives in exchange for victory. Unfortunately, neither side was victorious.

May 12 had begun with incredible success yet ended in a stalemate, with both sides mauling each other. The losses for the day easily totaled 10,000 men for the Union with roughly the same or more for the Confederates. Everyone who remained alive knew this was a battle that would be remembered as one of the most ferocious of the war. Indicative of the fighting, at about midnight a number of Union officers observed that a large oak tree in the center of the battle line had been cut down by Minié balls after 18 hours of fighting. It was one of the last living things to die that day.

Both sides were worn out. Late at night Lee pulled his men back to the line that had saved them earlier in the day. The men on both sides rested as much as they could, hoping there would be relief in the morning.

On the thirteenth, General Grant ordered skirmishers forward to find the line of the Confederate army once again. Skirmishing continued for most of the day as the general considered his next move. Finally, the commanders concluded that the new rebel line was too well defended to make another frontal assault, so General Meade ordered the V Corps to move around the Union army to the south. General Warren's objective was the Fredericksburg Road, about a mile due east of Spotsylvania Court House where he could attack Lee's right flank. The rains continued.[7]

At 8:10 P.M. Warren directed the corps to form up and move out with Griffin's division in the lead. Unfortunately, Griffin couldn't get under way until around 10 P.M.; and when his division finally did begin to move, it became the most difficult march his men had ever attempted. The roads were a mess, and the men were lacking rest and needed supplies.[8] During the night the V Corps' route again took them east to the Landrum House, then on to the Harris House where they reached Fredericksburg Road. At that point, the column moved south towards Spotsylvania Court House.

On Saturday, May 14, Griffin's troops halted at the Beverly House, a point about a mile and a half from Spotsylvania Court House. Because of fatigue and the fact that some men had become lost in the night, Griffin's entire division numbered only 1,000 to 1,200 men. General Meade ordered an immediate attack, but General Warren sent word to him that the planned assault would have to wait for the rest of his troops. Two hours later Warren advised Meade that the prospects of a successful attack continued to be poor as not all of his troops had arrived and those present were exhausted. A short while later, Warren reported that his corps consisted of Griffin's division, numbering 2,500, and Cutler's division of about 1,300 men.[9] The words of Napoleon seemed most appropriate: "The first qualification of a soldier is fortitude under fatigue and privation. Courage is second."[10] The regulars collected themselves and prepared for the next assault.

General Warren became concerned about a hill to the southeast of the Beverly House, which appeared to be in control of Confederate infantry and artillery. Identified as the Myers Farm, it appeared as though Brig. Gen. John R. Chambliss's Confederate cavalry and McGregor's battery had staked a claim to it. Despite the small size of their force, the rebels held a commanding view of the area. Griffin received orders to send a small force out to take the hill, and General Ayres's brigade was called upon for the task. The 140th New York, the 91st Pennsylvania, and the regulars went forward to attack the hill. The rebels were unable to hold off the superior firepower of the Yankees. Once the position was taken, Meade ordered Wright, who had moved his corps to the left of Griffin, to hold the hill as part of his position on the left flank. While all of the fighting around the Myers Farm continued, Meade canceled the planned attack on Spotsylvania Court House.

Later, with Meade and Wright at the Myers Farm, the Confederates mounted a successful counterattack. Both generals were lucky to escape capture as the rebels broke the Union lines and recaptured the hill. Meade immediately ordered Wright to retake the hill. Failing to retake it, Warren again ordered Ayres's brigade to move on the hill from the northeast. At around 6:30 P.M., Brig. Gen. David Russell's and Brig. Gen. James Ricketts's divisions of the VI Corps and Ayres's regulars moved up the hill in a handsome fashion only to find the rebels gone. Once the VI Corps arrived, Ayres was relieved, and his men returned to their position near the Beverly House and the Fredericksburg Road.

On the following day, a Sunday, it rained again, and the two armies skirmished in an attempt to locate each other's positions. The sporadic activity along the line in front of Ayres's brigade allowed the men the opportunity to improve their position. Later at night, the Federal lines extended further to the south across the right flank of Lee's army. Grant awaited the roads to become more passable before pressing the attack. Unfortunately, his strategy with respect to the other armies under his command was not going well. Early reports from other departments indicated that Maj. Gen. Nathaniel P. Banks had failed to reach his objective along the Red River, and Maj. Gen. Franz Sigel had been beaten at New Market in the Shenandoah Valley. While Grant waited in the rain, Confederate Gen. Pierre G. T. Beauregard defeated the Federals under the command of Maj. Gen. Benjamin F. Butler at Drewry's Bluff.

On Monday, May 16, 1864, it rained so hard that both armies were forced to suspend all operations for the day. This was a welcome relief to the soldiers who had been marching and fighting all the way from the Rapidan. Yet the spirit of the Union army remained high, and the thought that they had been given the chance to stand toe to toe with the rebels made each Union soldier stronger. Still, Grant requested the War Department in Washington to send more troops.

On the following day, the weather cleared, and the roads began to dry. A plan developed that on the next day, Hancock's II Corps would make an attack on the center of the Confederate line. With only minor skirmishing taking place the men on both sides to prepare themselves for the next engagement.

At about 4:30 A.M. on the morning of May 18, Hancock's Corps attacked the "Mule Shoe," as the old salient had been named, as ordered. Artillery boomed from the V Corps in preparation for the attack, which came up against a formidable force. By 8:30 A.M., on Hancock's recommendation, Meade called off the attack. Skirmishing continued throughout the rest of the day along the Federal line.

Later in the day, Grant ordered Meade to prepare orders for the southern movement of the army. The orders directed Hancock to move his corps south, followed by the VI Corps and the IX Corps. Warren's V Corps was to serve as a rear guard.

As the day wore on, reports from the other fronts continued to come in. General Grant received the news that Butler had been defeated and had headed back to Bermuda Hundred near Petersburg, Virginia. General Banks was returning to New Orleans from his defeat along the Red River, and Sigel had withdrawn from the Shenandoah Valley after being whipped at New Market. Grant took quick action by immediately relieving Sigel and Banks and became even more determined to destroy Lee's army.

Early in the morning on the nineteenth, Hancock's Corps moved south for Hanover Junction as a decoy in hopes that Lee would come out from behind his defensive position. If Lee went after Hancock, he would be out in the open where Grant would have a better chance of defeating him. As soon as Hancock's Corps left Spotsylvania, Wright's VI Corps began to march south; and, for the rest of the day, elements of the two armies faced each other. The pickets from both sides talked to each other and in some areas even exchanged coffee.

Lee, sensing the right side of the Union line might be vulnerable, ordered General Ewell to move around to test the Union position. Ewell moved through Harrison's farm, and around 4 P.M. crashed into the Union lines. At first panic struck the Federals, then the line held. Once the Union forces organized themselves, they began to move against Ewell forcing him back. It was all Ewell could do to keep his troops from being driven from the field. At dark he returned to the salient, and the battle was over.

May 20 was a Friday, and at 3 A.M. the Union army at Spotsylvania moved into the wooded area to their front to locate the Confederate lines only to find that Lee had moved to the south.

The following day the sun came out. The Army of the Potomac marched south with little or no resistance from the rebels. As the army reached Bowling Green, the advanced units searched in vain for signs of the Confederate army. Grant showed no sign of concern knowing that at some point Lee would have to face him, sooner or later.

Madison and the regulars recovered from the early days of the campaign with their numbers greatly reduced. When they had started for the front in late April, there had been a few more than two hundred men in the 11th U.S. Infantry regiment and slightly more than two thousand in the brigade. The 11th had lost about 140 so far with the rest of the regular units in about the same situation.

Promptly at 10 P.M. on May 21, the V Corps began its southward movement as Warren followed Hancock's route east to the railroad, then on to Guiney's Station.

May 22 was another beautiful spring day, and the spirits of the men lifted with each step they took to the south. For them, each step moved them farther away from the death and misery of the Wilderness and Spotsylvania. Leaving the enemy's front, the V Corps crossed the Po River at Guiney's Bridge and then advanced across the Ta River at Madison's Ordinary.[11] As they marched south on Telegraph Road, the men encountered small units of rebel cavalry sent to slow them down or to test their strength. After a long day's march the V Corps bivouacked near Dr. Filipo's House.[12]

Early the next morning the corps moved south then west until it reached the North Anna River at Jericho Mills where the enemy maintained a strong position on the west side of the river. The job of fighting their way across the river fell on Griffin's division. With the help of Union cavalry, the initial Federal units quickly advanced across the deep river and established themselves on the other side. Once there, the First Division continued the advance by driving the rebels back for almost a mile. Griffin's men had proven themselves as hard fighters over the past three weeks, and they easily held their position while the rest of the corps crossed the river. Once in position, the division hastily constructed a defensive position that helped them repulse several fierce attacks. By nightfall, the entire V Corps was well positioned on the west side of the North Anna River.[13]

On the twenty-fourth, Lt. James P. Pratt stood on the breastworks in front of the men of the 11th U.S. Regiment as he read a note of congratulations from General Meade regarding the previous day's fighting.[14] Later that night, the VI Corps joined Warren's Corps on the right, as both units began to expand their position by pushing further to the south and west. The V Corps held the position from the railroad down to the North Anna River, where part of the IX Corps occupied a small section of the line on the west side of the river and all of the east side between Ox Ford and Chesterfield Bridge. The II Corps positioned itself on the west and south side of the North Anna below the Chesterfield Bridge.

The next day began quietly until rebel skirmishers began to test for weaknesses, each attempt encountering stiff Union resistance. In some cases, the rebels were driven all the way back to their defenses. With the Confederate position as well fortified as the Union lines, a successful attack by either side appeared impossible.[15] As the enemy lines developed, General Grant and the Union army were confronted with a strategic problem—Lee's position, shaped like a *V*, with the point located at Ox Ford extended to the southwest. If Grant elected to attack, he would have to do so with his forces divided. Lee's position gave him a strategic defensive advantage by enabling him to hold off attackers on either side of the *V* with a minimum force. With all of his men inside the *V* he easily and swiftly could shift his forces to defend his position. Grant, on the other hand, felt confident in his position because Lee would have to turn his back on half of his forces in order to make an all-out attack. It was a dangerous situation for both, and for that reason, neither had the desire to mount a serious attack.

On May 26 the two armies stared across at each other in anticipation. The generals on both sides waited to see if the other would make a serious attack. Skirmishing continued throughout the day as the Union army tested the strength of the Confederate lines. As the day ended, Grant reverted to his old strategy—cut the Gordian knot by simply withdrawing his forces as he continued his movement to the south. It had rained all day, but that didn't prevent the generals from issuing the marching orders. At 8 P.M. Madison and the V Corps began to march again.[16] They marched by night to a point near the Mount Carmel and St. Paul's Churches where they hoped to outflank the rebel army.

The next day the V Corps made camp about two miles from Mangohick Church.[17] At about 10 A.M., the II Corps began to withdraw from its station south of the North Anna River. Lee wasted no time in ordering his army to move even before Hancock's II Corps left the area. He had successfully anticipated Grant's movement, and once again raced to the south.

On Saturday, both armies found themselves continuing to march south at a rapid pace, trying to establish position on the other. The V Corps crossed the Pamunkey River at Hanovertown in the late afternoon and established a camp near the Brockenbrough House. The right of the corps bivouacked near Mrs. Newton's house, while the left was anchored on the Totopotomoy Creek.[18] The men were tired, but their spirits were high. They had no idea when victory would come; however, they could tell by the voracity with which Grant kept attacking that another major engagement was imminent. With every new captive the Federals could see the worn, haggard look of the rebel soldiers. As the Union army progressed further to the south, the men became more confident, each feeling inside that the next battle could really be the last, for all it would take was a breakthrough and Lee's army would be destroyed. The men felt a sense of history knowing that the end was near, and everyone wanted to be there for it.

By midnight the entire Union army had crossed the Pamunkey River. The V and IX Corps crossed at Hanovertown, while the II and VI Corps forded about four miles upstream. Throughout the day, Madison and the others heard the distant roar of the fighting between cavalry units at Haw's Shop to their front. It had been a fierce fight with Maj. Gen. Philip H. Sheridan's men and infantry from the V and VI Corps winning the field, but not until Lee had secured valuable information about the location of the Union army. He knew that Grant wanted to flank him again, and with the crossing of the Pamunkey River, it appeared that the Union army would make a run at him at Atlee's Station.

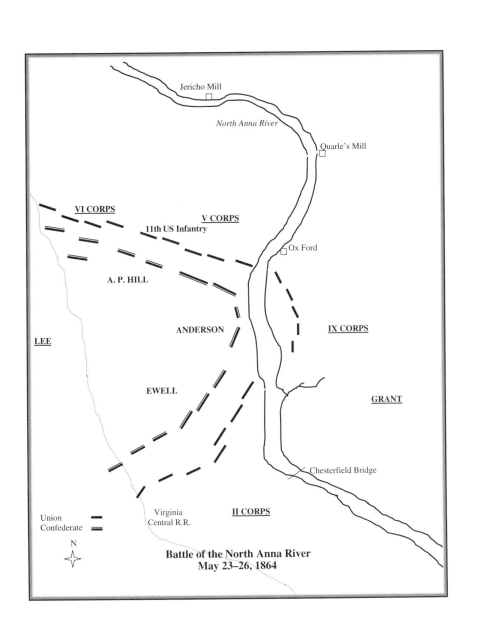

Jericho Mill

North Anna River

Quarle's Mill

VI CORPS

V CORPS

11th US Infantry

Ox Ford

A. P. HILL

ANDERSON

IX CORPS

LEE

EWELL

GRANT

Chesterfield Bridge

Union
Confederate

Virginia
Central R.R.

II CORPS

N

**Battle of the North Anna River
May 23–26, 1864**

At the close of the day, orders went out to the Union corps' commanders to continue the march to the Totopotomoy Creek several miles to the south. Lee, knowing the position of the Union army, began to search for a defensive position on the south side of the Totopotomoy to stop the onslaught of Federal troops.

On Sunday, the May 29, the V Corps camped at the Norman House near the Totopotomoy, where most of the troops had time to regain some of their strength while the rest of the army joined them. The army still remained on the move with tough demands put on each man who knew that it would not be long before they would again meet their rebel counterparts.

Later in the day Warren ordered Griffin's division to move toward Shady Grove on the other side of the river. With skirmishes occurring down the line, the division had made its way about a mile and a half down the road when they met heavy resistance. Fighting grew as the division pushed the rebels aside and crossed the river. One of the favorites of Madison's regiment, the faithful Lieutenant Pratt, went down with a shot through the heart.[19] The pressure increased as the two armies continued to skirmish. As the rebels gave way, their resistance continued to strengthen. At this point, the Union lines had reached within 10 miles of the capital of the Confederacy.

In the following days, the Union veterans had begun to see more and more men walking around in clean new uniforms, which indicated reinforcements. Untested in battle these soldiers were still badly needed. Unfortunately, the regulars didn't get many of the new men which left many of them to wonder whether anyone would be left when the work was finished. Suffering terrific losses, the Army of the Potomac regained much of its previous strength with the infusion of 40,000 new soldiers. Grant knew he could afford to lose men and supplies during the campaign while Lee's chances for reinforcements would never come close to his. He was right, because Lee was only only able to get about 10,000 men, about half as many as he had lost. In addition to the depletion of men, Lee had to deal with the loss of his commanders: Longstreet was still away recovering from the wound he had received in the Wilderness, and Ewell became so sick that he had to turn his command over to Gen. Jubal Early. Even Lee had become so sick that he had to be transported by carriage.

On the following day, Warren ordered Griffin to press on toward Shady Grove as the rest of the corps moved to the Via House, south of the Totopotomoy River. The rebels contested the Yankees' right to all of the roads, so moving forward took some effort. Everyone on the Union side knew, however, there were more rebels in front of them. The time grew nearer when the two armies would clash again.

With the V Corps on the left side of the Union army, the Federals had successfully crossed the Totopotomoy River and continued their way towards Mechanicsville, Virginia. They found themselves on familiar ground, as this was the same area they had fought during the Seven Days' Campaign in 1862. The regulars made their stand not too far from where they now stood. To Madison, it was all new terrain, full of marshes and swamps. Still, it didn't make much difference as long as the enemy was there.

To prevent further Union movement on his right flank, Lee ordered Early to attack the V Corps moving down Old Church Road. The objective of General Early's Corps was Bethesda Church, which stood at an intersection roughly three miles east of Mechanicsville. Early made his attack shortly after noon, but Warren quickly repulsed the fierce Confederate attack. The rebels came back a second time and were stopped again. The confidence began to build in Warren's men the same as it had when they repulsed repeated attacks during the first day's fighting along the North Anna River. Later in the afternoon, Early ordered a third attack, which met with the same fate as the other two before. After the engagement, General Warren reported losses of five hundred killed and wounded.[20]

Madison and the regulars, using any kind of loose material they could find, built a defensive position. Later in the day, Warren ordered a counterattack. It was almost successful, except for the timely arrival of the lead units of Anderson's Corps. Fighting continued into the night with both sides strengthening their positions. At midnight, the rebels made yet another unsuccessful attack against the V Corps.

Further to the south at a small river port on the Pamunkey River named White House, Union Maj. Gen. William F. "Baldy" Smith's XVIII Corps from Butler's Army of the James disembarked and marched to the west for the small settlement of Cold Harbor.

On May 31, approximately seven miles from Richmond, the two armies faced each other again. "Maybe this is the place we destroy them and move on to Richmond," thought many of the Union soldiers. The rebels attacked first with great force but were repulsed. The V Corps, with the IX Corps on its right, held a strong position.

Further to the south, Grant ordered Sheridan to move his cavalry to Cold Harbor as quickly as possible and to hold it at all cost. Sheridan with great skill reached the small village before the Confederates. Lee fully understood the value of Cold Harbor because it exposed his right flank.

He ordered Maj. Gen. Fitzhugh Lee to take his cavalry to Cold Harbor to secure a position for the infantry.

During the entire day, a cavalry duel ensued with Sheridan eventually proving victorious. Even though the younger Lee's forces could not hold Cold Harbor, he had stalled the Union advance.

As night fell, the VI Corps began a movement that took them back across the Totopotomoy behind the IX and V Corps to Cold Harbor. Grant was positioning his forces for another strike at the right flank of Lee's army. For his part, Lee ordered more troops to Cold Harbor in an effort to strengthen his right and to stop Grant's southerly movement. Both Grant and Lee knew the area south of Cold Harbor consisted of swamps, and this appeared to be Grant's last chance to outflank the Confederate line.

Chapter IX

The Battles of Cold Harbor and Petersburg

At daybreak on June 1, Madison stood with the regulars in front of Bethesda Church, looking westward along Mechanicsville Road. General Lee had again performed magic in finding and fortifying a position that enhanced his fewer numbers in men, and now attempted to drive the newly arrived infantry from the field. Activity became hot on the far left of the Union line where Wright's Corps had taken a position near Cold Harbor. Confederate Gen. Richard H. Anderson's attacked him as planned, but it was unsuccessful. The Union line held and was joined later in the day by General Smith's Corps, which filled the gap between Wright's and Warren's Corps. Hancock's Corps on the far right of the Union line received orders to follow Wright's route behind the line and take a position to the left of Wright's Corps. With the army in this position, Grant and Meade prepared for a major engagement.

On June 2, at 6:30 A.M., Hancock's Corps reached its destination tired and exhausted from a long, dusty night's march. Despite their exhaustion Grant ordered the corps to assault the Confederate line at 5 A.M. on June 3. In anticipation of the upcoming attack, Grant ordered Burnside's Corps on the right to withdraw to a position behind the V Corps, where it could provide support.

As Burnside's men began to move out, Lee ordered General Early to advance on the unoccupied right flank of the Union line north of Bethesda Church. Around three o'clock in the afternoon, Early ordered the divisions of Gen. Henry Heth, Maj. Gen. Robert E. Rodes, and Brig. Gen. John B. Gordon to attack. Their attack caught Burnside's men as they were pulling back, allowing the rebels to rapidly move forward. As the IX Corps fell back, it opened the way for the rebels to advance behind the exposed flank of the V Corps. Without warning, the entire right flank of the V Corps came under attack. The regulars, stationed on the far right of the line, immediately found themselves being enveloped. The fighting became furious as they fought their way back out of the rebel vice. As the drums beat other units of the corps fell in and came forward to meet the challenge. The fighting intensified and combat was close at hand on both sides. After three heavy Confederate attacks, the Union line had held. It was a slaughter with the 11th U.S. positioned on the far right of the line taking a terrible licking.

Many of the regulars wanted to counterattack before the rebels could fortify their new position, but no such order came forth. Instead, the men were ordered to construct new defenses and to prepare for the fight planned for the following day. As rain began to fall, the officers assessed the results of the battle and tried to piece together their remaining forces. Madison and Captain Cooley realized the 11th regiment had taken the brunt of the attack. In this one attack, Madison's old company lost 17 men either killed or captured.

Later that night, in brigade headquarters, General Ayres received word that an all-out attack was scheduled for 4:30 A.M. Grant planned to throw his whole army at Lee and, with any luck, create a hole in the line that would take lead to Richmond.

Madison was present as the company commanders received their orders. Everyone in the army now knew that to attack strongly defended field works was almost suicide, but each knew that they would make the attempt as ordered.

The rains continued on and off for most of the evening. The men's experiences from the past several weeks had brought a new reality to the war. Each soldier throughout the army knew that Grant would continue to fight until the war was won. Still, the thing most concerning for everyone continued to be, how to survive.

Madison, like the others, thought of victory but never dwelled on death and dying. His logic told him it could happen at any time or place, and he couldn't do a thing about it. He had attained his goal, to gain the respect of his brother officers and men. The stories of his bravery spread throughout the V Corps and the army. His tenacious fighting style and apparent total lack of emotion regarding the tempest around him immediately struck anyone who saw him on the battlefield. He was becoming a legend within the army as a fighter and a man of incredible and conspicuous valor.

As the sun came up, the men stood in battle line, as the order to attack was given. The entire V Corps moved out along a line with the other corps as Meade's massive assault began. The sound of gunfire became deafening as the Federals charged across the open field running

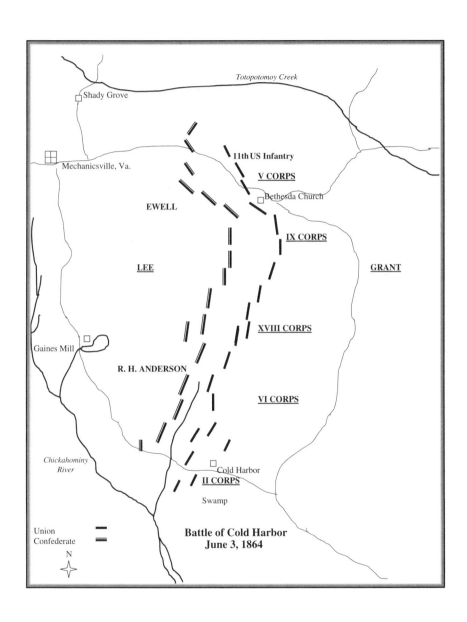

Battle of Cold Harbor
June 3, 1864

headlong into the face of well-fortified rebel forces whose fire cut into the Union lines. Most of the attack focused on the Union left with Hancock, but the fighting all along the line increased. As Madison and the V Corps engaged the enemy, they quickly realized that the rebels were firmly entrenched. Some early success had been made as Hancock's Corps hit the Confederate line hard, but the Confederate defenses and their determination were too much. As the wounded and disheartened began to stream back from the assault, Grant called off the attack. Some of the Union men made it to the enemy line only to realize that their comrades had withdrawn from the field, leaving them with no shelter or support. As many of them in front pondered their situation, they looked back over the field from which they had come, to see one of the most vivid scenes of carnage of the war. By 7:30 A.M., the Battle of Cold Harbor was over. In the first 30 minutes of the attack, the Union army had suffered eight thousand casualties with wounded and dead scattered along a five-mile path.

With the Union army behind its defenses, individual units began to make plans for saving those left on the field. It was hoped that a truce would be called so that stretcher-bearers could go forward to bring back the dead and wounded. Unfortunately, the order to pick up the casualties never came. During that long, hot day, the skirmishers continued to fire away as many gallant attempts were made to save those still left on the field. The rebel sharpshooters who took aim at anything that moved refused to let anyone leave that field alive.

Following most battles, it was the practice of opposing commanders to mutually accept a truce in order to collect the dead and wounded from the field. At Cold Harbor, this was not the case. The dead and wounded remained where they fell. General Lee, knowing the vast majority of dead and wounded in no-man's-land were Union, refused to allow a truce until General Grant unilaterally asked for one. The smell of the dead and dying filled the air adding to the misery. Madison continued to survey the battlefield during the lull. Knowing full well this was the price to be paid to preserve the Union, he contained his anguish and pain of the sight deep inside himself. He most likely remembered his speech at Brown University several years before when he had spoken of the "Responsibilities of the American Citizen." How could he have ever imagined that so many others felt the same, as he, and that they would be willing to give their lives for the preservation of the country?

The V Corps remained on the line at Bethesda Church until it was ordered to march six miles southward to a position behind the left of the

Union line. Here, the corps rested as Grant and Meade set about making plans for the next movement. As the days passed, the two armies continued to skirmish with Lee making a number of unsuccessful attacks on the Union line. During that time, more men on the field either dragged themselves or walked back to their lines. When a truce was finally arranged on June 8, the Union side found approximately two hundred men alive in no-man's-land. Cold Harbor had been a terrible battle and a setback in the drive to reach Richmond. The men had followed Grant all the way from the Rapidan and had given everything they had to break the Army of Northern Virginia with little to show for it. During the campaign, the Union lost almost one-third of its force. They reached a point no better than had been achieved two years earlier by McClellan. Ironically, the members of the regular infantry stood almost at the same point at which they had earned their reputation as tough fighters during the Battle of Gaines' Mills. With the Confederate army dug in to their front, Richmond seemed as though it was on the other side of the world. Ayres's brigade had been devastated, losing more than two thousand men in the 30 days of fighting. The brigade had been thrown into the thickest part of the battles, but time and rebel bullets had taken their toll. It was a running battle of attrition, and no one knew who was winning.

The rebels in even worse shape had been on the receiving side of everything that the Army of the Potomac had thrown at them. Outnumbered and outgunned, they had all they could do to hold off the determined Yankees. Tired, hungry, and worn out, the rebels had no choice but to keep fighting and winning, or the war would be lost. Only their determination and their love for Lee kept them going.

On June 6, General Warren reorganized his ravaged units by designating the Third Brigade, Fourth Division, as the First Brigade, First Division, and assigned Col. Joshua Chamberlain as its commander. Ayres's First Brigade, badly damaged, became the First Brigade, Second Division. The old regulars, what few remained, brought out their original white Maltese crosses of the Second Division. Madison was given command of Company H of the Second Battalion, 11th U.S. Infantry, but he had to wait until enough men arrived to fill its ranks.[1] Until that time, he remained as a battalion field commander.

During the reorganization, the regulars took control of Long Bridge and the Long Bridge Road, which crossed the length of White Oak Swamp. With the bridge and the road firmly in Union hands, Grant ordered the withdrawal of the Army of the Potomac south to the James River. On the night of June 12, the II Corps moved away from their entrenchment at

Cold Harbor, followed by the rest of the V Corps. That same night Smith's Corps withdrew to White House, where they boarded steamers for Bermuda Hundred. Later, the VI and IX Corps withdrew their positions and traveled south over to Jones's Bridge on the Chickahominy River. The following day, the army traveled in one of the most brilliant withdrawals in front of an enemy that has ever been attempted. Behind them, they left 54,926 Union dead, wounded, and missing in the wake of their path to Richmond. With more than seven thousand killed in 43 days of fighting, it had been a costly campaign, marking a new era in the conflict in which the Union commanders continued to press the fight no matter what the outcome of a single battle. The war was being brought to a close through hard, bloody fighting and sheer determination.[2]

Grant's plan all during the campaign attempted to get Lee's army out in the open, where he could bring all of his forces to bear. If that could be done, Grant believed he could be victorious and the war would be over. Prior to the withdrawal from Cold Harbor, Grant ordered his trusted General Sheridan north to the Shenandoah Valley to drive the rebel forces out of there and cut off the supplies flowing to the Confederate army. The other part of his strategy consisted of moving his entire army to the south side of the James River, then to advance on the rail center at Petersburg, Virginia. If successful, he would capture Petersburg and come at Richmond from the south; and, if that failed, he would at least cut off the vital rail lines that ran through Petersburg to Richmond and hold the city under siege. From there it would be only a matter of time until the end of the war. His plan worked masterfully as the II Corps reached the James River at Charles City Court House on the evening of June 13.[3]

By June 14, after two days of marching in the heat and choking dust, the Army of the Potomac reached the north bank of the James River. After all the soldiers had lived through, the peaceful James River made them feel as if they'd reached the Promised Land. For the first time since May 5, they were not under rifle or cannon fire. The quiet in the air became almost deafening. The men cleaned themselves, some for the first time in over a month, and relaxed. While the II, V, VI, and IX Corps arrived and revitalized themselves, Smith's XVIII Corps landed at Bermuda Hundred moving his corps into position in front of Petersburg to begin an attack. His men achieved success in driving the enemy back to within a few miles of the city. With little standing in his way, he apparently accepted a small victory of 15 artillery pieces and about three hundred prisoners rather than capturing the city.[4] While Smith contemplated his next move, farther to the north Lee faced another dilemma. The Confederate general had successfully prevented the Union army from advancing on Richmond, but now, he had lost track of it. Grant's brilliant movement away from Cold Harbor achieved its goal, and the Union army was in a position to take the advantage.

Early on the fifteenth, Hancock's II Corps ferried across the James at Wilcox's Landing. At 10 A.M., after hours of delay, the order was finally given to move the II Corps towards Petersburg. Once on the road, the II Corps moved rapidly to the west to join the XVIII Corps. Throughout the day, the men marched to the sound of cannon fire coming from Petersburg. By evening, Hancock's men took a position on the left of Smith's Corps. As Hancock's men took their position on the line, Burnside's IX Corps crossed the James on a pontoon bridge at old Fort Powhaton and marched toward Petersburg.

At 4 A.M. on June 16, the First and Third Divisions of the V Corps ferried across the James from Wilcox's Landing, while the Second Division, which included Madison and the Fourth Division, ferried across the James at Wind-Mill Point. Madison, refreshed from the lull in the fighting, dressed in his dark blue coat with vest and sky blue trousers. With his boots blackened, and his sword hanging from his side, he was ready for battle.

The soldiers had heard the cannonading of Petersburg for two days. Word came back regarding the rail center on the underbelly of the Confederate capital. At Petersburg, the Cockade City, four major railroads converged from the south to supply goods and materiel for the Richmond and Petersburg Railroad, which ran north to Richmond.[5] Petersburg, a relatively small town, was of strategic importance if General Grant wanted either to capture Richmond or, in the case of a siege, to cut off the major supply lines going into the capital.

Petersburg was strongly defended by a series of earthworks, which contained over 50 batteries and a line of interconnected trenches that took almost the entire year of 1863 to build. The earthworks were constructed by architect and builder Capt. Charles H. Dimmock, and at completion the defenses took on his name. The Dimmock Line wasn't an entrenchment hastily thrown together as had been the defenses at the Wilderness, Spotsylvania, North Anna, and Cold Harbor. This was the most formidable man-made position the Army of the Potomac had encountered thus far in the war. With batteries covering all approaches, the earthworks stood approximately 6 feet high and 20 feet thick for a stretch of 10 miles. In front of the works a 15-foot-wide, 6-foot-deep ditch had been excavated with slashing, abates, and gun pits. To help the defenders with their aim and to make an attack almost impossible, a field of fire had been cleared for more than half a mile in front of the breastworks.[6] As the bright moon shone down on them, the men of the V Corps thought about what lay before them as they took up the march to Petersburg. Madison's battalion was only a shell of its original size, and the thought of attacking the fortress seemed a daunting task. The men still kept up their spirits and resolved to go wherever ordered. Madison knew they would achieve either glory or death.

The IX Corps had reached the left of Hancock's Corps in the late afternoon of the sixteenth and had made a handsome advance through the works in front of them. For a time, it appeared as though the power of the Union army would overwhelm the defenders of the Cockade City, but a failure to follow up enabled the rebels to hold. Grant and Meade, both confident that a mass attack on the city would create a breakthrough, ordered all troops to the front.

The V Corps reached a position near Petersburg in the evening to settle in for some rest. The soldiers, accustomed to the hard, long marches, became adept at getting sleep along the way when they had a chance. All that night, the soldiers could hear the rumbling of cannons as they sent their deadly message to the enemy's camps. If they were successful this time, they would rip a hole in the defenses around Petersburg and send the Confederate army reeling. They had come through the tough fighting, some of the worst of the entire war, and now found themselves ready for the kill.

Once the V Corps reached the front, they marched to the left side of the Union line slowly crossing woods, swamps, and ravines requiring another night's march. The march took them along the outer earthworks of the Dimmock Line, which had been captured with great difficulty by the Federal troops the day before, and across Prince George Court House Road. Around 7:30 A.M. on June 18, the first elements of the V Corps arrived at Taylor's Farm where they were welcomed by heavy cannon fire from the rebels. By early afternoon, the V Corps extended its position from south of the Taylor farmhouse to a point just west of the Avery Farm, Blackwater Swamp, and a cut for the Norfolk and Petersburg Railroad. With the arrival of the V Corps, everyone hoped this would be the final attack on Petersburg.

General Warren aligned his corps with General Crawford's Third Division to the north, next to the left flank of the IX Corps. To the left of Crawford stood Griffin's First Division, and on the left of Griffin's division

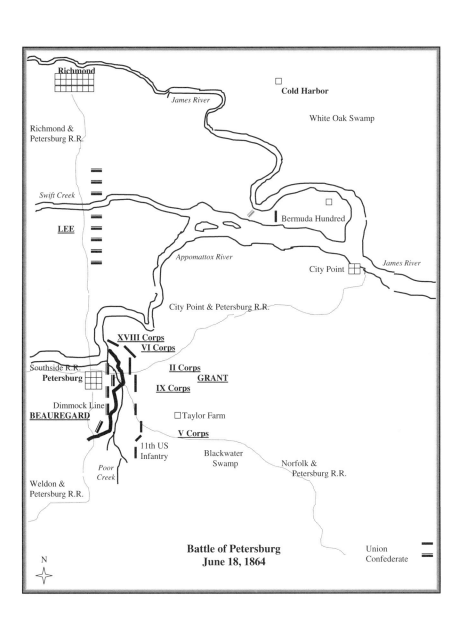

Richmond

James River

Cold Harbor

White Oak Swamp

Richmond &
Petersburg R.R.

Swift Creek

LEE

Bermuda Hundred

Appomattox River

City Point

James River

City Point & Petersburg R.R.

XVIII Corps
VI Corps

Southside R.R.
Petersburg

II Corps

GRANT

IX Corps

Dimmock Line
BEAUREGARD

☐ Taylor Farm

V Corps

11th US
Infantry

Poor
Creek

Blackwater
Swamp

Norfolk &
Petersburg R.R.

Weldon &
Petersburg R.R.

**Battle of Petersburg
June 18, 1864**

Union
Confederate

N

was Cutler's Fourth Division. Ayres's Second Division held the south side of the line on Cutler's left.

The First Brigade, Second Division, commanded by Col. Edgar M. Gregory and consisting of the 5th New York, the 140th New York, the 146th New York, and the regulars, was positioned to cover Cutler's left flank. The balance of Ayres's division manned the abandoned rebel earthworks on the left to prevent any Confederate flanking action. As Ayres's regiments formed, the officers and men moved forward to a rise between Blackwater Swamp and Poor Creek to stage for the advance. On their left could be seen the remains of the southern edge of the advanced Dimmock Line, which extended to the west toward the city. To Ayres's front was an open field that ran the full length of the Union line down a slight slope to Poor Creek. On the other side of the creek, the ground rose until it reached the innermost earthworks of the Dimmock Line. The truly remarkable Confederate defenses were planned with rifle and cannon emplacements that covered the entire field before the Union army. The rebels welcomed the newly arrived Union troops to a continuous and astonishing display of firepower. Looking at the rebel position, the officers and men of the V and IX Corps knew how difficult the attack would be. The Confederate cannons continued to fire throughout the afternoon in an attempt to keep the Federals from advancing.

As field commander, Madison looked out over the scene and realized to move forward would be suicidal. He could see the fear and fatigue in his men's eyes and faces and knew that it would take everything he had to get them to advance. They had marched a considerable distance without rest to arrive at a point from which they would soon be called upon to attack. The breastworks before him stood as a fortress, and the enemy cannon fire proved both strong and accurate. Madison's battalion found itself in the usual, honored position of the right of the brigade. Word from the commander had already been issued for a coordinated attack at 3 P.M., and all the available men prepared for the advance.

The regulars had been beaten badly over the past 40 days, still they remained eager to do their part in battle. It was a spirit instilled years before by General Sykes, and it carried on with unflinching discipline. With their numbers greatly reduced, they were at the end of human endurance continuing only by the most determined forces of will and pride. The battle line for the regiment was formed with Madison taking the prescribed position, behind and centered on the right side of the line. The cannon from the Confederate gunners discharged a murderous fire.

Being well within range, even the small arms fire from the rebel sharpshooters found their mark. Still, the men of Ayres's division, under fire for three hours, maintained their position.

Madison called to his men to stand firm, over the sound of exploding shells and canisters. There was no place to hide in the open area around them, and the Confederate gunners drew deadly aim on their attackers. With every shot, the earth moved and the air became filled with shell fragments, cordite, and death. Yet, the regulars stood steadfast with grit and determination. Suddenly, a spherical-case shot landed in the midst of Madison's line, killing seven men outright, and wounding many others.[7] The explosion destroyed almost half of the unit while sending the remaining men in all directions. The cries of the wounded with the roar of the bursting shells filled the air as everyone attempted to find shelter. Madison quickly surveyed the situation to find the battalion severely damaged. He saw some of his men beginning to withdraw; and it appeared that the entire right side of the battalion's line was evaporating. His mind raced through the possible results of this devastating chain of events. Looking to his right he saw Chamberlain's First Division rushing toward Poor Creek, followed by Cutler's men. If his men stayed where they were, Cutler's men would be cut to pieces in a crossfire. If they moved forward, many would die in the assault. The cannon shells continued to rain down with killing effect. Madison instantly decided to move out in front of his men.

His men turned to see him standing alone before them, unnerved by the sound and fury surrounding him. Madison stood facing his men as if on a parade ground during drill. They would not let him advance without them. Case shot continued to explode around him, while Madison remained as firm as a rock. Cutler's division was being cut down and Madison knew the only hope of continuing the attack was to advance. He looked for a signal from Colonel Gregory as his men began to reform their line behind him. The entire battle line along Poor Creek erupted in fire and smoke.

Suddenly, Madison thought that he saw a signal from an aide, John Parke, directing him to immediately order his men to advance into the valley.

Holding his sword high in the air as he turned and pointing it toward the enemy, Madison ran forward. As the Confederate artillerymen accelerated their firing, the ground seemed to lift around him. Madison continued to move down the slope with the brave souls of the battalion following. It was truly an inspiring sight as the lone captain led the force into the face of death. Suddenly, Madison felt the sharp pain of a bullet ripping through his chest. After being shot, he took ony a few more steps before his body collapsed to the ground. The men who followed him into the valley were soon sent reeling.

The assault of the Second Division lasted only a few minutes because of heavy artillery fire. With a successful attack most unlikely, Ayres sent word to his commanders to halt the assault.

As Madison lay on the bloody field in front of his men, he knew it was impossible for help to get to him. He resolved that this would be where his life ends for his beloved Republic. He could feel the life pouring out of the hole in his chest before he passed out.

General Ayres requested that as soon as possible troops be sent forward to recover the body of Captain Cutts. At dusk, the firing from the rebel position slowed enough for the men to safely venture out onto the field. The dead and wounded lay all around as the stretcher-bearers took to their task. Madison was soon placed on a stretcher along with his sword and carried to the safety of the Union line. As they inspected his wound, officers and soldiers alike called for transportation to get him to the surgeons. His condition appeared hopeless, and everyone knew it was only a matter of time before the wound would take his life.

Word quickly spread as to the valiant charge, and that the "Hero of the Republic" had received a mortal wound.[8] By order of the commander, they placed him in an ambulance and, with an honor guard of cavalry, rushed to headquarters at City Point.[9]

Once there, the doctors observed that a Minié ball had struck the left side of his chest, passed completely through his body, and exited several inches from his spine. His life was in peril, and everyone knew that he had little chance of living. Upon learning of his wound, his old friend Gen. Rufus Ingalls came to see him. He feared for the young man's life and would do anything in his power to help him. Ingalls had kept track of Madison's exploits and had learned of the title that had been bestowed upon him. Madison required better medical treatment, which meant he had to be transported to the hospital in Washington as soon as possible.

Colonel Chamberlain arrived at the hospital a short time later with a bullet wound to the hip and stomach. His chances for survival appeared slim as well. He soon underwent surgery to help repair his bladder. Chamberlain had gallantly led the First Brigade of the First Division to Poor Creek before being struck down. Now, the two fraternity brothers lay near each other while the surgeons tried to save their lives. As quickly as they came together, they soon went their separate ways. On June 19, Madison was transported by the U.S.A. hospital steamer *George Leary* to Washington, D.C.[10] On the following day Chamberlain shipped out on the hospital steamer *Connecticut* to a hospital in Annapolis, Maryland. For the two gallant men of the V Corps, their march through Virginia appeared at an end.

Madison reached the military hospital in Washington on June 20 where he found himself in the care of his family and military surgeon, Dr. Basil Norris. Upon observing his wounds the doctor noted:

> *His wound was a gunshot wound (rifle ball) of the left side. The ball entered between the eighth and ninth ribs on a line below the axilla, fractured the ninth rib, penetrated the lung, and made its exit between the ninth and tenth ribs at a point about one inch from the spinal column.*[11]

Dr. Norris elected to let it heal naturally. This allowed the doctor and family to monitor the healing process while minimizing the chance of infection. A month later the doctors declared Madison out of danger.

In early August, the wife of his former commander, General Griffin, visited him. The Griffins, longtime friends of the Cutts family, also lived in Washington, D.C. Mrs. Griffin maintained an interest in Madison because he served in the same division as her husband, and she regularly visited Mrs. Cutts. This time, she came to share a letter written by her husband. Madison's heart swelled as she read the general's comments about him.

> *I asked Gen. Ayres today how Capt. Cutts was getting along, and he replied he understood he was out of danger, and added he had made his mark as a gallant officer in this campaign.*
>
> *I doubt whether any officer of the regulars has been so specially gallant and attentive to duty as Captain Cutts, and it was a subject of universal remark before he was wounded or thought he was going to die; still, it would not have surprised anyone who had known his father.*[12]

To Madison, honor was everything, and to receive such noble comments from his commander struck him as the greatest compliment he could ever have hoped for.

As Madison recovered, he eagerly read the reports of the continuing siege of Petersburg and of the further attempts to break the Confederate line. The most interesting news related to General Burnside's attempt to blow a hole in the Confederate line so that his troops could break through. The reports from his friends in the field and newspaper accounts indicated that the Battle of the Crater, as it was known, had been a spectacular debacle. Its chance of success had been marginal from the start. Beyond this, Burnside's incompetence and the inability of his staff to coordinate the attack became quite obvious. Madison listened to the reports with feelings of redemption as he had been recognized as a hero, while his former commander was relieved of duty.

He felt saddened when he learned of the almost complete destruction of the regulars at the Weldon Railroad. In Grant's push to cut off Petersburg's supply lines in the South, he had ordered the V Corps to the Weldon Railroad, just three miles south of the city. Apparently, heavy fighting on August 18 and a massive Confederate counterattack by Gen. A. P. Hill on the following day nearly wiped them out. In a situation resembling a tidal wave, the regulars and remnants of Madison's battalion became engulfed as the units attempted to absorb the impact of Hill's attack. The gallant Capt. Joshua Fletcher had relieved Captain Cooley as commander of the 11th U.S. Infantry and proudly served the regiment by holding firm inspite of losing half of his 206 men.

As he reflected on the war, Madison realized that the strongest, the bravest, and the most gallant men had given their lives to save the Union. They were the ones who wouldn't let the Republic fall and it is they who should be long remembered for their honor and devotion to duty. He swore to himself that he would remember them forever and always honor the sacrifice they had made.

As time went on, he learned of the attempts of the Union army to sweep around the right flank of Lee's command. Grant continued to cut off the supply lines running north while stretching Lee's line. He knew that eventually the thinning Confederate line would break, and the city would fall.

At the end of September, news arrived of another westward movement of the V Corps and the subsequent battle at Chapple House. Although successful, the regulars had paid a heavy price. Madison couldn't help thinking about the officers and men of his regiment and battalion who had started out from Alexandria, Virginia, earlier in the year. Only a few remained, yet Madison longed to return to them.

His health steadily improved, and Dr. Norris eventually advised him that there was nothing more he could do. He indicated to Madison that although his ribs and wound were healing quite well, a great deal of damage had been done to his left lung. The doctor cautioned Madison that the wound would have a lasting effect, and that he should resign from the army. Madison heard the words from the doctor yet paid no attention to them. He was young, he knew he would recover, and soon he would be rejoining his battalion. On September 26, Madison decided to repay Lincoln's kindness by writing him a letter describing his service to the Army of the Potomac. In his letter he thanked the president and provided copies of the documents and letters that told of his extreme gallantry in battle. In concluding his letter he wrote, "Having been sent home from the field, as then generally believed mortally wounded, in front and in advance of my battalion, in a driven assault upon the enemy's works, I do not think, Mr. President, that if again called upon for higher and more important service, I shall be found the last—where I should be the first."[13]

As time passed, he continued to regain his strength. It had been a time of rest and a time to be with his mother and sister. They both rejoiced in seeing him alive.

In early October, the family received word of the death of Aunt Rose. She had been in England as an ambassador for the Confederacy and her fundraising had produced large sums of money for the South and greatly supported the Cause. With the siege of Petersburg and Sherman's relentless drive on Atlanta, Rose had longed to be home with her comrades. She hoped that by returning with a large amount of gold, she could somehow help with the purchase of war materiel. She booked passage on the blockade-runner *Condor* ; unfortunately, the Federals identified her when the ship stopped in Halifax and made plans to intercept the ship, as she was en route to Wilmington, North Carolina. On September 30, the *Condor* ran aground as she approached the harbor. With the Union ship bearing down on her, it was apparent that the *Condor* and passengers would be captured. Not wanting to return to a Federal prison, Rose and two men elected to row their way ashore, but waves rocked the boat sending them overboard. Because she had been carrying a large amount of gold within her undergarments, Rose quickly drowned. Her body washed up on the beach near Fort Fisher on October 1, and she immediately became a martyr. Her body was buried a few days later in Wilmington with full military honors. Madison's mother and sister were filled with grief when they received the account of her death. For Madison, there was no feeling of loss as he had seen the deaths of many noble souls on the battlefields of Virginia.

In the late fall of 1864, Gen. Winfield S. Hancock, who was forced to relinquish his command of the II Corps because of his lingering Gettysburg injury, petitioned the War Department to form a new corps made up solely of veterans. He hoped to establish an elite unit filled with only the finest of men—men who were no longer in the service but who had proven themselves in battle. With the strength of the veterans in his corps, Hancock would have a force that could accomplish any assignment the army gave him. Upon hearing rumors of the establishment of the new corps, Madison applied for a position. Soon after, he received word that Hancock had recommended that he be made a colonel of his own regiment. Unfortunately, the Department of War turned down Madison's request, saying that the concept of a veteran corps was created to bring veterans back into the army; since he remained in active service, he did not qualify.[14]

As soon as he could, Madison joined his battalion at Camp Parole, Maryland. Glad to be back with the regulars, he looked forward to returning to the rest of the army.

On December 12, 1864, Madison proudly acknowledged his promotion to the rank of brevet major. But just four days later he discovered that officers of lesser rank during the previous campaign had been awarded higher brevet promotions. Upon further investigation, his name was not included in a list of names of officers who had fought at the Battle of the Wilderness. Never being inhibited, he immediately wrote a letter to Brig. Gen. Lorenzo Thomas at the War Department, requesting a correction to his record. Unfortunately, he would have to wait for the issue to be resolved.

As December 1864 came to a close, the regulars were ordered back to Petersburg. Despite continual suffering from his wound, on January 2, 1865, Madison reported for duty with the 11th U.S. Infantry Regiment at City Point, Virginia. He was assigned to the position of commander of the 11th U.S. Infantry, serving as part of the provost guard for General Grant. In early February the unit became provost guard of the Army of the Potomac stationed at the headquarters of General Meade.

Early in the morning of March 25, 1865, City Point roared to life from the sounds of guns at the front. Word quickly spread that the rebels had broken through the Union line at one of the main Union redoubts known as Fort Stedman.

In a bold move, Lee ordered General Gordon to make a concentrated assault on the Union line due east of Petersburg. Lee planned to drive deep behind the lines to inflict as much destruction to Union supplies as possible. He intended to take pressure off his ever-thinning defenses and to force Grant to cease his flanking actions to the west. General Gordon broke through at Fort Stedman and the lesser posts directly to the north and south. Fortunately, Union soldiers quickly came to the support of their brothers. Madison, always anxious to battle the rebels, took the initiative by ordering the provost guard to board a train for the front. They arrived at Fort Stedman in time to participate in the counterattack that recaptured the fort and forced the rebels back to their own lines. By late morning, the Union line was completely restored. For Grant and the visiting President Lincoln, the incident appeared little more than heavy firing, but to Lee it showed the Union army numbered far more than he imagined. The Battle of Fort Stedman proved to be the last engagement Madison would fight in the Civil War. The hard-nosed Col. Edmund Schriver became incensed at Madison for taking the provost guard to the front. He ordered Capt. Alfred E. Latimer to place Madison under arrest and to take command of the guard. Upon learning of his arrest, Madison stated in a letter of protest that he would always come to the aid of his fellow soldiers despite the consequences and the meanness of his commander. After the heat of the battle had settled down, the charges were dropped; yet, Captain Latimer remained in command of the provost guard.

Grant continued to apply pressure to the right flank of Lee's line, knowing it was only a matter of time before a breakthrough would happen. When that occurred, Petersburg would fall, and the fall of Petersburg meant the fall of Richmond. On April 1, while General Sheridan's cavalry and the V Corps mounted an attack on the rebel right at Five Forks, Virginia, the Confederate line broke. With this single successful action, the entire defense of Petersburg and Richmond collapsed. The destruction of the Army of Northern Virginia became reality.

By nightfall, Lee ordered the evacuation of Petersburg and sent word to the capital that he could not prevent the Union army from moving on Richmond. Grant ordered a massive attack on Petersburg for the following morning with the intent of destroying Lee's army.

The next day the Confederate army began retreating to the west, being hotly pursued by the Federals. Everyone knew the war was rapidly coming to an end. In hopes of having a regular army unit on hand at the time of surrender, the 11th U.S. Infantry along with the remnants of the other regular units was ordered to proceed west. Madison took up the march hoping he would be there for the end. Events quickly unfolded as the Union army rapidly moved in for the kill.

April 3 brought news that the first Union troops had entered Richmond. With each new message from the front, it appeared the rebels would not go down without a fight. But everyone knew the end was near. Three days later, a large detachment of Confederate forces made a stand at Sailor's Creek, Virginia. Although they fought hard, the tired and starving rebels didn't stand a chance.

By April 8, Madison and the 11th U.S. Infantry reached Appomattox Court House, Virginia, where Madison remained near General Meade's headquarters. Awestricken by the speed with which the end had come, the following day he felt a sense of disbelief with the surrender of Lee's army.

On April 10, Madison awoke to the silent sound of peace. The war would soon be over and the Union preserved. Shortly after the surrender at Appomattox he learned that Frederick Winthrop had been killed on April 1 at Five Forks. Winthrop's death brought to mind all who had been killed in the long, hard struggle.

Several days later, the 11th U.S. Infantry joined the other United States Regular Army units in a triumphant march into Richmond. Their mission was to maintain law and order in the once proud rebel capital.

Late at night on April 14, Madison learned the president had been shot. In a state of disbelief, he recalled the tremendous turn of events of the past four years and how President Lincoln had responded to them. He also thought with pride of his own relationship with the president and how he had risen to the president's expectations.

On June 2, 1865, while routinely going about his duties, Madison received his promotion to the rank of lieutenant colonel, a position of which his father and the great Stephen Douglas would have been proud. He had upheld the model of life described on graduation day at Brown many years before. He had been called the Hero of the Republic. His courage had enabled him to fulfill his pledge, honor his family, and take his place in history with others who gallantly gave of themselves for their country. The great American experiment had been preserved, and through the pain of his wound, he had steadfastly remained at his post until the final bugle had sounded. The War of the Rebellion was over.

Chapter X

Reconstruction

Shortly after the close of hostilities, the 11th U.S. Infantry received orders transferring them to New York City for recruiting duty. The War Department had determined that the United States needed a strong regular army and therefore ordered the regulars to rebuild their units.

New York City, the largest and fastest growing city in the United States, was so populated that it proved difficult just to get around. The streets, cluttered with horses, carriages, and endless numbers of people, made life challenging yet exciting. With the war at an end, unemployment on the rise, and veteran soldiers having difficulty returning to civilian life, New York provided fertile ground for recruiting new soldiers.

Madison, wearing the rank of a lieutenant colonel on his shoulders, remained in Washington as a recorder for the newly created Confederate Archives. The assignment gave him an opportunity to renew some old acquaintances with retired officers and civilians living in the city, to continue his recovery process, and to think about his future. The wound had healed leaving a permanent hole in his back and severe damage to his lung. Often the pain served as a reminder of his charge down the hill in front of Petersburg.

While on assignment, Madison made a decision to remain in the army, for he loved the service, its honor, and its tradition. He had left many friends on the battlefields of Virginia and Maryland. He came to realize his place in life was to continue to serve his country.

At the conclusion of the war, a great debate erupted over what to do with the Southern states. The matter of secession and slavery had been settled at the cost of 600,000 lives, yet the struggle remained. Pres. Andrew Johnson, loyal to the principles of Lincoln, "with malice toward none, with charity for all," took the position that the war had settled the issue as to whether states could secede from the Union. Johnson wanted the Southern states to quickly reestablish their governments, take the necessary action to adhere to the laws of the land, and resume their place in the Federal government. The resolution seemed simple enough except politics, hatred, and distrust in Congress and in the Southern states made the president's position impossible to achieve. The Southern states, deliberately slow in responding to the laws of suffrage for the new freemen, made voting in the South a major issue. It appeared as though voting for representatives was being delayed until the aristocracy could be assured of victory. While the Southern politicians struggled to regain their power, the politicians in the North feared that the new South would be as difficult to deal with as the old one. Some claimed, all that was won as a result of the war could be lost. Eventually, Congress took the position that the Southern states were no longer part of the Union, which meant they had to fully comply with the law before they could be readmitted to the United States. The ensuing struggle between the president and the Congress lasted for many months.

Madison lost interest in politics. He joined his unit in New York, where the people were bustling with life. He had no ill will towards the South or the Southern people. A difference of opinion had led to the war and he realized that once passions reached a point as they had in early April 1861, only a war could settle the matter. He also knew that many families had been split by the war, as in his own case, and that every effort should be made to bind the country together again.

In January 1866, Madison gave his sister in marriage to Brig. Gen. Robert Williams. Williams from Culpeper, Virginia, had served in the Union army throughout the war. Adele, very much in love, longed to start a family. Her wedding seemed akin to a storybook marriage that would last a lifetime.

Following the wedding, Madison rejoined his regiment in New York. In March, he received word from Capt. Eugene Carter, 8th U.S. Infantry, requesting that he write an account of his activities during the war. He documented his actions and gave recommendations for several officers who served under him during the war.[1]

In July, Madison and the 11th U.S. Infantry, after successfully accomplishing their assignment in New York, returned to Richmond. They maintained a military presence in the city while conducting training and drills.

On July, 26, 1866, Congress passed an act that provided a pension at the highest rank for those disabled in the war. This was a generous gift by a grateful nation, and many took advantage of the government's generosity. With the passing of the new law, many of Madison's friends and associates urged him to take the pension, but pride and love of the military way of life would not permit him to become a ward of the land, which he fought so hard to preserve. With his only wish to remain in the military and serve his country, Madison refused to retire or accept the disability pension.[2]

On September 21, the 11th U.S. Infantry was formally renamed the 20th U.S. Infantry Regiment. Madison officially maintained his regular army rank of captain, yet retained the rank of brevet lieutenant colonel.

On October 1, he returned to Washington to work on a special military board to review the practice of awarding brevets. While on assignment, the feud between the Congress and President Johnson came to a boil. During the fall elections, a majority of radical Republicans entered Congress and immediately began to initiate their own approach of reconstructing the South. Their position embraced the idea that in order for the Southern states to "reenter" the Union, they had to pass stringent laws regarding suffrage of the new freemen and of men who had fought for the South during the rebellion. Since the Southern states, except Tennessee, had resisted attempts at reform and lacked good-faith efforts to adhere to even the more lenient approach of President Johnson, the radicals took charge. With strong popular support in hand, they moved swiftly to strengthen the demands on the South. Just prior to the end of the Thirty-ninth Congress, both houses overrode the president's veto of the Military Bill, which essentially ordered the military to occupy and maintain control of the South. The law divided the South into five military districts:

I. Virginia.
II. North Carolina and South Carolina.
III. Georgia, Alabama, and Florida.
IV. Mississippi and Arkansas.
V. Louisiana and Texas.

The duties of the commanders of each district were to protect the people and their property, to put down any civil insurrection, violence, or disorder, and to punish offenders. In order to secure law and order, the commander of the district could either monitor civilian courts or establish military commissions. With the Military Bill and the military occupation of the South, the rapid assimilation of the Southern states into the Union remained a long way off.[3]

Madison worked on the special board, while the political turmoil continued to build. He spent time with his mother until the board concluded its business, then returned to Richmond for further orders. Soon after his arrival, his regiment was ordered to the Fifth Military District in New Orleans commanded by Maj. Gen. Philip H. Sheridan.

In January 1867, he arrived in New Orleans, ready for an assignment that would provide him with an opportunity for greater responsibility. As one of the senior officers in the regiment, he anticipated a challenge in some high station within the district. But trouble greeted him right from the start. Madison received orders to take command of the outpost at Shreveport, Louisiana. He had been assigned the worst area in the whole district—an outpost, ripe with discontent and rabble-rousers. His years of experience in the regiment made him the only one who had a chance at handling both green troops and the resistant local population. It, indeed, was a thankless job.

Disappointed, Madison swallowed his pride, accepted his assignment, and set off to do his duty.[4] With three companies from the 20th Infantry, Madison traveled by steamer to Port Shreveport arriving there near the end of the month.

The post at Shreveport was located on the Red River in the heart of Louisiana and included subposts at Marshall and Jefferson, Texas. The fort consisted of a series of whitewashed buildings and a flagpole. The area had a nasty reputation for unruly locals and an abundance of scoundrels from the North trying to take advantage of them. The hot, humid climate bred malaria, and for a man with one lung, the setting had all the markings of a living hell.

Upon arrival, he found conditions in far worse shape than he ever had expected. As he and his troops marched into the post, he noticed the slovenly attitude of the guards manning the entrance. Once inside, he became appalled at the deterioration in the buildings and grounds and wondered how it could ever have reached this state. All military order had seemed to have disappeared.

Following the exchange of command, Madison immediately ordered small detachments to Marshall and Jefferson to relieve the troops there. He ordered his command to put the fort into perfect shape and begin operations. While making his initial rounds, he discovered that a nearby shantytown, consisting of women of questionable character, had been constructed a short distance from the post. He quickly ordered the shanties off limits and forbade his troops to go there. The fort was put into order and, after a concerted effort on his part to address the fears of the locals, the people from Shreveport began to recognize a positive change. Since his men were inexperienced, Madison found himself spending a great deal of time working with the officers and men regarding standard procedures and drill. Since he would tolerate nothing less, he drove his men to make Shreveport the best post in the district. He conducted the military's business within his region and with the civilian population, using as a guide fairness, justice, and moderation. The townspeople seemed grateful, and they often expressed their pleasure in having Madison in command. They felt comfortable having an efficient commander and well-disciplined troops stationed nearby.

His time at the new post was tough, and he had to work long and hard hours in order to maintain the command. His wound never let him forget his limitations and the pain was often excruciating. In addition, he contracted malaria, and his health began to deteriorate. His options for relief were limited to either painkillers or drink. Fearing the loss of his mental faculties to morphine, his only recourse was to occasionally indulge in whiskey.[5] He knew also of the powers of drink and always felt that its dulling effect on the senses made a man less effective. He had seen what it could do to a man who used alcohol to disguise the horrors of war. But when the pain in his chest became overwhelming, he requested from the post surgeon, Dr. Chandler B. Brayman, a proportion of whiskey and quinine to comfort him enough to sleep. It became a balancing act to drink just enough to produce sleep without taking him into a condition of drunkenness. Most of the time, his strong will and disciplined character prevented this from happening; but even with all of his strength of constitution and character the drink would occasionally overtake him.

Dr. Brayman, a sad sort of man, was dirty, careless, and unkempt in his personal appearance, and an incompetent in his profession. Madison likened him to a little schoolboy who, not having a mind of his own, would follow after the others, doing their bidding. He took pity on the doctor often providing him with comments aimed at self-improvement. They messed together and talked about how the military worked and what Dr. Brayman would have to do to adjust. Along with all of his other flaws of character, Brayman liked to play with fire, and that concerned Madison a great deal. He once said that if Dr. Brayman were 40 miles into the woods that's where a fire would be.[6]

On March 1, Madison returned to his headquarters in great need of rest and comfort following a trip with the Reverend Father Pierre into the backcountry.[7] He wasted no time in paying a visit to the post surgeon for relief. The doctor gave Madison the whiskey he needed, but unfortunately this was one of the times that drink got the better of him; and, he retired to his room slightly under the influence of the whiskey. Later that night a fire broke out in Dr. Brayman's residence. The physician sounded the alarm and rushed into his commander's quarters to warn him. As the quarters burned, Madison found himself standing in the middle of the parade ground in nothing more than a nightshirt. He was angry, for he had warned Dr. Brayman a number of times to be careful. The following morning, Madison had the doctor placed under arrest for a short period of time. Although their relationship outwardly seemed cordial, Madison thought the doctor a fool.

On March 8, the tranquillity of the post was again destroyed by the screams of two women running into the fort with most of their clothes ripped from their bodies. In between their cries it was determined that soldiers had destroyed their shanty. Madison's fears of his men visiting the shantytown had come true, and a grave matter of discipline seemed close at hand. A detail was ordered to go to the shantytown and arrest the offending soldiers. The detail soon returned to the post with the drunken Corporal Garland and Private Wright. An enraged Madison couldn't believe they would disobey direct orders, and he instinctively knew that this matter would require swift and severe punishment. With a number of troops standing around him, Madison ripped the chevrons off Corporal Garland. Suddenly, the two soldiers became violent, unruly, noisy, disrespectful, and insubordinate.[8] Their insolence reached such a state that Madison had no choice but to use force. Without hesitation, he struck Garland in the mouth with his fist and sent him to the ground. Disregarding the consequences of his actions he immediately ordered the two to be bucked, gagged, and tied to the flagpole. While that was taking place, he ordered the regiment to stand in formation. With the two in position, Madison spoke to the troops reminding them that they were duty-bound to obey orders. The shantytown had been placed off limits because of the concern for both the soldiers and the residents. Madison indicated that he had struck the uncontrollable soldier knowing clearly that he had committed a breach of military law; yet, he had no regrets and made no apologies. Following his remarks, the troops were ordered to parade around the two delinquent soldiers, demonstrating to everyone the extent he would go to maintain military discipline.

While the troops marched, Dr. Brayman protested the treatment of the two soldiers but to no avail. At the conclusion of the march the two prisoners were taken to the stockade. Madison returned to his quarters and called for Dr. Brayman to set his broken right hand.[9]

The officers and men apparently agreed with him, as no voices of protest were heard from either the officers or the men; it became clear that his actions had quickly reestablished discipline.

Life on the post soon returned to normal. Dr. Brayman, longing to return to his home in Brighton, Massachusetts, resigned from the army on March 25, 1867. His parting comments to Madison seemed cordial, and he indicated that he regretted not being able to learn more from him. For Madison it was just a matter of losing another officer, and after an amiable parting he went on about his business.

Madison's duties consisted of monitoring the federal agencies as well as the state and local governments. He was required to oversee the legal system to ensure its fairness and smooth operation. To do his work, he frequently traveled a circuit between Shreveport, Marshall, and Jefferson. As time went on, he became more confident in his officers and troops, and the local inhabitants grew to admire his judgment and his ability to maintain order. In writing his report to headquarters regarding the condition of his command, he indicated that the situation seemed much improved with the local population and despite the ill feelings of the people, law and order had come to the territory. He concluded his report by saying,

> *the influence of this command has been exerted to promote good feeling, to accelerate an improved and improving tone of political sentiment, and to illustrate by character, conduct, example, and act that the power of the Government is to be used for the peace, harmony, and happiness of the entire country.*[10]

Madison was proud of his accomplishments, his men, and the command. He now realized that General Sheridan had not sent him to Shreveport as punishment but as an honor. Truly, this was the most difficult area within the most difficult military district of the South. He had made his mark as an efficient officer with just about every possible hope of success against him. Madison continued to meet with his officers or sent them letters to remind them that doing their duty required maintaining order as well as developing a harmonious relationship with the public.[11]

Often, his words were put to the test. On June 19, the steamer *Live Oak* with a cargo of 250 bales of cotton, 3,500 hides, and 25 passengers ran aground several miles west of Shreveport. The ship's commander traveled to Shreveport where he found the only steamer in port, the *Cotile,* being held by the sheriff. The sheriff agreed to release the vessel if White could arrange insurance in case of damage or loss. Not finding any support from the Southwestern Insurance Company or leading citizens, he finally went to the military. Situations like this were not normal at the post; but since his arrival, Madison often found it necessary to make decisions with little or no direction from headquarters. Confidently taking matters into his own hands and against the wishes of those who held legal claim to her, Madison authorized the release of the *Cotile* for the rescue of the *Live Oak*.

On the following day the *Cotile* pulled the *Live Oak* free. The crew and passengers were so happy to have been rescued that they published a letter in Shreveport's *Caddo Gazette* thanking Madison for his fast action and his kindness. The passengers wrote: "Such officers as Colonel Cutts sent among the people of the South will do more for reconstruction and good will than all other measures combined."[12] He was proud of himself and honestly felt that no other post commander in the South had developed the level of rapport with the people that he had established since his arrival. Although there continued to be some kind of event or mischief going on within his region, he and his men were confident that they could handle whatever came their way. Madison knew the territory and, like any good warrior, knew what action was necessary to maintain command. He and his officers had treated the people fairly, and they had responded accordingly. But looming throughout his region there existed a bigger issue that plagued the entire South.

With the advent of reconstruction, many came southward in order to seek their fortunes. They figured that since the Southern people had squandered their money on the rebellion, it was their good fortune to reap the spoils. The South was crawling with them, "carpetbaggers" and scoundrels who, in the name of the "Union" or "loyal men," sought any opportunity to take advantage of their fellow man. On the political side they were referred to as "Massachusetts Democrats," or "Radical Republicans," and in the South they caused problems. These people who Madison looked upon as the exact opposite of everything he stood for were not gentlemen, nor did they serve any purpose other than their own. He had no use for them and would not tolerate their ill treatment of the Southern people or their contempt for the law. He kept his political views to himself and judged all men by their own merits; yet once a rascal broke the law, Madison took immediate action, for the restoration of law and order was paramount.

Unfortunately, the political climate of the army was such that an officer either supported the "Union" and the "loyal men" or he was considered an outcast. For that reason, many looked the other way when unjust acts were committed by the Northerners. The officers knew it was the kind of situation that could destroy a man's career. Madison cared little for army politics. Having proved his loyalty in battle, he, like his hero Don Quixote, would never compromise his honor no matter how many were against him.

During the last days of June, Madison found himself in Jefferson, Texas, investigating a report about the administration of justice in that area. While there, he met with the deputy collector of the U.S. Internal Revenue, who informed him that he had been approached by Dr. B. H. Peterson regarding a scheme to circumvent paying taxes on cotton. Peterson, a typical Northern scoundrel, spent much of his time purchasing cotton and other merchandise for shipment back to New Orleans. Peterson assured the deputy collector that his illegal transactions had the protection of Maj. Gen. Joseph A. Mower, Internal Revenue Commissioner E. A. Rollins in New Orleans, and all of the officers between Shreveport and Washington. Upon hearing the information and knowing the reliability of the source, Madison immediately ordered the arrest of Dr. Peterson. Following his arrest, Peterson was held for transfer to New Orleans for trial. Ironically, on June 29, Madison found himself traveling toward Shreveport on the steamer *T. D. Hines* with the recently arrested Peterson. Since it was an evening voyage, Madison took the liberty to relax in the salon and did so by sharing a few drinks with the passengers. While he enjoyed some free time in the salon, Peterson suddenly lashed out at him with a verbal assault. In an effort to discredit Madison, the doctor brought up the incident in Cincinnati and his subsequent court-martial claiming that Madison had disgraced himself and should have been thrown out of the service. His merciless attack was made public for all to hear. The doctor's comments infuriated Madison; yet, he maintained his presence of mind and military bearing, took control of the situation, and placed Peterson into confinement.

Returning to the salon, Madison apologized to the patrons and then retired to his room. He was struck by the fact that even a low-life scoundrel in Louisiana knew about the embarassing incident in Cincinnati. He hated Dr. Peterson, General Burnside, the miserable heat of Louisiana, and himself. Realizing the incident would never go away, he sat quietly in his room as the ship moved on to Shreveport.

The next day, Madison had Peterson brought to him in the salon, where the two men had a more civil conversation. Dr. Peterson apologized for his comments and behavior and asked Madison to let him go indicating this incident would not go well for Madison once his superiors became aware of his arrest. Dr. Peterson indicated his friends in high places in the military and the civilian government would never permit his being brought to trial. If Madison would allow him to walk away from the boat, there would be no further problems. Madison, true to his nature, refused and ordered a detail of guards to accompany Dr. Peterson to New Orleans.

Soon after Peterson arrived in New Orleans, as predicted, he was immediately released from custody. General Mower, after a short consultation with his chief of staff, quickly ordered Madison's arrest. With Peterson's release and Madison's arrest, General Mower clearly had some sort of business relationship with the doctor, and Madison would be made to pay the price for interfering.

Learning from his friends in New Orleans of possible legal problems looming over Madison, Dr. Brayman sent a note to him requesting payment for his equipment destroyed in the March fire. Madison sent a letter back to Brayman indicating that his equipment had been lost by his own carelessness and that he could not, in good consciousness, permit the government to honor his claim. On July 10, after receiving Madison's reply, Dr. Brayman wrote a letter of indictment to Sen. Charles Sumner of Massachusetts, informing him of the beating that Madison gave to his two soldiers and called Madison a drunk, a hater of Republicans, and "an unabashed scoundrel."[13] Senator Sumner, one of the most powerful of the radical Republicans, forwarded Dr. Brayman's letter to the War Department demanding action.

In the meantime, on July 17, Col. Joseph A. Von Schrader, acting assistant inspector general, District of Louisiana, arrived in Shreveport and placed Madison under arrest for his treatment of Dr. Peterson. Bewildered that Peterson had been so right about his close connection with General Mower, Madison immediately wrote a statement regarding Dr. Peterson's arrest:

> *I arrested Doctor Peterson because I believe that under the color of great names, including those of Brevet Major General Joseph A. Mower and E. A. Rollins, Commissioner of the Internal Revenue, he had sought and does seek to perpetrate a fraud upon the Internal Revenue of the government. I further state that by the release of the alleged conspirator and fraudulent scoundrel Peterson, because apparently of his influence with military and civil authorities of the government without investigation of any kind whatever, instantaneous and authoritative by Brevet Major General Joseph A. Mower, and my*

subsequent arrest upon the mere exparte statement of an infernal scoundrel. I believe the honor and integrity of the army, and the welfare of the country are imperiled.[14]

When Madison had finished his note he calmly handed it to Colonel Von Schrader. As the colonel read the note, both men knew the implications of Madison's comments, and there was no question that the problems Madison had with the arrest of Dr. Peterson were magnified by his apparent lack of respect for his commanding officer. The colonel relieved him of duty and confined him to the post under house arrest.

Upon learning of his arrest, Gen. Lorenzo Thomas, adjutant general of the army, wrote a letter to General Sheridan requesting that Madison be released.

August 8, 1867

Maj. Gen. P. H. Sheridan
Commanding the Fifth Military District, New Orleans.
Please relieve Colonel Cutts from arrest and reinstate him in his command. He is a capable and good officer who, if he errored at all, has had in view the best interests of the government. Order him to New Orleans to communicate in person with you. You will be perfectly satisfied with his explanation.

L. Thomas
Adjutant General of the United States Army[15]

Madison returned to the command of his post and awaited orders to report for the court-martial.

On September 22, 1867, he finally received the charges that had been brought against him. He passed the time in Shreveport in the midst of heavy rains and yellow fever, both of which took a terrible toll on his health. The army continued to delay the trial as it attempted to develop a stronger case against him.

Finally, the court-martial for the charges involving the arrest of Dr. Peterson began on January 14, 1868, in New Orleans. Madison was brought to trial on three charges. The first charge was conduct unbecoming an officer and a gentleman. It questioned his authority to arrest Dr. Peterson and his subsequent treatment of the accused while being transferred from Jefferson, Texas, to Shreveport. The second charge, being drunk, was a violation of the Article of War 45. The third charge was for conduct prejudicial to good order and military discipline. Madison was accused of disrespectful language toward his commanding officer for the letter he wrote at the time of his arrest. When asked how he pleaded to the charges, Madison defiantly stated "not guilty" to all charges and specifications.

The trial became protracted because the judge advocate could not get Dr. Peterson to appear before the court. Madison knew they wouldn't find him and that he wouldn't dare participate in the trial. The trial continued for several months while prosecutors attempted to locate Dr. Peterson. During this time, Madison met and befriended Lt. William Magee. The young man was an interesting fellow, and although they came from different walks of life, Madison liked his spirit. Both shared a commonality of being extremely brave and honorable men.

Magee had joined the 33rd New Jersey Volunteer Regiment at age 17 on July 28, 1863, as a drummer. He served his regiment with honor and won great recognition on December 7 and 8, 1864, for rallying his regiment at the Battle of Murfreesboro, Tennessee, and, in the face of great danger, personally capturing a cannon. As a drummer, he had become the favorite of his commander, Maj. Gen. Lovell H. Rousseau, and the governor of New Jersey, who after the war encouraged him to continue his education. In addition, they sponsored him for special recognition for which Magee received the Medal of Honor. He liked being in uniform far more than being in school, and with the help of his supporters Magee enlisted into the 20th U.S. Infantry Regiment in late 1867 as a second lieutenant. Upon arrival in New Orleans, he took an immediate interest in Madison. The two often spoke of the war, the situation in the South, and Madison's legal problems. The most common elements between the two were probably their uncanny ability to see things as they are and their directness of action. In Madison's case, he had no choice other than to arrest the errant Dr. Peterson. His integrity would not allow him to act in any other manner no matter what the consequences. The same held true for Magee, for he would not compromise himself or his values for anyone. The only difference between the two was in their level of education. Since there weren't many around who understood the true circumstances surrounding his court-martial, Madison enjoyed Magee's company and inquisitive mind. The young lieutenant soon idolized Madison and often asked for his advice on military matters.

On April 1, the Peterson trial came to a close. Madison read his statement of defense to the court, which indicated that by every principle of law when a witness refused to appear in court to face the accused, the court had no choice but to acquit the defendant. The court disagreed and passed judgment upon him. The court found that Madison did have the authority to arrest Dr. Peterson, but found him guilty of being drunk while on the steamer and guilty, with the exception of the third charge, of disrespect for his commanding officer. As a result of their findings, the court recommended that Madison be cashiered from the army. Madison's legal experience told him that the judgment of the court was lacking and that the only legitimate charges didn't warrant being discharged. He was confident that the members of the court would not let this judgment stand without a more realistic recommendation.

On February 5, while still involved in the Peterson court-martial, Madison received charges in a new case against him brought by Dr. Brayman. Madison had always been a man of solid self-esteem and confidence, yet with notification of the second trial, his faith in the army and his fellow man began to weaken. The charges filed against him developed as a result of Dr. Brayman's letter to Massachusetts Senator Sumner. It became clear to Madison that had he allowed Dr. Peterson to go when asked at Shreveport, and had allowed Dr. Brayman to be paid for his medical equipment as he had requested in mid-July, neither would have come forward and the charges against him would never have been filed. But to do that would have sacrificed everything Madison stood for. For him it was easy to see that Peterson was a crook, and Dr. Brayman, a selfish young man, who thought nothing of destroying a life for a bag of medical supplies.

On May 8, 1868, the Brayman court-martial began. In this trial Madison was charged with "conduct unbecoming an officer and a gentleman," to which he pleaded "not guilty" to the charge and all of the specifications. This charge carried with it eight specifications, alleging Madison was drunk on March 1, 1867, he had acted in an ungentlemanly way towards Dr. Brayman, and he struck Corporal Garland. Madison knew there were some shreds of fact in the charges, yet he considered them greatly exaggerated and of little merit. He could not deny that he had struck an enlisted man; other officers had done so under far less serious circumstances. In addition, the political climate of the times placed him on the opposite side of popular opinion. Since he had taken an interest in the people of the South, he became branded a rebel, which made him fair game for anyone who was connected to the "Union" men. Madison continued to believe his enduring character and his devotion to honor and duty would guide him through the impending storm. He found it hard to believe that a man of honor could be forced to endure such disgraceful proceedings at the hands of such despicable people. However, he remained strong in his faith in the law and his brothers in the officer corps that right would prevail.

On May 15, Madison received word from the commander of the Fifth Military District confirming the findings of the court in the Peterson case and forwarded the decision on to the judge advocate office in Washington for final approval. There was no indication of any further recommendations of the court. This couldn't have come at a worse time. Madison was in a battle for his military life, and his health had deteriorated due to malaria and exhaustion from efforts to produce a strong legal defense.

The Brayman trial lasted until the latter part of May. During the testimony, Dr. Brayman retracted many of his original statements regarding Madison's alleged language, and in many cases, other witnesses presented testimony that directly conflicted with statements made by Brayman. Some points of fact, however, could not be disputed. As in the Peterson trial, it appeared that threads of fact had been exaggerated beyond reality by the prosecution and the entire proceedings were designed to destroy him. This condition led him, in his summation, to bring to the court's attention the writings of Napoleon, who had found himself in a similar situation before a court.

> *You have deprived me of my functions; you have arrested me and declared me suspected. I am thus ruined without being condemned; or else, which is much more correct, I am condemned without being heard.*
>
> *In a revolutionary state exists two classes—the suspected and the patriots. When those of the first class are accused, they are treated as the common law of safety provides. The oppression of those of the second class is the ruin of public liberty. The judge must condemn only after mature deliberation and when a series of unimpeachable facts reaches the guilty.*[16]

Clearly, Madison believed that he had proven beyond any doubt that Dr. Brayman had perjured himself throughout the trial. But in the same sense, he knew he had become a marked man who would inevitably be found guilty. When the officers of the court returned with their findings, they found Madison guilty of a lesser charge of "conduct to the prejudice of good order and military discipline." With this, the court sentenced him to be suspended from rank and half-pay proper for nine calendar months and to be confined to the limits of the post during the period of his suspension.[17] He had been convicted for striking an enlisted man, but his actions were not uncommon for officer at an outpost. He understood the sentencing and quickly resolved to adhere to the wishes of the court.

On May 25, Madison arrived at regimental headquarters at Baton Rouge and reported to his old commander, Gen. George Sykes.[18] He had shared some uncomfortable times in late 1863 when he arrived in Virginia just prior to the Mine Run Campaign. Sykes was unforgiving and a tough commander. Sykes had become a bitter man, with his past successes forgotten and no real future left for him in the army; he was short on patience and long on discipline. As Madison stood before him, Sykes had very little to say. He expected Madison to resign from the service. When Madison refused, he indicated that he would see to it that his sentence was carried out to the letter of the law and that there would be no mercy should Madison fail to adhere to his sentence. Madison had been given a short rope in which to conduct himself, and it was clear that his nine-month sentence would go slow and hard.

During the time of his trial, William Magee had developed problems of his own. Some of the officers of the regiment had protested his being commissioned as an officer and declared him unfit for the position. Magee had been brought before a council for testing in order to determine if he understood military law and order. Although Madison had helped him, there wasn't enough time and William failed the test. As the two met in Baton Rouge, Madison started to serve his sentence, and William waited for the final disposition of his test.[19] It was not a happy time for either man.

Soon after his conversation with General Sykes, Madison was shocked to see Chandler Brayman back in uniform. He had rejoined the army as a surgeon and had been assigned to the regimental headquarters in Baton Rouge. Maddened beyond belief, Madison would have killed the scoundrel outright if not for Magee holding him back.

That night, May 25, they went to the officers' quarters, opened a bottle of whiskey, and both drank until the bottle was empty. Madison, for the first time in his life, drank himself into an uncontrollable condition with little regard for anyone or anything around him. All he could think of was Brayman, and when Magee passed out, Madison decided to go looking for the surgeon.

In a state of intoxication, Madison went to the home of a friend of Brayman's, Captain S. M. Morris, pounded on the door, and yelled for Brayman to come out. Captain Morris's wife and several other women became deeply distressed as he entered the house and continued to call for Brayman. Not finding him at the Morris's home, Madison went next door to the quarters of Lt. John Gae. Mrs. Gae refused to let him search her home for the cowardly doctor. Madison returned to his quarters only after being arrested by the sergeant of the guard. It took him a little over a week to get an audience with General Sykes to explain his actions. The general, not in any mood to listen to Madison's comments, requested Madison's resignation on the spot stating that with the recommendation of the court in the Peterson case it was just a matter of time before he would be cashiered out of the army. Furthermore, Madison's recent behavior would result in another court-martial, which would go very hard on him. In Sykes's mind, there was no way Madison could remain in the service. Sykes offered Madison one opportunity to save his honor by submitting his resignation. Madison, believing his brother officers had forsaken him in the Peterson case, wrote a letter of resignation on June 7, 1868. For Madison, the whole purpose for his living was gone. With bitterness he wrote:

> *Baton Rouge, Louisiana*
> *June 7, 1868*
>
> *General,*
> *I have the honor to tender my resignation as Captain 20th Infantry, U.S.A.*
>
> *I am General*
> *Your obt. servant*
> *J. M. Cutts*
> *Bvt. Lt. Col. U.S.A.*
> *Capt. 20th Infy* [20]

On June 19 his resignation became official. The following day, almost seven years to the day after receiving his commission as a captain in the regular army, Madison found himself a civilian. It was the saddest day of his life, for he had loved the army, passing up numerous opportunities in civilian life to remain in uniform. He had been born and nurtured into a life of service to his country, and while in the military he had served in the Great War with honor and distinction. Unfortunately, his previous deeds became lost in the difficult times of the postwar era and Reconstruction. With bitterness, he dressed in civilian clothes, packed his bags, and bid farewell to his friend William Magee. With nothing else to do, he passed through the gates of the post for the last time. At age 30, after attaining the rank of brevet lieutenant colonel and gaining the admiration and respect of all who fought with him, his life as a soldier had come to an end.

Epilogue

Madison left the South at his earliest opportunity and headed for Chicago. He traveled up the Mississippi where he stopped in St. Louis to visit his former employer, Basil Duke, Esq. The younger Duke had also survived the war, having surrendered to the Union army on May 10, 1865. When Madison told Basil he was going to Chicago, the older gentleman provided him with a letter of introduction and the names of lawyers to add to his list of contacts.

Madison stopped in Springfield, Illinois, where he, like many others, stood before the grave of Abraham Lincoln, a man whom he was proud to have known. He felt he had proven himself worthy of the president's kindness.

Madison then continued on to Chicago and visited the monument of Stephen Douglas. In silence, he shared with his brother-in-law the beauty of an army on the move and the ugliness of war. With a soft touch of the monument and his story complete, he walked away knowing he had fulfilled his commitment to his dear friend.

He stayed at the Tremont for some time while he reestablished himself. Between Stephen Douglas's old acquaintances and those of Duke, locating work was not difficult. Chicago, as lively now as before the war, offered him a good chance to pull together his life. Inside he was still sick from malaria and was deeply depressed.

Soon after his arrival, he received a letter from Willie Magee informing him of the death of Dr. Brayman. Magee explained that Dr. Brayman had become somewhat of a hero among the Massachusetts officers at Baton Rouge. Speaking brashly about his run-ins with the famous Colonel Cutts, all agreed with the doctor that Madison had done grievous things to him and that the doctor had handled himself like a gentleman. Magee knew better. On a day in August, shortly after Madison left the army, Magee learned from General Sykes that Dr. Brayman had penned a note to a local citizen falsely accusing him of being a thief. Upon hearing this news and to protect his honor, Magee confronted Brayman. The discussion between the two became heated as Magee thrashed him with a strip of cowhide. Fearing Brayman was going for his gun, Magee pulled out his own revolver and accidentally fired. Brayman died about 30 minutes later from a gunshot wound to the stomach.[1]

Madison smiled on learning the news. He knew that Magee, as simple as he was, was not an individual to be taken lightly. Obviously, Brayman had made his final mistake. There had been no telling how many people Dr. Brayman had damaged in his short life, but clearly his downfall occurred when he met William Magee. Unfortunately, Magee ended up being court-martialed for manslaughter and spent a year in prison before being discharged from the service.

Madison entered a dark phase of his life during his time in Chicago. The malaria had become worse reaching its maximum debilitation. His will to fight the dreaded disease had been effected by the broken heart he suffered at the hands of the army and his brother officers. Through sheer determination, Madison was able to work though still in pain, and on May 26, 1869, he passed all the necessary requirements and was authorized to practice law in the state of Illinois.[2] He maintained a practice while continuing to battle the debilitating effects of malaria. Finally, at the insistence of his friends, associates, and doctor, Madison returned to Washington to regain his health.[3]

Recovery from his physical wounds continued to be slow but steady due to the loving care of his mother. Like many young men who had fought in the war, he had lived the most glorious years of his life at an early age and now found himself lacking in direction. The future appeared to have little to offer; yet, Madison regained his constitution and strong religious beliefs, which led him to stop drinking. One day while visiting with Father McQuire, pastor of St. Aloysius Church, he indicated that he might like to try teaching. The priest knew many educators and offered to see what, if anything, might be available. Soon after their conversation Madison applied for a professorial opening at Seton Hall University in East Orange, New Jersey and in the fall of 1871 was appointed to the position of professor of history, rhetoric, and oratory. He enjoyed the opportunity to return to college and work with the young students. He was a strict teacher who held the students to high standards, and worked hard to force them to think and develop their minds. While employed at Seton Hall he had an occasion to communicate with Senator Sumner regarding

the circumstances surrounding his previous relationship with the senator as it pertained to the Dr. Chandler Brayman case. The senator responded, and eventually Madison was given an opportunity to meet with
him. The senator admitted that he could not recall the situation, but if he
had known then of Madison's high degree of character, he certainly would
not have supported Brayman's claim. The short meeting proved to be of
great value to Madison. The senator's comments brought to a close a sad
event in Madison's life. Again he proved that honesty and character ultimately wins over evil. At the same time and at the urging of his old friend
Francis Dickman, Madison decided to take a wife.[4]

At a social function in Washington he immediately fell in love with
Mary E. Wheeler, the daughter of Thomas and Rose Wheeler of Baltimore. Mary, a young beauty with a family heritage similar to Madison's,
was related to the famous Confederate Maj. Gen. "Fightin'" Joe Wheeler,
who had a distinguished military career prior to and during the Civil
War. The other side of her family had a connection with the politically
active Harrison family.

On July 10, 1872, Father McQuire married Madison and Mary in
St. Aloysius Church.[5] Following the wedding, Madison and his new bride
returned to New Jersey where he continued to teach. While there, he
thought about returning to the practice of law. In December 1872 at the
calling of the "jealous mistress," he resigned his position at Seton Hall
and returned to Washington, D.C.

Madison developed a new look on life and energetically moved forward to build his legal practice. After so many years of sickness and ill
health, he regained direction in his life. Madison established his office at
505 Seventh Street along with many of the other lawyers of the day.[6]
Despite his continued disability from his war wound, he approached
the law and his future with new determination. In September 1873,
Madison, thinking about his wife and the impending arrival of their
first child, completed an application for an invalid pension claim. He
received an award of $20 per month for his disability.

On October 28, 1873, his first child, Douglas Aloysius, was born.
Douglas, named after his beloved brother-in-law, died after only nine
months of life. One year later, Mary Elizabeth was born, followed by Douglas II in 1876. During this time, the country had settled down from the
war. Rutherford B. Hayes, a former war companion, was elected president of the United States; and upon his election, Madison remembered
the days at South Mountain.

President Hayes quickly consolidated his political strength and in 1877 he ordered the withdrawal of military forces from the South. With this single act, Reconstruction and the War Between the States came to an end. In that same year, Mary gave Madison another son, Madison Aloysius, and two years later, another son, Leo Merit.

On February 8, 1880, Madison learned of the death of Brevet Maj. Gen. George Sykes, who died at Fort Brown, Texas, with few remembering his name or his gallant leadership during the Rebellion. Madison felt that he had been treated harshly by the strongly regimented commander yet admired his fighting spirit. As Madison thought of his passing, he was reminded that anger and ill feelings toward others often destroy a man's soul. Maybe, that's what had happened with Sykes.

In August, Madison was devastated with the loss of Madison Aloysius; nevertheless, he had little time for mourning his son's death. Mary was with child; and later that year, a bright little girl, Adele, was born. While his family continued to grow, he struggled to find a position that would accommodate his ill health. In July, Douglas II passed away, leaving the family once again distraught over the loss of a child.

In 1882 with his health and financial stability weak, he secured a position in the surgeon general's office. His family now had grown by one more with the birth of Alice Salome. Although his income seemed sufficient to sustain the family, his new position at the surgeon general's office provided a welcomed relief.

He continued to practice law to supplement his income, yet with an income of little more than $1,400 per year the family lived a modest life. An old wound was opened on September 13, 1881, when he learned of the death of General Burnside. Despite Burnside's cordial letter of apology and admiration, Madison never forgave him because Burnside had tried to ruin him even though Madison was correct in his assessments and legal opinions. What Burnside had done was unforgivable, and Madison felt little pity upon learning of his death.

On December 1, 1883, he applied unsuccessfully for another position in the government, an appointment to the Office of the Librarian of the House of Representatives for the 48th Congress. Several distinguished persons, including Brig. Gen. H. W. Slocum, Maj. Gen. William S. Rosecrans, William Holman, and Maj. Gen. George W. Getty, endorsed his application.[7]

In 1884, another son, Charles Haywood, came along bringing the number of children in the family to five. It was a difficult time for the family, yet they lived a modest and happy life in the center of Washington. Madison continued to serve his country as best he could.

Arthur Douglas was born in 1886, followed by a son, Horace Mellon, in 1888. The family of seven children seemed about all that he and Mary could manage. They frequently moved from one location to another in order to keep their finances under control. The children often heard stories of the war from Madison; and on occasion, he permitted the children to put their little fingers into the hole in his back where the near-fatal shot had passed. As he spoke of the war, he talked about the campaigns and the dear fellows who had given their lives. He rarely ever spoke of his own actions in respect for those who had died.

In 1889, his daughter Adele passed away, leaving the family heartbroken again and reminding Madison and Mary that life was not easy for the children. On April 5, Mary gave him another son, James Madison III. Living on a moderate income with seven growing children, Madison looked for additional assistance from the government. He pleaded to Congress for a pension under the Disability Act of 1866. Bound and determined, he immediately set out to obtain a bill in Congress to provide for his relief. Letters were written to his military comrades asking for their support, which came quickly. Madison received glowing reports about his devotion to duty and bravery on the battlefield from many of the most notable officers of the Union army. These letters were used as the foundation for his case. While researching his claim, he had the opportunity to review the returns from the War Department regarding his military service.

In May 1889 while at the War Department on other business, Madison casually asked a clerk to retrieve the court documents relating to the Peterson case. To his astonishment as the clerk read aloud the recommendation of the court, Madison learned that Sykes had lied and that the court had recommended the remission of the sentence. He was shocked and surprised to learn, after 22 years of believing his brother officers had forsaken him, all charges against him would have been dropped. In his case, the president would certainly have remitted the sentence and Madison would have been permitted, contrary to Sykes's statement, to stay in the service. With this revelation and vindication, he vigorously pursued his request for a pension.

As he continued to prepare his case for relief, it occurred to him that he might have enough justification to warrant consideration for the country's highest military honor. On September 29, 1890, he wrote an application to Maj. Gen. John M. Schofield, commander of the United States Army, in which he requested to be considered for the Medal of Honor. Ironically, this was the same John Schofield who along with

Nathaniel Lyon commanded the "Wide Awakes" in St. Louis before the war. Madison's valor in battle had been widely recognized by those who served with him and, with their support, he thought it was quite possible to obtain this honor. In concluding his application Madison wrote:

> *Such a medal, if honorably deserved and gracefully bestowed, would be the proudest legacy, surpassing riches, which a soldier could hand down to his children, and as I have five sons who will otherwise commence life poor, I hope it will be self evident that no mere personal motive prompted this communication.*[8]

Along with his request, he enclosed the letters from men who had known and fought with him during the war.
Exhibit 1,

Camp Parole
Annapolis, Md.
Dec. 13, 1864

Captain,

> *I take pleasure in adding testimony to that you have already received for your services rendered during the last campaign. Your services on the 5th and particularly on the 8th and 12th of May at Spotsylvania are entitled to the highest praise for the gallant manner in which you conducted yourself—rendering important aid as commander of the right wing of the regiment, also on the 18th of June in front of Petersburg, where you were conspicuous as acting Field Officer and wounded while in front of the right wing of the battalion; encouraging the men by your own example to stand firm and I hope that you will receive a proper acknowledgment for your services. You have already been recommended for brevets for the actions mentioned.*
> *Very respectfully,*

Your obedient servant
F. M. Cooley, Capt. 11th Infantry
Bvt. Lt. Col. USA

Exhibit 2,

New York
March 12, 1890

To Bvt. Major J. M. Cutts
Capt. 11th Infantry

It affords me great pleasure to recommend Col. J. M. Cutts, having known him personally while connected with the 9th Army Corps. A brave and accomplished officer whose faithful services during the late war entitle him to the kind consideration of his fellow men in general. I sincerely hope that his wishes to be retired will meet with the approval of the Senate and House.

> *Edward Ferrero*
> *Late Major General USA*

Exhibit 3,

> *Fremont, Ohio*
> *March 14, 1890*

During the Antietam Campaign, I served in the same corps with Col. Cutts, and have sufficient information of his services throughout the War to be well assured that it was of decided merit.

I am confident that he deserves the relief that Congress is asked to afford and I trust sincerely it will be granted.

> *Rutherford B. Hayes*

Exhibit 4,

> *Governor's Office*
> *U.S. Soldiers' Home*
> *Washington, DC - March 18, 1890*

Col. J. Madison Cutts
Washington

Dear Sir:

I have read the abstract of your service in the Army with great interest and cheerfully add my testimony to the mass of evidence to your distinguished services during our acquaintance in the War of the Rebellion.

I remember your activity and great usefulness in the fights at South Mountain and Antietam, particularly where, as aide-de camp to General Burnside, you contributed so much to success and I may safely say that no staff officer habitually exposed himself to danger in carrying orders and gaining intelligence more than yourself. In my humble judgment you are richly deserving with the rank of Captain at least.

> *Yours truly,*
> *O. B. Wilcox*

Exhibit 5,

Forest Glen, Md. - April 10, 1890

Dear Colonel:

I have read with deep interest the very high testimonials of distinguished officers and ex-officers of the Army with whom you served during the late War for the preservation of the Union and fully concur in all that has been said in your behalf.

During the Maryland Campaign, which resulted in the Battles of South Mountain and Antietam, I was Chief of Artillery of the Left Wing of the Army of the Potomac. You rendered most efficient aid to me in selecting positions for the artillery and subsequently in conducting the batteries to the positions selected.

In the Virginia Campaign under Maj. Gen. Burnside, your services were active and dangerous in carrying orders and gaining intelligence of the movements of Gen. Lee's Army. No staff officer on Gen. Burnside's staff rendered more efficient or valuable services than yourself. After the Battle of Fredericksburg (sic), I have but little personal knowledge of your services, as the division I commanded was detached for service in Eastern Virginia, but from information derived from others, I learned they were highly distinguished, until you were wounded. Supposed at the time mortally at the head of your regiment in front of Petersburg. Your services during the War were eminent and honorable, deserving the highest consideration.

I do most sincerely hope that Congress, as a simple act of justice, will grant the relief you ask.

> *With high regard.*
> *Truly yours,*
> *Geo. W. Getty*
> *Bvt. Major Gen. U.S.A.*
> *Colonel retired*

Exhibit 6,

Washington, D.C.
May 20, '90

It affords me great pleasure to add my testimony to your gallantry on the field of battle and to your high soldierly character when we served together in the Army of the Potomac.

*The records of the War Dept. shows this, all your brother of-
ficers were witnesses of it. Such being the case, a generous country will not refuse its aid, only asked for when broken down by
wounds and disease incurred battling for its existence.*

*I sincerely wish you success, and I haven't the slightest
doubt that you will achieve it. No one has a better claim and
few as richly deserved of their country.*

Truly your friend,
D. B. McKibben
Bvt. Brig. General U.S. Army [9]

The general called for an investigation. On October 29 in the memo-
randum to Madison, the investigator concluded his report with the statement, "It would appear from the evidence of Captain Cutts' distinguished
services and personal gallantry in action that he was entitled to a Medal
of Honor and would probably have received one had he applied for it at
the time."[10] General Schofield took this information to the secretary of
war along with Madison's application. Knowing Madison as a gentleman
of the highest honor and likening him to a gallant knight of old, Schofield
felt his valor on the battlefield should not be confused with the events
that followed the war.

On December 6, 1890, the Committee on Military Affairs listened
intently to Madison's presentation of his military service. After some discussion, the committee hearings ended with a unanimous decision to bring
the Bill for the Relief of Colonel Cutts to a vote of the House.[11] On February 26, 1891, the House of Representatives unanimously passed the bill
for his relief, therefore eliminating the need for the medal in connection
with the bill before Congress. Schofield believed Madison deserved the
highest recognition possible for his valor on three separate occasions:
the Battle of the Wilderness, the Battle of Spotsylvania, and the Battle
of Petersburg. On April 4, 1891, Schofield wrote to the secretary of
war:

Respectfully submitted to the Secretary of War.

*In view of the very favorable report of the military com-
mittee of the House of Representatives, dated December 22,
1890, and of the action of House thereon, and of the many
strong testimonials by distinguished officers of the Army to
the gallant and meritorious services rendered by Col. Cutts,
and especially to the fact that the court martial which had
sentenced him to be dismissed from the service unanimously*

*recommended the remission of that sentence, there would be
no valid objection to the granting to Colonel Cutts the medal
of honor heretofore applied for by him for distinguished bravery in battle.*

JM Schofield
Major General Commanding[12]

On April 8, the acting secretary of war, upon hearing the general's
firm convictions in the matter, sent his response back to General Schofield.

*War Department
April 8, 1891*

*Let the medal be issued as recommended by the Major General
of the Army.*

SA Grant
Acting Secretary of War[13]

The secretary of war had approved Madison to be the first officer
ever to receive a triple Medal of Honor. Never before had an officer in any
of the military services of the United States received such an honor. It
was an honor not to diminish the glory of those who had previously received it, yet to recognize the extraordinary heroism of James Madison
Cutts.

On May 2, 1891, Madison was awarded the Medal of Honor. The
inscription on the back of the medal read:

*The Congress to Capt. James M. Cutts, 11th Infantry, for gal-
lantry at Wilderness, Spotsylvania, and Petersburg, 1864*

Delighted with Madison's honor, Mary and the children each immediately laid claim to the medal, but Madison insisted that it belonged
to each of them. He, however, insisted his mother be the first person to
wear it. He removed the medal from its maroon velvet case, walked over
to his mother, and gently pinned it upon her dress.

After the initial celebration, Madison once again remembered all of
the people, battles, and destruction of the war. Even after all of the years
gone by, he still thought of the events as if they had occurred only days
before. He could smell the air and hear the sounds of battle. Except at his
trial in Cincinnati, he had maintained his vow never to speak openly of
his actions under fire. He was awarded the highest form of recognition a
soldier could receive, which would forever identify him as a brave and
gallant soldier.

His life quickly returned to the routine of work, family, and the
passage of his bill for relief. As Madison continued to gather information

to support his case, he began to recognize a level of resistance swelling from within the Senate. To obtain his pension he needed the full support of both houses of Congress.

To commemorate the receipt of his medal, Madison joined a group of other Medal of Honor winners and helped organize the Medal of Honor Legion. Elected the organization's first historian, Madison worked tirelessly on its behalf.[14] He was active in the Lafayette Post of the Grand Army of the Republic, the Oldest Inhabitants Association of Washington, D.C., and the Columbia Historical Society.

On March 5, 1892, another son, Harold Schofield, was born, bringing the number of children in the family to eight. More good news arrived on July 25 when he learned the Senate passed a bill to pay him in arrears for army pay. He was close to getting his retirement pension if only the House passed the Senate bill. Unfortunately, the House did not pass the Senate version of the bill, and he was forced to keep trying.

The following year a prayer had been answered when Madison was given a position in the judge advocate general's office at the War Department. He was assigned to room 299 of the War Department, which he shared with R. W. Fish.[15] The position required hours to review the legal cases pending in the military judicial system. His office, located next to the executive mansion, was not far from his childhood home on the opposite side of Lafayette Park. He took the Pennsylvania Avenue trolley to and from work every day and maintained an excellent work record. He had returned to his element and there he found happiness.

While he continued his fight with Congress, he lost his greatest ally on February 16, 1895, when Madison's mother passed away. She had nursed him back to health on several occasions and cared for him as a dedicated mother. Madison had loved her dearly and at her funeral, a lock of her silver hair was placed in an envelope in order to keep a part of her with him, always.[16] Her body was laid to rest alongside of his father at the Oak Hill Cemetery in Georgetown.

On February 25, 1895, Madison had an opportunity to state his case for relief before the Senate Military Affairs Committee. He provided much the same information he had presented to the members of the House. Unfortunately, a minority report took exception to his military record. The minority report stated that despite his gallant behavior on the battlefield, the actions leading to his court-martial—drunkenness and the use of foul language—were unforgivable. As a result, the bill never made it out of the committee. It was a devastating blow to Madison. Refusing to quit, he continued to improve upon his argument. In the end, he never achieved the full approval of Congress.

Later that spring Madison traveled to Philadelphia to celebrate the fourth anniversary of the Medal of Honor Legion. The organization included 125 Medal of Honor winners out of 165 known survivors. The banquet at Dooner's, one of Philadelphia's finest hotels, was attended by many dignitaries. When asked to tell his story of bravery to a reporter, Madison remained true to the promise. He refused leaving the reporter to write:

> *Colonel J. Madison Cutts, historian of the Legion, did no little service in helping to make the history which the Legion has elected him to write. A brother-in-law of Stephen Douglas, he was a brave soldier and won his medal for distinguished service in three of the hardest fought battles of the war. His medal is a triple one and modestly tells its own story; for the Colonel won't.*[17]

Madison, an active member of the Columbia Historical Society, was held in the highest esteem and honored by that organization when they requested him to present a paper on his great-aunt, Dolly. Madison used it as an opportunity to share the life he had enjoyed with his beloved aunt.

On May 2, 1898, his paper was presented to the society and to an honored guest, William McKinley, the president of the United States. He spoke of all he remembered about the grand lady and of his personal relationship with her. Most important was her account of the saving of General Washington's picture.[18]

The following year Madison lost his sister,[19] Adele, who had been a major part of his life and one whom he had always loved. After her marriage to Robert Williams, Adele had settled into the life of a soldier's wife traveling with Robert to Leavenworth, Kansas, the headquarters for the Department of the Platt, where he was involved in the Indian Wars. Later, she returned to Chicago when Robert accepted a position with the Department of the Missouri. During this time, she had raised three boys and three girls. She had kept in communication with Madison all during their adult lives, and with her death, Madison felt a great loss.

As time passed, Madison became afflicted with Bright's disease, a debilitating disease that caused severe damage to the kidneys. In his last years, he had become increasingly disabled; yet, being the honorable man that he was, Madison continued to do his duty for his country and his family.

On Thursday, February 19, 1903, Madison left his home following lunch to return to his office at the Executive Office Building. As he stepped onto the trolley, as he had done so many times before, he fell unconscious to the floor. The driver stopped the trolley, while several passengers came to his aid. An ambulance took him to the emergency hospital, where Dr. Robert Perkins, after completion of his examination, found Madison to be in a urasmic coma brought on from severe intestinal nephritis. Madison was dying from kidney failure. He remained in the hospital unconscious with his family by his side until his death on Tuesday, February 24, 1903, thus ending the life of one of America's greatest soldiers and a proud man, who had achieved the status of legend on the battlefields of the Civil War.

Madison, an extraordinary man who understood the meaning of life, freedom, history, honor, bravery, and glory, never spoke about or flaunted his achievements. His character spoke for itself, and those who knew him clearly understood and admired him. In all of American history, there are only a small number who accepted their role in life and achieved great deeds despite the obstacles in their way. James Madison Cutts was such a man.

When the ravages of war and sickness finally won their battle, not only did the country lose one of its greatest heroes, the world also lost a great gentleman soldier. Committed to honor, truth, and devotion to duty, Madison demonstrated the responsibilities of a good citizen by his personal example. In doing so, he joined the ranks of all of the great men who gave of their fortunes and lives for the United States.

Following his death, Dr. John R. Wright, an embalmer and undertaker on Tenth Street, prepared his body for the funeral.[20] There it was placed in a rosewood casket with silver mountings with his name engraved on the nameplate[21] and then transported to his home at 534 Twentieth Street, NW, for viewing. At 9 A.M. on the following day, Rev. Father O'Connell conducted a full mass at St. Joseph's Church, and then officiated at the funeral.[22]

From the church, a large hearse and four carriages carried the body and the family to Arlington National Cemetery. The pallbearers, E. Thomas Brown, B. W. Reiss, Luke Kelly, John Fish, W. W. Brown, Nathaniel Shatswell, J. Edmond Brown, and Robert Wormersley, all members of Madison's favorite organizations, carried the casket to his grave.[23] Under full military honors, J. Madison Cutts, Jr., the Hero of the Republic, was laid to rest.

In his youth, Madison had charted a course, which provided direction for the rest of his life. He elaborated on the way an American citizen should conduct their life in his commencement address at Brown University when he said, "...Republican virtue of the past and the present teaches as its most important lessons, Patriotism, Integrity, and Self Denial." He lived his entire life by this rule and, like a modern-day Don Quixote, used honor and truth as his shield. His life was a testament to the adherence of principle, for all who knew him, worked with him, and fought with him there was no denying his strength of character.

On March 23, 1903, Madison's associates from the Encampment no. 69, Union Veterans Legion, unanimously adapted a resolution with respect to their departed comrade. In it they resolved: "That in the death of Comrade Cutts, the Country has lost a patriotic and good citizen, the church a faithful devotee, and this Encampment an efficient, courteous and zealous member." In their final words, Madison's comrades quoted an old refrain as their simple but greatest form of tribute:

His life was gentle; and the elements
So mixed in him, that nature might stand up
And say to all the world — This was a man.[24]

Addendum

Brown University, Commencement Address 1857.

The Personal Responsibilities of the American Citizen

From the citizen in his individual capacity, have ever emanated influences affecting the welfare of nations and the happiness of men. If the contrary be asserted, we point along the vista of the past to the glorious triumphal arches, which the gratitude of man, at each successive step of his progress, has reached in memory of the majestic influence and the glorious deeds of individual men. If proof is required by the American mind, we point to the examples of Washington. If the memory of Washington deserves to be cherished in the grateful hearts of his countrymen; if his character be worthy of all admiration and of all imitation, it is not because he can be favorably compared with Peter the Great, with Frederick the Great, or with Napoleon the Great; but it is because of his influence upon his own country in the development of our institutions, and of freedom which we now enjoy. It is because of his influence during the progress of the Revolution, in the formation of the Confederacy, in the development and adoption of the Constitution. It is because without that influence the American Revolution never could have been conducted to a successful result; it is because without that influence the Confederacy never could have been formed; it is because without that influence the Constitution never could have been developed and adopted, it is because without that influence the Constitution, once adopted, never could have been carried into successful operation. These are the considerations which give to the memory and to the character of Washington a greatness, which is lasting, a dignity, a grandeur, a sublimity.

175

If then such be the influence which individual men have in all ages and in all countries exerted, there comes a time, when in view of the position he occupies, and of the advantages he enjoys, every American Citizen must needs reflectingly consider his Personal Responsibilities.

From the very nature and constitution of our Republic, most weighty responsibilities are imposed upon every one of its citizens upon the fulfillment of which their safety and prosperity—both individual and national—ultimately depend.

Ours is a system of government which gives importance and consideration to every man, because he is a man: which proclaims all men to be free and equal: which discards force, for it is enthroned in the heart: which rests on the free utterance of thought, on freedom, on reason, on reflection: which makes Humanity-its Law giver and its oracle and acknowledges the common mind to be the true material for a commonwealth. In such a government duty, like death, enters every abode and summons its inmate to service of his country. The citizen must not be confined within the solitude of his own heart. He must exert an influence over his fellow countrymen; to them he owes everything, from them he must expect everything. He is not born to live alone, nor has he his destiny in his own hands. He is responsible for the exercise of his powers and his faculties in the service of the whole community. How can the American Citizen faithfully discharge his responsibilities, if he refuses to serve his country? The highest praise which the father of eloquence could bestow upon a Roman Citizen, was that he had served well his country and been a benefit to the Republic. Our early fathers did not hesitate to pledge their lives, their fortunes and their sacred honor in the service of their country. The brightest star in the history of the world, scorned not to shed its wisdom, and its guiding light over the infancy of our Republic. Let Americans be guided by the glorious example of the father of his country. Let them partake of the wisdom of our Washington, for it comes from the "oracles of God" and shall gladden and enrich the American heart.

Montesguieu, the publicist, has wisely said that Republics are preserved by virtue, and Monarchies honor; but it is no less true that the Republican virtue of the past and the present teaches as its most important lessons, Patriotism, Integrity, and Self Denial.

The American citizen should allow on consideration to take precedence of patriotism. It alone can impart unity and harmony to the dissatisfied and divided interests of our country. To the American citizen belongs the noble task of leading the world on to freedom, by the beauty, the glory, and the dignity of his example. Proud of being a citizen of the Republic, the love of country should be the highest elevation of his mind. His views should be large, generous, and comprehensive. His whole country should be dear to his heart, as any single part of it. Present glory should not be the only object of his existence his visions should be projected and his aspirations invoke the future. He should live not for himself, but for posterity, should aim not to aggrandize, but to establish. Forgetting personal considerations regardless of the ties of blood or of kindred, he should give his heart and his hand to the defense of the Republic and should mercifully discountenance all who, guided by ignorance or by passion, propose measures destructive to freedom or universal to peace and prosperity of the country. From the recollections of the past so glorious, from the associations of the present to inspiring, from the hopes of the future, so big with mighty promises, the American Citizen can gather patriotism which shall lift his mind above all passion and prejudice and preserve it from all the dangers of corruption, which shall elevate his soul and quicken his imagination, which shall give harmony, beauty, and sublimity to his entire character and impart to the discharge of his duties a dignity and grace, which can come from no other source. How can the American Citizen faithfully discharge his responsibilities if he fails to cultivate an ardent love of his country?

Integrity and a disinterested public spirit are the very life of our Republic. The integrity of the American Citizen must be derived from a desire of well being and a consciousness of his own dignity; and integrity inculcated by education "the keystone of a state," the "chief defense of nations," and strengthened by religion which can alone give dignity to man, and power and enduring greatness to nations. When education shall have taught the citizen the true aims of objects of his existence, shall have trained him to uphold and govern the Republic, and have made him intelligent, free, and active.

*The Goddess of Reason will give place to the Goddess of vir-
tue, and religion will teach him how to subject his intellect
and his passions to Christianity and to the laws, will give him
true ideas of his own well being and dignity, such as the Chris-
tian religion alone can teach, will vanish from his mind the
false and exaggerated notions of perverted schools and make
him a good citizen every way worthy of the praise, the admiration, and the reverence of his fellow men. Before his in-
flexible honesty, demagogues shall fear and tremble; clothed
in integrity, let rulers thereafter, or the masses rage, neither
the chorus of popularity, nor entreats of friends, the eulogies
of the multitude, the threats of enemies, the whole world
raised against him, can change his decision. Reason, moderation, prudence, and good sense will be his inseparable
conscious. The public good will be the favorite test which he
applies to everything; whatever does not promote this, he will
reject as useless, whatever is opposed to it he will repudiate
as pervious. He will not seek to conciliate individuals, nor
dread the powers of a party, for integrity has raised him to
all his dignity, his nobleness, and his grandeur and lifted him
above the consumptions of life, for he can stand alone in the
greatness of his conduct, solitary in the sublime elevation of
his intellect, in the entire purity of his heart. If ever the time
comes when brothers shall take arms to fight each other, when
the strongest ties that can bind a people together are broken
and displaced, the patriot and the man of integrity must stand
forth alone, and whether armed with the sword, or clothed
in the resistless power of his eloquence must and stem the
torment that may threaten to destroy our beloved country.
How can the American Citizen faithfully discharge his responsibilities, if he be found wanting in integrity?*

*Governed by laws, the freest in the world, a corresponding
exercise of self control is required of every American citizen.
Federal laws and self government are his distinguishing dignity and prerogative. Voluntarily subjecting himself to a government founded upon the safety and happiness of the whole
community, the American citizen must be convinced that no
great good can be permanently secured except by grievous and
oft repeated sacrifices. He must be ever ready to perform their
highest act of moral courage by making sacrifices for the*

public good. He must consider himself as a member of an as-
sociation having for its object the welfare and happiness of all,
the benefits of which require of him some sacrifices in return.
When self control and self denial shall no longer influence
the American heart, the floor of the Senate Chamber may at
any time be made to drink the blood of America's best, purist,
and noblest sons, shed by the guilty hand of the coward and
the assassin. Popular assemblies will by demagogues be made
the pretext and the occupation for disseminating views and
sentiments disloyal to the Union and for implanting in the hearts
of the people, a spirit, contrary to the spirit of the Constitu-
tion. Against such evils as these it is the manifest duty of every
citizen to contend. It is his duty to practice self denial and to
teach to the people self control. The moment the word dis-
union passes his lips, the moment that thoughts unworthy of
the loyal and true American stain the purity of his mind, that
very moment does he become a traitor, guilty of the basest
ingratitude to a country which has nourished and protected
him, worthy of the indignant scorn and the withering con-
tempt of his fellow countrymen, worthy of the direct punish-
ment an outraged humanity can inflict. Distant, far distant,
immeasurably distant be the time when such principles shall
become universal; when thoughts like these banish self con-
trol and self denial from the American mind, then shall we
soon pass away, then will our National existence be no longer
possible.

But we have no fear of so dire, so dreadful, so untimely
result provided a spirit of lofty patriotism, a spirit of manly
integrity, a spirit of courageous self denial become the ruling
and all pervading elements in the American character. In that
glad day members of the Congress shall no longer go to the
National Capitol to represent the peculiar passions and preju-
dices of those at home, they shall no longer consider them-
selves as the children of particular states, sent to represent
particular interests, but regarding themselves as the offspring
of that nobler parent the Union, they shall lend all their ener-
gies to the promotion of the general welfare and the increase
of the general harmony. The language in which their noble
efforts will then find utterance will be borne swifter than eagle's
wings, to the utmost limits of the world. It will speak to the
oppressed and enslaved and no longer in the language of fiction,

will tell there of a land where liberty and equality dwell among men, it will speak to the barbarians and savage tribes of the earth and tell them of the glorious civilization which here presides, of the knowledge, the truth, the light here enjoyed. It will gather them all under the American banner of our common country, and under it will they contend for the liberties of men, and thus will the cause of humanity be ultimately secured.

All this glorious future can be, must be, and shall be ours, where every American citizen feels, recognizes and fulfills his Personal Responsibilities.

James Madison Cutts, Jr.[1]

Notes

PREFACE

1. Carl Sandburg, *Abraham Lincoln, Vol. 1* (New York, N.Y.: Hartcourt, Bruce and World, Inc., 1953), 581–82.

CHAPTER I

1. Cecil Hampden Cutts Howard, *Genealogy Cutts Family in America* (Albany, N.Y.: Genealogy Society of Utah, Salt Lake City, Utah, 1892).

2. Allen W. Eckert, *Wilderness Empire: A Narrative by Allen W. Eckert* (Boston, Mass.: Little, Brown and Company, 1969), 58.

3. Cutts Family Records, Library of Congress, Manuscript Division.

4. Currently the site of the Dolly Madison House, Washington, D.C.

5. Anne Hollingsworth Wharton, *Social Life in the Early Republic* (Philadelphia, Pa.: J. B. Lippincott Company, 1903), 143–44.

6. James Madison Cutts, *The Conquest of California and New Mexico by the Forces of the United States in the Years 1846 and 1847* (Albuquerque, N.Mex.: Horn & Wallace, 1965), preface.

7. Currently the site of The Supreme Court of the United States.

8. Isabel Ross, *Rebel Rose, Life of Rose O'Neal Greenhow* (New York, N.Y.: Harper & Bro. Publishers, 1954).

9. Ibid.

10. Mary Cutts, Letter to Wm. Carry Poland, President of Brown University (Providence, R.I.: Brown University Archive, circa 1903), 4.

11. James Madison Cutts, Jr., *Dolly Madison* (Washington, D.C.: Columbia Historical Society, 1900), 25.

12. Ibid.

13. Ibid.

14. Cutts Letter, National Archives, Military Records Division, Washington, D.C.

15. Howard, *Genealogy Cutts Family in America*, 545.

16. Cutts, *The Conquest of California and New Mexico by the Forces of the United States in the Years 1846 and 1847*, preface, by George P. Hammond.

17. Mary Cutts, Poland Letter, 4.

18. Austine Cassini, "These Charming People," (Washington, D.C.: Newspaper article, October 5, 1947).

19. Robert W. Johannsen, *Stephen A. Douglas* (New York, N.Y.: Oxford University Press, 1973), 541.

20. George Johnson, Jr., *Rose O'Neale Greenhow and the Blockade Runners* (Rose Distributor, 1995), 44.

21. Ibid., 47.

22. James Madison Cutts, Jr., Letter (Washington, D.C.: Cutts Family Collection).

23. Cutts File, E. S. Otis Letter (National Archives, Military Records Division, Washington, D.C.: *Congressional Records*, February 25, 1891), 3002.

24. St. Aloysius Church, Informational Leaflet, Washington, D.C.

25. Robert W. Johannsen, *Stephen A. Douglas* (New York, N.Y.: Oxford Press, 1973), 778.

26. Robert W. Johannsen, *The Letters of Stephen A. Douglas* (Urbana, Ill.: University of Illinois Press, 1961), 503.

CHAPTER II

1. Marshall D. Hier, "Basil Wilson Duke, Legend Made Vivid," *The St. Louis Bar Journal* (St. Louis, Mo.), vol. 43, no. 21 (fall 1996): 45–46; (Directory, Missouri Archives, 1860), 576.

2. Library of Congress, Manuscript Division, Douglas Papers (Washington, D.C.).

3. Brown University, *The Historical Catalogue of Brown University 1764–1934* (Providence, R.I.: Brown University, 1936), 204.

4. Margaret Leech, *Reveille In Washington* (New York, N.Y.: Harper & Brothers Publishers), 68.

5. Cutts, Jr., Letter (National Archives, Military Records Division).

6. Robert W. Johannsen, *Stephen A. Douglas*, 871–72.

7. Cutts, Jr., Letter (National Archives, Military Records Division).

8. Abraham Lincoln, Letters (Washington, D.C.: Library of Congress, Manuscript Division).

9. Rebecca D. Larson, *Blue and Gray, Roses of Intrigue* (Gettysburg, Pa.: Thomas Publications, 1993), 12.

CHAPTER III

1. John Michael Priest, editor in chief, *From New Bern to Fredericksburg, Captain James Wren's Diary* (Shippensburg, Pa.: White Mane Publishing Company, Inc., 1990), 30. Also see, David C. Learned, Letters to His Sister, Entry for May 18, 1862 (Washington, D.C.: Library of Congress, Manuscript Division).

2. Ibid.

3. Court-martial Records (Washington, D.C.: National Archives, Military Records Division, microfilm 1105, vol. 2, KK49).

4. Thomas Yoseloff, *Battles and Leaders of the Civil War, From Sumter to Shiloh* (New York, N.Y: Thomas Yoseloff, Inc., 1956), 660–69.

5. *The West Point Atlas of American Wars* (New York, N.Y.: Frederick A. Praeger , Publisher, 1959), maps.

6. Court-martial Records, *J. Madison Cutts Court-martial, Cincinnati* (Washington, D.C.: National Archives, Military Records Division).

7. Ibid.

8. Thomas Yoseloff, *Battles and Leaders of the Civil War, Vol. II*, 583–84. Also see Cutts Military Records File, Cutts Letters, National Archives, Military Records Division.

9. *The West Point Atlas of American Wars* (New York, N.Y.: Frederick A. Praeger, Publisher, 1959), 65.

10. John C. Waugh, *The Class of 1846* (New York, N.Y.: Warner Books, 1994), 370.

11. Thomas Yoseloff, *Battles and Leaders, Vol. II*, 631.

12. Ibid., 648–49, 660, 682–83.

13. Court-martial Records, *J. Madison Cutts Court-martial, Letter of Defense* (Washington, D.C.: National Archives, Military Records Division), 49.

14. Cutts Military Records File, *Congressional Records* (Washington, D.C.: National Archives, Military Records Division).

15. Ibid., 5.

16. Ibid.

17. Ibid.

18. Cutts, Jr., Letter (Washington, D.C.: National Archives, Military Records Division).

19. Cutts, Jr., *Letter of Defense*, 49.

20. Thomas Yoseloff, *Battles and Leaders, Vol. III* (New York, N.Y.: Thomas Yoseloff, Inc., 1956), 137–36.

21. Cutts Military Records File, *Congressional Records*, Fifty-Third Congress, Third Session, Senate Speech of Hon. Jacob H. Gallinger, N.H., February 25, 1895.

22. *Congressional Records* (Washington, D.C.: National Archives, Military Records Division).

23. Cutts Military Records File, *Congressional Records* (Washington, D.C.: National Archives, Military Records Division).

24. Cutts Military Records File, "Bill for the Relief of Bvt. Lieut. Col. Madison Cutts," *Congressional Records* (Washington, D.C.: National Archives, Military Records Division), 2.

25. Cutts, Jr., *Letter of Defense*, 76.

26. Cutts Military Records File, *Congressional Records*.

27. The Military Commision was made up of Brig. Gen. C. P. Stone, Brig. Gen. J. J. Abercrombie, Brig. Gen. Silas Casey, Brig. Gen. John Buford; Col. George Willard and Col. Augustus Gibson; Lt. Col. Joseph Hoskins; Maj. Charles Whiting and Maj. Julius Hayden; and Capt. J. B. McIntyre and Capt. E. M. Baker. National Archives, The Court-martial of Major Delancey Floyd-Jones.

28. Major Delancey Floyd-Jones, Court-martial File (Washington, D.C.: National Archives, Military Records Division).

29. William Marvel, *Burnside* (Chapel Hill, N.C.: University of North Carolina Press, 1991).

CHAPTER IV

1. Court-martial Records, *J. Madison Cutts Court-martial, Cincinnati* (Washington, D.C.: National Archives, Military Records Division).

2. Francis Haseltine, Letter to Captain Pell (Washington, D.C.: National Archives, Military Records Division, 11th U.S. Infantry Correspondence, Entry 1374).

3. *J. Madison Cutts, Jr., Court-martial, Cincinnati* (National Archives).

4. Haseltine, Letter to Captain Pell, Entry 1374.

5. Cutts, Jr., Cutts Letter (National Archives).

6. Alfred H. Guernsey and Henry M. Alden, *Harper's Pictorial History of the Civil War* (New York, N.Y.: The Fairfax Press, 1866), 646.

7. *J. Madison Cutts, Jr., Court-martial, Cincinnati* (National Archives).

8. Ibid.

9. Ibid.

10. Ibid.

11. Ibid.

12. Ibid.

CHAPTER V

1. *J. Madison Cutts, Jr., Court-martial, Cincinnati* (National Archives). The officers of the commission were: Brig. Gen. G. Clay Smith, U.S. Vols.; Brig. Gen. J. Ammon, U.S. Vols.; Col. Mark Munday, 23rd Kentucky Vols.; Col. S. B. Griggsby, 24th Kentucky Vols.; Lt. Col. J. U. Elroy, 20th Ohio; Acting Assist. Inspec. Gen. John Walkup, 118th Ohio Vols.; Lt. Col. Henry Howard, 2nd Maryland Vols.; Maj. J. M. Wright, Assist. Adj. Gen. of Vols.; H. P. Burnet, 2nd Ohio Cavalry, judge advocate.

2. Ibid. The witnesses were: Maj. Gen. A. E. Burnside, Commanding, Dept. of the Ohio; Maj. Gen. Joseph Hooker; Maj. Gen. William B. Franklin; Maj. Gen. John G. Parker; Brig. Gen. Daniel P. Woodbury; Brig. Gen. Samuel Sturgis; Brig. Gen. J. D. Cox; Brig. Gen. Rufus Ingalls; Brig. Gen. Henry J. Hunt; Capt. Joseph O'Keife, of Brigadier General Buford's staff; Capt. John Dahlgren, son of Commodore Dahlgren, can be heard of from his mother living in Washington; Maj. N. H. McLean, Asst. Adj. Gen.; Maj. W. P. Anderson, Asst. Adj. Gen., of General Burnside's staff; Lt. Col. Lewis Richmond; Lt. Col. E. R. Goodrich; Maj. L. J. Van Buren; Capt. Philip M. Lydig; Capt. E. M. Neil, Asst. Adj. Gen.; Capt. C. S. French; Dr. W. H. Church; Col. R. D. Cutts; A.D.C. Gen. Henry Halleck; Mrs. J. Madison Cutts; and Mrs. Stephen A. Douglas.

3. Ibid., 58.

4. Daniel R. Learned, Letters #600, July 8, 1863, 4.

5. *J. Madison Cutts, Jr., Court-martial, Cincinnati* (National Archives), 61.

6. Daniel R. Learned, Letters.

7. Alfred H. Guernsey and Henry M. Alden, *Harper's Pictorial History of the Civil War*, 532.

8. *J. Madison Cutts, Jr., Court-martial, Cincinnati* (National Archives).

9. Charles G. Hutton Court-martial Records (Washington, D.C.: National Archives, Military Records Division).

10. *J. Madison Cutts, Jr., Court-martial, Cincinnati* (National Archives).

11. *The Collected Works of Abraham Lincoln, Vol. VI, 1862–1863* (New Brunswick, N.J.: Rutgers University Press, 1953), 538–39.

12. Cutts Letter (National Archives).

13. Abraham Lincoln, Letters, Library of Congress.

CHAPTER VI

1. Timothy J. Reese, *Sykes' Regular Infantry Division, 1861–1864* (Jefferson, N.C.: McFarland & Co., 1990), 4.

2. 11th U.S. Infantry Regiment, Regimental Report (Washington, D.C.: National Archives, Military Records Division).

3. Reese, *Sykes' Regular Infantry Division*, 262.

4. Ibid., 268.

5. 11th U.S. Infantry Regiment, Regimental Report.

CHAPTER VII

1. Reese, *Sykes' Regular Infantry*, 309.

2. *The War of the Rebellion: A Compilation of the Official Records of the Union and Confederate Armies*, ser. 1, vol. 36, pt. 1 (Washington, D.C.: Government Printing Office, 1902), 553.

3. John Michael Priest, *Nowhere to Run* (Shippensburg, Pa.: White Mane Publishing Co., 1995), 6; also see *OR*, ser. 1, vol. 36, pt. 1, 555–57.

4. Robert Garth Scott, *Into the Wilderness* (Bloomington, Ind.: Indiana University Press, 1988), 18.

5. Ibid., 53.

6. Priest, *Nowhere to Run*, 79.

CHAPTER VIII

1. William D. Matter, *If It Takes All Summer* (Chapel Hill, N.C.: University of North Carolina Press), 67.

2. Ibid., 108.

3. *OR*, ser. 1, vol. 36, pt. 1, 549.

4. Cutts, Jr., Letter (National Archives).

5. 11th U.S. Infantry Regiment, Regimental Report (Washington, D.C.: National Archives, Military Records Division).

6. *OR*, ser. 1, vol. 36, pt. 1, 554.

7. Ibid.

8. Matter, *If It Takes All Summer*, 279.

9. Ibid., 283.

10. David G. Chandler, *The Military Maxims of Napoleon* (New York, N.Y.: Macmillan Publishing Co., 1988), 74.

11. *OR*, ser. 1, vol. 36, pt. 1, 550.

12. Ibid.

13. Ibid.

14. Reese, *Sykes' Regular Infantry*, 313.

15. *OR*, ser. 1, vol. 36, pt. 1, 550.

16. William H. Powell, *The Fifth Army Corps* (Dayton, Ohio: Morningside House, Inc., 1984), 664.

17. *OR*, ser. 1, vol. 36, pt. 1, 550.

18. Powell, *The Fifth Army Corps*, 664.

19. Reese, *Sykes Regular Infantry*, 313.

20. *OR*, ser. 1, vol. 36, pt. 1, 82.

CHAPTER IX

1. Cutts, Letter (National Archives).

2. Powell, *The Fifth Army Corps*, 677.
3. Ibid.
4. Ibid., 697.
5. The Southside Railroad, The Weldon and Petersburg Railroad, The Norfolk and Petersburg Railroad, and the City Point Railroad.
6. Thomas J. Howe, *The Petersburg Campaign, Wasted Valor, June 15–18, 1864* (Lynchburg, Va.: H. E. Howard, Inc., 1988), 26–27.
7. Cutts Military Records File, *Congressional Records*.
8. Ibid.
9. Ibid.
10. James Madison Cutts, Jr., *Medical Records* (Washington, D.C.: National Archives, Military Records Division).
11. Ibid.
12. Cutts Military Records File (National Archives, Military Records Division).
13. Ibid.
14. Ibid.

CHAPTER X

1. Cutts Military Records File (National Archives, Military Records Division) (Capt. Joshua Fletcher, Capt. David Hazzard, Capt. Edward Ellsworth.
2. Ibid., *Congressional Records*, 32.
3. Alfred H. Guernsey and Henry M. Alden, *Harper's Pictorial History of the Civil War*, 822.
4. Cutts Military Records File, *Congressional Records*, 18–19.
5. Ibid., 23.
6. Ibid., 147.
7. Ibid.
8. Ibid., 23.
9. Ibid., 24.
10. James Madison Cutts Court-martial, *New Orleans – Peterson* (Washington, D.C.: National Archives, Military Records Division), 138.
11. Ibid.
12. "Letter from the Passengers of the Live Oak," *Cado Gazette* (Shreveport, La.: June 21, 1867).
13. Cutts Military Records File, *Congressional Records*.
14. James Madison Cutts Court-martial (Washington, D.C.: National Archives, Military Records Division).
15. Cutts Military Records File, *Congressional Records*.
16. James Madison Cutts Court-martial, *New Orleans – Brayman* (Washington, D.C.: National Archives, Military Records Division).
17. Ibid.
18. Cutts Military Records File, *Congressional Records*.
19. Ibid.
20. Cutts Military Records File, *Congressional Records*.

EPILOGUE

1. Cutts Military Records File, *Congressional Records*, 28.
2. State of Illinois, *Certificate*, James Madison Cutts IV Collection, Washington, D.C.
3. Cutts Military Records File, *Congressional Records*, 8.
4. James Madison Cutts, Pension Records (Washington, D.C.: National Archives, Military Records Division).
5. Ibid.
6. John Claggett Proctor, "Seventh Street Half a Century Ago," *The Sunday Star*, January 25, 1931, The Columbia Historical Society, Washington, D.C.
7. James Madison Cutts, Jr., Letters of Endorsement (Washington, D.C.: James Madison Cutts IV Collection).
8. Cutts Military Records File, *Congressional Records*.
9. Ibid.
10. Medal of Honor Report (Washington, D.C.: National Archives, Military Records Division), 3.
11. Cutts Military Records File, *Congressional Records*, 28.
12. Ibid., Scholfield Letter.
13. Ibid., S. A. Grant Letter.
14. *Certificate*, James Madison Cutts IV Collection, Bethesda, Md.
15. James Madison Cutts, Jr., Pension Records (National Archives).
16. Lock of Ellen O'Neale Cutts' Hair, Harriet Cutts Lundquist Collection, Saratoga, Calif.
17. "Union Medals of Honor," *Philadelphia Record*, April 10, 1893, Philadelphia, Pa.
18. Cutts, Jr., *Dolly Madison*, 28–72.
19. Mary Cutts, Letter to Wm. Carry Pollard, president of Brown University, Brown University Archives.
20. Invoice from Dr. John R. Wright, embalmer and undertaker, dated February 26, 1903, James Madison Cutts IV Collection, Washington, D.C.
21. Ibid.
22. "Obituary of James Madison Cutts, Jr.," *Evening Star* Newspaper, Washington, D.C., February 25, 1903.
23. "Obituary of James Madison Cutts, Jr.," *The Washington Times* Newspaper, Washington, D.C., February 26, 1903, buried, Arlington National Cemetery, Section 3, Grave 1371.
24. "Encampment No. 69, Union Veterans Legion, Resolution, March 21, 1903," Harriet Cutts Lundquist Collection, Saratoga, Calif.; Edgar L. Masters, Spoon River Anthology, The MacMillan Company, New York, N.Y., 1916, No. 6 Cassius Hueffer.

ADDENDUM

1. Cutts, Jr., "Brown University Graduation Speech, 1857," (Washington, D.C.: Library of Congress, Manuscript Division, Cutts Family Records).

Bibliography

Abbott, John S. C. *History of the Civil War in American.* Vol. 2. New York, N.Y.: Henry Bill, Publisher, 1866.

America's Medal of Honor Recipients, Complete Official Citations. Golden Valley, Minn.: Highland Publishers, 1980.

Bates, David H. *Lincoln in the Telegraph Office; Recollections of the United States Military Telegraph Corps during the Civil War.* New York, N.Y.: The Century Company, 1907.

Block, Eugene B. *Above the Civil War: The Story of Thaddeus Lowe.* Berkeley, Calif.: Howell-North Books, 1966.

Brown, Dee Alexander. *The Bold Cavaliers: Morgan's 2nd Kentucky Cavalry Raiders.* Philadelphia, Pa.: J. B. Lippincott Company, 1959.

Carr, Clark E. *Stephan A. Douglas.* Chicago, Ill.: A. C. McClurg Publisher, 1909.

A Catalogue of the Law School of the University at Cambridge, for the year 1859, Cambridge. Cambridge, Mass.: Sever and Francis, 1859.

A Catalogue of the Law School of the University at Cambridge for the Academic Year 1858–59, First Term, Cambridge. Boston, Mass.: John Bartlett, 1859.

Catton, Bruce. *The Centennial History of the Civil War, Volume Three, Never Call Retreat.* Garden City, N.Y.: Doubleday & Company, Inc., 1956.

Coleman, Penny. *Spies! Women in the Civil War.* Cincinnati, Ohio: Betterway Books, 1992.

Cutts, James Madison. *The Conquest of California and New Mexico, by the Forces of the United States, in the years 1845 and 1847.* Philadelphia, Pa.: Carey and Hart, 1847.

Cutts, James Madison, Jr. *Dolly Madison.* Washington, D.C.: Columbia Historical Society, 1900.

D'Aquilar, Lt. Gen. Sir George C. *The Military Maxims of Napoleon.* New York, N.Y.: MacMillian Publishing Company, 1988.

Dennett, Tyler. *Lincoln and the Civil War in Diaries and Letters of John Hay.* New York, N.Y.: Dodd, Meade & Company, 1930.

Duke, Basil W. *Reminiscences of General Basil W. Duke, C.S.A.* Freeport, N.Y.: Books for Library Press, 1969.

Dyer, Frederick H. *A Compendium of the War of the Rebellion, Vol. 2.* Dayton, Ohio: Morningside, 1979.

Dyer, John P. *Fightin Joe Wheeler.* Baton Rouge, La.: Louisiana State University Press, 1941.

Eckert Allen W. *Wilderness: Empire: A Narrative.* Boston, Mass.: Little Brown and Company, 1969.

Foote, Shelby. *The Civil War: A Narrative, Red River to Appomattox.* New York, N.Y.: Random House, 1974.

Fox, William. *Regimental Losses in the American Civil War, 1861–1865.* Albany, N.Y.: Albany Publishing Company, 1889.

Greenhow, Rose. *My Imprisonment.* London, U.K.: Spottiswood and Company, 1863.

Heitman, Francis B. *Historical Register and Directory of the United States Army, Vol. 1.* Washington, D.C.: Washington Printing Office, 1903.

Howard, Cecil Hampden Cutts. *Genealogy Cutts Family in America.* Albany, N.Y.: Genealogy Society of Utah, 50 East N. Temple, Salt Lake City, Utah, 84150, 1892.

Howe, Thomas J. *The Petersburg Campaign: Wasted Valor, June 15–18, 1864.* Lynchburg, Va.: H. E. Howard, Inc., 1988.

Johannsen, Robert W. *Stephen A. Douglas.* New York, N.Y.: Oxford University Press, 1973.

Johannsen, Robert W. *The Letters of Stephen A. Douglas.* Urbana, Ill.: University of Illinois Press, 1961.

Johnson, Allen. *Stephen A. Douglas, A Study in American Politics.* New York, N.Y.: Da Capo Press, 1970.

Johnson, George, Jr. *Rose O'Neale Greenhow and the Blockade Runners.* Canada: George Johnson Publisher, 1995.

Judson, A. M. *History of the Eighty-third Regiment, Pennsylvania Volunteers.* Erie, Pa.: B.F.H. Lynn Publisher, 1865.

Kane, Harnet T. *Spies for the Blue and Gray.* Garden City, N.Y.: Hanover House, 1954.

Kinchen, Oscar A. *Confederate Operations in Canada and the North.* North Quincy, Mass.: The Christopher Publishing House, 1970.

Larson, Rebecca D. *Blue and Gray: Roses of Intrigue.* Gettysburg, Pa.: Thomas Publications, 1993.

Leech, Margaret. *Reveille in Washington, 1860–1865.* New York, N.Y.: Harper & Brothers Publisher, 1941.

Long, E. B., editor. *Personal Memoirs of U. S. Grant.* New York, N.Y.: DaCapo, 1982.

Lord, Francis A. *Civil War Collector's Encyclopedia; Arms, Uniforms, and Equipment of the Union and Confederacy.* Harrisburg, Pa.: Stackpole, 1963.

Lord, Francis A. *They Fought for the Union.* Harrisburg, Pa.: The Stackpole Company, 1963.

Lowry, Don. *No Turning Back: The Beginning of the End of the Civil War March -June 1864.* New York, N.Y.: Hippocrene Books, 1992.

Lucas, Dr. Jay, and Col. Harold W. Nelson. *The U.S. Army War College Guide to the Battle of Antietam.* New York, N.Y.: Harper & Row Publishers, 1987.

Lyman, Theodore. *Meade's Headquarters, 1863–1865: Letters of Colonel Theodore Lyman from the Wilderness to Appomatox.* Boston, Mass.: The Atlantic Monthly Press, 1922.

Marvel, William. *Burnside.* Chapel Hill, N.C.: University of North Carolina Press, 1991.

Milton, George F. *The Eve of Conflict, Stephen A. Douglas and the Needless War.* Boston, Mass.: Houghton Mifflin Company, 1934.

Nicolay, John C. *Abraham Lincoln.* The Century Company, 1914.

Pennypacker, Isaac Rusling. *General Meade.* New York, N.Y.: D. Appleton Press, 1901.

Porter, Gen. Horace, L.L.D. *Campaigning with Grant.* New York, N.Y.: Konecky & Konecky, 1992.

Powell, William H. *The Fifth Army Corps.* Dayton, Ohio: Morningside House, Inc., 1984.

Quinquennial Catalogue of the Law School of Harvard University, 1817–1934. Cambridge, Mass.: Published by the Law School, 1935.

Ray, J. P., comp. *The Diary of a Dead Man: Letters and Diary of Ira S. Pettit.* Philadelphia, Pa., and Wilson, N.Y.: Eastern Acorn Press, 1981.

Reese, Timothy J. *Sykes' Regular Infantry Division, 1861–1864: A History of Regular United States Infantry Operations in the Civil War's Eastern Theater.* Jefferson, N.C.: McFarland & Company, Inc., 1990.

Rhea, Gordon C. *The Battle of the Wilderness, May 5–6, 1864.* Baton Rouge, La.: Louisiana State University Press, 1994.

Root, The Honorable Elihu, Secretary of War. *The War of the Rebellion: The Complete Army Official Records of the American Civil War.* Washington, D.C.: Government Printing Office, 1902.

Ross, Ishbel. *Rebel Rose, Life of Rose O'Neale Greenhow, Confederate Spy.* New York, N.Y.: Harper & Brothers Publishers, 1954.

———. *The President's Wife.* New York, N.Y.: G. P. Putnam's Son, 1973.

Sandburg, Carl. *Abraham Lincoln One Volume Edition.* New York, N.Y.: Hartcourt, Brace & World, Inc., 1953.

Schott, Joseph L. *Above and Beyond – The Story of the Congressional Medal of Honor.* New York, N.Y.: G. P. Putnam's Son, 1963.

Scott, Robert Garth, editor. *Fallen Leave: The Civil War Letters of Henry Livenmore Abbott.* Kent, Ohio: Kent State University Press, 1991.

Seymour, Digby Gordon. *Divided Loyalties, Fort Sanders and the Civil War in East Tennessee.* Knoxville, Tenn.: University of Tennessee Press, 1963.

Shannon, Fred Albart, Ph.D. *The Organization and Administration of the Union Army, 1861–1865, Vol. 1.* Cleveland, Ohio: The Arthur H. Clark Company, 1928.

Smith, J. L. *History of the 118th Regiment, P.V., Corn Exchange Regiment, Antietam to Appomattox.* Philadelphia, Pa.: Map Publisher, 1905.

Steere, Edward. *The Wilderness Campaign.* Harrisburg, Pa.: The Stackpole Company, 1960.

Temple, Wayne C., Ph.D. *Stephan A. Douglas, Freemason.* Bloomington, Ill.: The Masonic Book Club, The Illinois Lodge of Research, 1982.

Trudeau, Noah Andre. *Bloody Roads South, The Wilderness to Cold Harbor, May - June 1864.* Boston, Mass.: Little, Brown and Company, 1989.

Yoseloff, Thomas. *Battles and Leaders of the Civil War, Vol. 1, From Sumter to Shiloh.* New York, N.Y.: Yoseloff Inc., 1956.

———. *Battles and Leaders of the Civil War, Vol. 2.* New York, N.Y.: Yoseloff Inc., 1956.

————. *Battles and Leaders of the Civil War, Vol. 3, Retreat from Gettysburg.* New York, N.Y.: Yoseloff Inc., 1956.

————. *Battles and Leaders of the Civil War, Vol. 4.* New York, N.Y.: Yoseloff Inc., 1956.

————. *Campaigns of the Civil War, Vol. 5.* New York, N.Y.: Yoseloff Inc., 1963.

Wallace, Willard M. *Soul of the Lion, A Biography of General Joshua L. Chamberlain.* Gettysburg, Pa.: Stan Clark Military Books (Thomas Nelson & Sons, New York, N.Y.), 1991.

Wells, Damon. *Stephan A. Douglas: The Last Years, 1857–1861.* Austin, Tex.: University of Texas Press, 1971.

Wharton, Anne Hollingsworth. *Social Life in the Early Republic.* Philadelphia, Pa.: J. B. Lippincott Company, 1903.

Wilkerson, Warren. *Mother, May You Never See The Sights I Have Seen, The Fifty-seventh Massachusetts Veteran Volunteers.* New York, N.Y.: Harper & Row Publisher, 1990.

Williams, T. Harry. *Hayes of the Twenty-third: The Civil War Volunteer Officer.* New York, N.Y.: Knopf, 1965.

Woodbury, Augustus. *Ambrose Everett Burnside.* Providence, R.I.: N. B. Williams & Company, 1882.

Index

First names are listed where known.